THE LIFE .

COLO1

THE LIFE AND DEATH OF COLONEL BLIMP

Michael Powell and Emeric Pressburger

Edited
and with an Introduction by
IAN CHRISTIE

faber and faber

First published in Great Britain in 1994
by Faber and Faber Limited
3 Queen Square London WC1N 3AU

Photoset in Sabon by Parker Typesetting Service, Leicester
Printed in England by Clays Ltd, St Ives plc

A CIP record for this book is available
from the British Library

ISBN 0-571-14355-5

2 4 6 8 10 9 7 5 3 1

Contents

Acknowledgements

The script which forms the basis for this book is held in the Powell and Pressburger collections of the British Film Institute's Special Collections Unit, a part of Library and Information Services. Stills are from BFI Stills, Posters and Designs, a department of the National Film and Television Archive, by courtesy of the Rank Film Distributors. 'Blimp' cartoons and newspaper extracts are reproduced by permission of the London Evening Standard. Transcripts of Crown copyright records in the Public Record Office appear by permission of the Controller of Her Majesty's Stationery Office.

I am deeply grateful to Thelma Schoonmaker-Powell and to Kevin and Andrew Macdonald and Angela Gwyn John for the generous access they have granted to both Michael Powell's and Emeric Pressburger's papers, and for their permission to quote from these. Their encouragement to explore the context of the film and their practical help has also been invaluable.

Thanks are also due to Laurence Hayward, who first alerted me to the Churchill file on *Blimp*; to Julian Rees, for the Walbrook–Churchill information; to Markku Salmi, for his help with the credits; to Clyde Jeavons and David Meeker of the National Film and Television Archive, and especially the latter for his contribution to establishing the print history of *Blimp*; to Janet Moat of the BFI Special Collections Unit; to Melanie Tebb, Christine Gordon, Isabel Christie, Sylvia Mulvey and especially Patsy Nightingale, for valued help of various kinds; and finally to Walter Donohue and David Watson at Faber for their unwavering devotion to this project.

Introduction
A Very British Epic

I shall be sent for soon at night.
FALSTAFF IN SHAKESPEARE'S *Henry IV Part 2*

What we call the beginning is often the end
And to make an end is to make a beginning.
The end is where we start from.
[...]
History is now and England.
T. S. ELIOT, 'Little Gidding', 1942

The Life and Death of Colonel Blimp has had a career that would be unusual for any film, and must be unique in the history of British cinema. Conceived at the height of World War II, when film industries throughout the world were producing either escapist entertainment or rousing propaganda – and often trying to combine these in the same film, with varying degrees of success – *Blimp* dared to raise awkward questions in a puzzling form: questions about the calibre of Britain's military leadership and about its readiness for 'total war'; about the history of German militarism and how this differed from Nazism. Worst of all, perhaps, from a contemporary standpoint, the only military action it showed was ironic or downright ignoble.

'What is it *really* about?' demanded a contemporary critic, with an exasperation which valuably reminds us that this now-acclaimed film was and remains something of a conundrum.[1] For a work based on a bitingly satirical conception, it proved remarkably benign, not to say romantic, about the English ruling caste. And for all its length and decades spanned, we learn remarkably little about either Britain's or Germany's public history between 1900 and 1940. At a time when not only films but all kinds of public expression were required to be clear and positive in their meaning, *Blimp*'s greatest sin was to be open to different interpretations; to hint (as the same critic acutely judged) 'that it has something much bigger to say'.

From our latter-day perspective, it is tempting to link *Blimp* with *Citizen Kane*, a near neighbour in time and method. These two startlingly original studies of age, friendship and frustration openly revelled in cinema's ability to problematize a 'career'. But a more apt comparison might be with Welles's misunderstood and ruined *Magnificent Ambersons*.[2] For this too attempted a 'portrait of an age', built around a foreshortened, unenlightened character. And, like *Blimp*, it is a film of shadowy interiors and enigmatic vignettes – the very antithesis of a typical concise, informative 30s 'biopic'.

The makers of *Blimp* did indeed feel they had 'something to say' and knew that they had to find an original form. They had no previous experience of working in colour (then considered as much a new frontier as sound had been a decade earlier) and very little of dealing with history. Innocent, more or less, of the conventions of such films, they set about creating a 'crazy quilt of Technicolor'. The result, to their astonishment, ran almost three hours – an inadvertent epic.[3]

In many ways it was to be the most personal film that Michael Powell and Emeric Pressburger would ever make. Personal, in

1 C. A. Lejeune, *Observer*, 13 June 1943. See p.56 below.
2 Welles's *The Magnificent Ambersons*, made two years after *Citizen Kane* in 1942, was cut from 131 to 88 minutes by RKO before release.
3 Powell, in *A Life in Movies* (London, 1986), claims that they were surprised by the running time of the film, p. 418.

the sense that they patched into it so much of their own differing histories, making of its broad, simple story an allegory of their improbable partnership in wartime Britain, as well as a thoughtful contribution to the armoury of wartime propaganda.[4] Powell has described his own Edwardian English childhood in the richly evocative early part of *A Life in Movies*; and Kevin Macdonald's forthcoming biography of Pressburger will greatly extend our understanding of how closely Pressburger drew on his immigrant's experience, first of Germany and then of Britain, to create Theo's pivotal 'point of view'.[5] For if the Blimpish Candy is essentially static, empty, uncomprehending (Spud's nickname for him, 'Wizard', manages to combine a topical reference to the MGM musical, a reminder of that character's compensatory façade *and* a clue to one of the films that no doubt most inspired *Blimp*'s structure), it falls to Theo to witness, to learn and to interpret.

Because it grew from Powell and Pressburger's own experience and concerns – the anecdotal starting point was a scene (eventually cut) in *One of Our Aircraft is Missing* in which an old crew-member reminds his young comrades that he too was young once – the storm of controversy may well have come as a surprise to them. It should not have. From the point at which David Low's 'Colonel Blimp' became the armature for their project, it could have been anticipated that this would attract hostility. Low's iconoclastic cartoon character was described in his *Times* obituary as 'a rotund, bald, fierce gentleman who formed the mouthpiece for the most reactionary opinions'. Running in Beaverbrook's *Evening Standard* throughout the 30s, the Colonel was a scourge of establishment hypocrisy and self-interest. After the early reverses of the war, he had become a hotly contested symbol in the debate on Britain's ability to withstand the Axis. The parliamentary debate of February 1942

4 On British wartime propaganda, see my '*Blimp*, Churchill and the State', in *Powell, Pressburger and Others*, ed. Ian Christie (London, 1978), pp. 114–16.
5 Kevin Macdonald, *Emeric Pressburger* (London, 1994).

which promised a new coordination of the war effort turned on Stafford Cripps's claim that: 'From now we have said good-bye to "Blimpery".'[6]

Others, outside government, were not so sure. Low continued to pillory through the Colonel the Establishment's belief that its interests were identical with those of the nation. In the same year, Robert Graves published an essay, 'Colonel Blimp's Ancestors', prompted by 'the uncomfortable feeling that the British Army contained far too many pig-headed officers, left-overs from the First World War'.[7] Little wonder that the new Secretary of State for War, James Grigg, showed so little sympathy for Powell and Pressburger's project. The terms in which he wrote to Churchill, about its potential to 'give the Blimp conception of the Army officer a new lease of life at a time when it is already dying from inanition', show how sensitive officialdom was to the mere mention of Blimp.

All the more so, perhaps, because it seemed to many that Churchill himself embodied 'positive' Blimpish qualities. An American general, based in London, confided to his diary in 1940:

what I really think, which is that Churchill's strength and the reason he refuses to give ground anywhere is because he himself is a Blimpish character.[8]

To General Lee, as to Powell and Pressburger, it seemed obvious that Blimpism was by no means wholly negative. On to Low's swingeing satire, they had grafted other values: steadfastness, loyalty, gallantry, honour, hospitality. Clive Candy, as he eventually emerged, is as much Addison and Steele's archetypal English gentleman, Sir Roger de Coverley, as he is the

6 Reported in *The Times*, 26 February 1942. See p. oo below.
7 Reprinted in his 1949 collection *Occupation: Writer*, in the preface to which this phrase appears.
8 Raymond E. Lee, *The London Observer: A Wartime Journal 1940–1* (London, 1972).

anachronistically chivalrous Don Quixote – with elements of Falstaff (ever waiting to be 'sent for' to give service to his country) and perhaps even the long-suffering Oliver Hardy, forever finding himself in a 'mess' not of his making or comprehension.

Priding themselves on their up-to-date grasp of propaganda techniques, it seemed obvious to The Archers that, having anatomized the menace of Nazism in *49th Parallel* and celebrated the value of resistance under occupation in *One of Our Aircraft*, they should next commemorate the 'death' of Blimpery, by showing its embodiment literally defeated by the 'new army', even as he tries to cling on to the last vestiges of power in the Home Guard. A kind of 'how we fight', after their versions of 'why we fight'; and something of a *mea culpa* for the years of appeasement.

The extent to which they underestimated official 'Blimpery' became clear when Cabinet papers of the period were opened in the 70s. These show how Churchill took a close personal interest in trying first to have the film halted and then to obstruct its export. From James Grigg's letters to Powell and his later briefing to Churchill, it is clear that nuances of how films 'mean' and how audiences 'read' – which *are* addressed in the markedly more sympathetic Ministry of Information report and in Brendan Bracken's contribution to the debate – cut little ice with the ultimate authorities.[9]

There is, perhaps, a glancing parallel to be drawn with the Soviet attitude to cinema under Stalin. Film was in some sense 'real' for Stalin, as the director Grigori Kozintsev discovered at a Kremlin screening, which helps explain Stalin's obsessive desire to control what appeared and did not appear on Soviet screens, including his own portrayal by a series of actors.[10] Churchill seems to have have had a similar belief in the magical 'reality' of

9 See pp. 31–6, 41, 48–51 below.
10 One of the most vivid accounts of Stalin's film viewing habits is by Grigori Kozintsev. An extract is translated in A. Konchalovsky and A. Lipkov's *The Inner Circle* (New York, 1991), p. 28.

film, happy that it should portray inspirational stories from the past (Korda's *Lady Hamilton* appears to have been his favourite film, and he was understandably enthusiastic about a planned screen biography of his ancestor the Duke of Marlborough), but outraged that a cinematic Blimp should question his will to win the war. We do not know his detailed reaction to the actual film, except that it was negative. But there is an account of his visit to Anton Walbrook's theatre dressing room, when the latter was appearing in *Watch on the Rhine* at the time of *Blimp*'s première.[11] According to a friend of Walbrook's, the Prime Minister stormed into the actor's dressing room at the interval and demanded: 'What's this film supposed to mean? I suppose you regard it as good propaganda for Britain?' Churchill was apparently far from mollified by Walbrook's answer, that he thought 'no people in the world other than the English would have had the courage, in the midst of the war, to tell the people such unvarnished truth'.

We can hear in this the same justification that Powell and Pressburger used both during and after the film's stormy passage. For them, the theme was obvious:

> Englishmen are by nature conservative, insular, un-suspicious, believers in good sportsmanship and anxious to believe the best of other people. These attractive virtues, which are, we hope, unchanging, can become absolute vices unless allied to a realistic acceptance of things as they are, in modern Europe and in Total War.[12]

The film, both as originally planned (in the more didactic terms of Pressburger's first outline) and in its final, more romantic version, seems to mourn Blimp's death, without questioning its necessity. What, its authors wonder, will replace the Blimpish

11 This and the following quotation are from an obituary article by Curt Reiss, *Die Weltwoche*, 21 February 1964 ('The Last Charmeur: the Eight Careers of Adolf Wohlbrueck').
12 Powell's draft letter to Grigg, p. 28 below.

virtues? And it was of course this speculation that led to their next two films, *A Canterbury Tale* (about letting go of the past, without forgetting it) and *A Matter of Life and Death* (about rebuilding the idea of 'Britishness' after a war won only with American aid, which would spell the end of Empire).

The publication of background and contextual material inevitably raises questions about what the film we know 'might have been'. From Powell's letter to Wendy Hiller – a superbly self-confident manifesto for the independence that The Archers had just begun to enjoy under Arthur Rank's enlightened patronage – we gather that one early conception was of an 'empire' film, perhaps inspired by Korda's imperial ambitions (Powell had actually researched 'Burmese Silver', from a script by Vansittart, for him in the Far East). In the face of wartime restrictions and, apparently, Wendy Hiller's unwillingness to travel, this was replaced by a studio-based film in which both 'imperial' space and time are represented by such tokens as stuffed animal heads and snapshots – indeed by 'absence'.

Another theme which survives only marginally in the final film is the situation of women, as it had begun to change in the early years of the century and was drastically affected by two world wars. Pressburger's notes indicate the extent of his research into suffragism and the status of women, suggesting a potentially more significant trajectory for the triple female role. According to Powell, it was only Wendy Hiller's pregnancy that led to the very young Deborah Kerr being cast at the last moment, which no doubt modified the balance among this trio of characters.[13] In the light of Wendy Hiller's strong perform-ance two years later in *I Know Where I'm Going* it is tempting to believe that she could have given more depth and 'modernity' to the roles, but against this must be set their underlying conception as different manifestations of Clive's 'ideal'. Since

13 *A Life in Movies*, pp. 408–9.

Olivier's letter (pp. 21–4) makes clear that if he had played Candy he would have encouraged a sharper, more satirical account of Blimpery – indeed one closer to Low's polemic – we can deduce how much the film's elegiac tone stems from its enforced casting, without necessarily being able to imagine a coherent alternative.

We learn also from the correspondence during production why the only extant script is entitled 'The Life and Death of "Sugar" Candy' (p. 28). Removing 'Blimp' from the title represented one of the concessions offered by Powell and Pressburger in June 1942, in a last-ditch effort to secure War Office cooperation, both for casting and military resources. When these offers were spurned, there was nothing to be lost – and much gained – by reverting to the original title approved by Low.

There remains disappointingly little detailed evidence about what lay behind Arthur Rank's steadfast support for a production which had not only attracted so much official hostility but must also have seemed risky in almost all other respects. Pressburger's diary for early 1942 records Rank promising definite support for two films, one of which would be *Blimp*; while Powell records in *A Life in Movies* how, later that year, Rank not only backed the casting changes but, when asked what kind of film he was looking for, said 'quite simply and seriously: "like Colonel Blimp"'.[14] There is no suggestion that Rank requested any modifications to the film after the agreed May 'vetting' by the War Office and Ministry of Information (reported in Cabinet minute 10 May 1943); and, despite what must have been continuing pressure from Whitehall, he ensured that it was energetically promoted across the Odeon circuit and eventually exported to the United States. Churchill's known opposition was even used as publicity – 'see the banned film' – which uncomfortable fact Bracken quoted in his efforts to

14 *A Life in Movies*, p. 419.

persuade Churchill to relent (p. 50). Rank, for all his own innate conservatism, seems to have been a loyal and tenacious supporter.

One other episode from the film's post-production history is worth mentioning here, since it has tended to loom larger than it perhaps should in accounts of the film's reception. E. W. and M. M. Robson were two tenacious campaigners against the anti-patriotism and 'anarchy' which they saw on all sides at the height of the war. In 1944 they published a pamphlet provocatively titled *The Shame and Disgrace of Colonel Blimp*, which gave what they believed to be

> chapter and verse from the actual material of the Powell–Pressburger film ... proving point by point and up to the hilt, that the substance of all Powell–Pressburger's work was a rabid anti-Britishness which was almost pathological in its intensity.[15]

Although *Blimp* drew the heaviest fire from the Robsons, it should be noted that they also found the entire Archers' œuvre guilty of 'black-hearted bitterness against Britain', together with films by Asquith and Del Guidice. Why then should these fanatical forerunners of Mrs Whitehouse be regarded as representative of any significant body of contemporary opinion? The only possible answer is that their obsessive search for evidence of the Archers' supposed anti-Britishness and crypto-Nazism does in the end amount to a kind of unhinged textual analysis. Devoid of humour, irony or proportion – for example, they read the POW camp encounter of Clive with Theo as 'Germans ... turning their backs on Blimp wearing the King's uniform' – their extensive writings on Powell and Pressburger stand as a kind of reductio ad absurdum of The Archers' ambiguities and shock tactics which more judicious critics puzzled over.

---

15 This summary is from their subsequent book, *The World is My Cinema*, published like the earlier pamphlet by 'The Sidneyan Society' (London, 1947), p. 65.

When *Blimp*, like some relic of ancient British industry, was rescued from its truncated, derelict state by the National Film Archive and re-presented to a public which had for the most part not been born when it first appeared, the result was a wave of near-unanimous acclaim. The year was 1985, celebrated as 'British Film Year' and coming after the latest in a long series of drops in cinema attendances which threatened the final demise of cinema in Britain. It was inevitable, if ironic, that *Blimp* would be hailed as a 'revelation', proof that British films had once been rich, ambitious and, above all, British. Some reviewers happily wallowed in the very sentiments that Low had once targeted. David Butler, a biographer of Mountbatten, wrote in the *Daily Mail* (19 July 1985):

> Alternatively [*sic*] lifting the spirit and touching the heart, it sweeps one back to a time when there was real grace, and decency, and heroism, when the Empire was a source of pride and when to have been born British was to have won first prize in the lottery of life.

More measured responses are quoted later (pp. 60–3). But few reviewers in 1985 could resist the revelation of Churchill's diehard hostility, and so it was largely celebrated as a victory *against* the Blimps. Few were able, or minded, to probe once again Lejeune's question: What is it *really* about?[16] The question, of course, will prompt different answers in different times. And what will it be when *Blimp* has finally acquired the status of a classic, venerated almost as much in America and Europe as in Britain?

While resisting the temptation to offer one simple answer, we can perhaps start from the idea of *loss* – a theme that was understandably not considered paramount in 1943. Throughout *Blimp*, with all its curious transitional devices that elide time and space, while also reiterating experiences (coming back to an

16 Paul Taylor was an exception, taking Lejeune as his starting point (p. 62 below).

empty house that's never quite 'home'; the club that is more home-like than home, while actually recalling the ambience of public school; the War Office, shown like a headmaster's study), there accumulates an acute sense that Clive has never held on to anything, perhaps never really *experienced* anything. Bandaged like the Invisible Man after his duel, he gestures in a parody of communication – but this is little different from his unbandaged self. Going to the theatre with Edith's sister, he sees only how another has substituted for him, and found a happiness that constantly eludes him. His courtship of Barbara, like the search for Cinderella after the ball, is a formal pursuit of an ideal which can never be possessed in reality. We hear that they were happy together, but crucially we do not *experience* this interlude in a life which is otherwise blighted by the emotional inhibition that was an inevitable consequence of 'the White Man's burden'.

Kipling – the author of that notorious phrase and for many a symbol of imperial arrogance – was in Powell's view a much misunderstood figure. Particularly influential on Powell was his mysticism, an idiosyncratic blend of Eastern influences and English pantheism, which coexisted with all his bustling practicality. But even more relevant to *Blimp* is Kipling's 1904 story 'Mrs Bathurst', which offers one of the earliest attempts by a major artist to capture the novelty and strangeness of the film spectator's experience. A group of sailors are reminiscing and their talk turns to a boarding house keeper whom several of them knew in New Zealand, and the obsession with her that eventually destroyed another sailor, Vickery. The catalyst for Vickery's obsession is a film, in fact a simple 'actuality' of passengers leaving the Great Western mail at Paddington, shown in a Cape Town cinematograph programme entitled 'Home and Friends for a Tickey'. In it, he and his shipmates see a woman they all believe to be Mrs Bathurst.

There was no mistakin' the walk in a hundred thousand. She came forward – right forward – she looked out

straight at us with that blindish look which Pritch alluded
to. She walked on and on till she melted out of the picture
– like – like a shadow jumpin' over a candle, an' as she
went I 'eard Dawson in the tickey seats be'ind sing out:
'Christ! There's Mrs B!'[17]

What Kipling discerned was the peculiar *intimacy* of the filmic
experience, together with the fascination of its repeatability.
Like a victim of Freud's 'repetition compulsion', the hapless
stoker returns nightly to see that 'shadow' on the screen around
whom he has woven an obsessive personal mythology. In *Blimp*,
our attention is drawn to the suggestibility of perception by
Clive's remark about the Indian rope-trick – no one sees it who
is not already expecting to – just when we, literally, experience
his fateful 'recognition' of the Eternal Edith amongst the Yorkshire nurses. We learn in comic mode from his batman that
Clive has long been obsessed by this image. What gives the
theme filmic force and originality in *Blimp* is the conception of a
triple role played by the same actress. In a device which antici-
pates the theatrical disguises of *The Tales of Hoffmann*, we are
seduced into sharing Clive's fantasy of an 'eternal recurrence'.

Like in the films of Ophuls (with whom Pressburger worked
at the outset of both their careers), from *La Signora de tutti* to
Lola Montes, The Archers' work offers a close engagement
between the material and the means of narration. The dramatic
shape and structure of the film clearly underpin its main theme.
So, while circular repetition has an ironic or tragic connotation
in Ophuls, here it serves to focus our attention as much on what
is *not* being shown as on what is. Powell's anecdote about
improvising in the one domestic scene between Clive and Barbara, which he made turn upon Clive's endearing 'emptiness', is
revealing. The film's repeated emotional pattern is perhaps best
described as mock-heroism or bathos, from the opening 'raid on

17 Rudyard Kipling, *Traffics and Discoveries* (London, 1904), p. 356.

London', a parody of war, to the Broadcasting House skirmish. Clive constantly girds himself for action, only to find that the battle is elsewhere, and that friends and foes are not what they appear. Victory appears Pyrrhic, while we in turn experience Clive/Blimp's defeats, reluctantly, as victories – for *realpolitik*, for worldly wisdom and for modernity. Hence, for us too, the sense of loss; of a life, both individual and national, condemned to cyclic repetition – until death, madness or perhaps epiphany (as in *A Canterbury Tale* and *A Matter of Life and Death*) interrupts the cycle.

Such ideas of recurrence were widely fashionable in the 30s and 40s. J. W. Dunne's popular *An Experiment with Time* (1927) intrigued and perhaps inspired more writers than were willing to acknowledge it; while the esoteric philosophy of Gurdjieff, as interpreted by Ouspensky, proved a more reputable influence on writers as diverse as Isherwood, Huxley and Greene. J. B. Priestley's 'agnostic' acknowledgement of Ouspensky's *A New Model of the Universe* as a source for the second of his 'time' plays, *I Have Been Here Before* (1937), is probably a good barometer of how such exotic ideas were put to use by seemingly mainstream artists. James Hilton's *Lost Horizon* and *Good-bye Mr Chips*, both as books and films, communicated an anxiety about ageing and offered consoling fantasies of transcendence which clearly struck a chord with the popular audience. More austerely, T. S. Eliot's wartime *Four Quartets* are permeated by a Christian fascination with the paradoxes of time.

Like many of their contemporaries, without professing any specific theory, The Archers shared these mildly metaphysical concerns. They believed that the Great War had marked a watershed, that the post-war world was tainted by a loss of chivalry and grace, and that a new attitude or understanding was urgently needed. Powell spoke of the 'inconsequence' of pre-war English life; and Eliot pronounced what could stand as an epitaph for Clive and his generation:

Twenty years largely wasted, the years of *l'entre deux guerres* –
Trying to learn to use words, and every attempt
Is a wholly new start, and a different kind of failure.[18]

Theo, in the film, has suffered and learned from his suffering. He has lost everything, but is still richer than Clive, who knows only soldiering and service to his country. But the country that will be rebuilt on the ruins of Clive's house will be different from the one that has been his only true love. Or will it? This was the great question that would preoccupy Powell and Pressburger, along with many of their contemporaries, for the remainder of the decade, and beyond.

IAN CHRISTIE

18 'East Coker', from the *Four Quartets*, written in 1940.

DOCUMENTS
The Blimp Files

"Almost every Government department sent delegations to view the
film and give their own impressions.
When all the reports were in, they were
solemnly collated and examined. Great
decisions were made"—
*OUR SPECIAL CORRESPONDENT
ON THE BLIMP CRISIS*

WHITEHALL'S EVENING OUT   *(Copyright in All Countries.)*

Private

THE LIFE AND DEATH OF COLONEL BLIMP*
FIRST OUTLINE
Emeric Pressburger

1. Turkish Bath. Blimp meets a fellow officer with whom he served for eight months in a blockhouse in the Boer War. They sing to each other the Wagner aria.† An old man who wants to sleep doesn't succeed to stop them. They talk about an article Blimp wrote in *Times* and the other fellow wants to show a letter to Blimp. It came from Germany, from the sister of the young man's niece's governess. Finally the old man, seeing it is no use trying to sleep, decides to give up. It's pointed out that Blimp wanted to rest as in the evening he goes to the theatre with two young ladies who want to invite him to [their] estate. The two young officers are leaving the Turkish bath. At the entrance they meet the annoyed old fellow, who is a general (?). The general starts to shout at them: 'You young fools. You should be ashamed of yourselves. There's a war on and you are disturbing the peace in a Turkish Bath. That's what makes the citizens antimilitarists; while their sons are dying in South Africa, the officers are having a grand time in London.'

* From a manuscript in the Pressburger papers [n.d.], written in pencil as was EP's custom. Original layout has been preserved and all round brackets are in the MS, with square brackets reserved for editorial interpolation.
† The chosen aria remained Wagner into the typed script, although reference in the Berlin café scene to the 'Troubador' (*Il Trovatore*) suggests it was still undecided at this stage.

3

Suddenly, as the wind blows the coat of Blimp, the general realises it is a VC on Blimp's chest. Startled, he asks: What is that? – we learn about Blimp's South African war exploits.

Nothing else remains for the General but to ask: why this singing? We learn about the blockhouse and the record. The general goes as a loser.

2. War office. Blimp reports with letter addressed to his friend. He wants action. He knows the fellow Kaunitz. He wants to go to Berlin. General thinks he is crazy. 'My good man, leave it to our diplomacy. You wouldn't like diplomats to fight in your unit, would you?' 'Yes, I would.'

We learn about the contents of the letter, and about Blimp's returning to South Africa in 4 weeks' time. He should enjoy his time until then.

We learn about the general idea of war. We had reverses, but what does that matter? We are going to win all right, no matter this year or the next.

3. Her Majesty's Theatre. Blimp sleeping. We learn ladies left in third act as he fell asleep. Blimp very angry. The invitation is of course over now. He goes to club.

4. Last night in club. His luggage is packed, as his man thought Blimp was going to the country. He has a talk with a char-woman and decides to go to Berlin. He sends a telegram to girl, telling her that she should leave message in Hotel Adlon for him how he can contact her.

5. Little salon of Adlon. Blimp in mufti comes in. She is waiting for him. They are alone. We learn that she has lost her position. She explains the 'Alldeutscher Verband', which had up to now the holding down of the Poles. In 1895, a book was published, 'Grossdeutschland und Mitteleuropa in dem Jahr 1850'. Her first talk about 'Herrenvolk'.

We learn that she, Edith Hunter, lost her job. Now she is trying to get home with the help of the Consulate.

Blimp thinks he should call at the Consulate, where he has a young friend from public school.

Before he goes they make an appointment in the Café Kurfurstendamm ... where she knows Kaunitz goes every night, sitting at the Stammtisch with 'Alldeutsch' crowd.

British Embassy. Blimp meets silly young man. He is terribly [self-]important. They talk about women. He is terrified when he hears why Blimp came to Berlin. He reports to the First Secretary. He has a heart-to-heart talk with Blimp, telling him to lay off. The Prince of Wales is coming to settle everything. Blimp of course agrees.

Café Kurfurstendamm. Blimp all the same has to go to the Café for his appointment with Edith. They sit on balcony. Below the Stammtisch. A band (salon band) plays on balcony (programmes with repertoire of orchestra and numbers).

Edith tells him about herself. She doesn't want to marry, but what can a girl do? She mentions her idea [of] teaching English in Germany and learning German to teach it in England. As Blimp says he has to go back, she gives her opinion about it.

In the middle of this Kaunitz arrives. He can't see Blimp, but this one recognises him all right. Yes, he is the wretched skunk who was prisoner for four weeks in the blockhouse. Blimp sees him sitting there and making the rituals of drinking beer.

Blimp sorry he can't do anything but at least he wants a joke. He asks through the girl to ask the band to play the part from the Troubador. As if bitten by a mosquito, Kaunitz turns towards the band. He asks a waiter to stop the band. The band leader tells the waiter: it has been requested. Waiter goes back to Kaunitz. Now he goes himself to the band. Here he learns from which table the request came. He looks towards Blimp and recognises him. He goes to Blimp's table and waves to his companions to come up. Three Burschenschaftsbrüder come up. Kaunitz shouts to tell them and later the whole café that Blimp is one of the criminal aggressors against the Boers.

Edith [illegible]. Blimp says he is a traitor and a liar. As the Bursch. intervene and say that Kaunitz is one of theirs.

Blimp gets angry. One of the men understands English. Somebody says that in the Alldeutscher Verband there are officers of the German Army. Blimp, in the heat of the discussion, says they can be ashamed too. General consternation.

British Embassy. In the First Secretary's room sits also the Military Attaché. Outside, each time the door opens, we catch a glimpse of two Uhlan officers. The young diplomat who talks German comes with the news.

The two Uhlans come to enquire whether Blimp [can give satisfaction]; they want to challenge Blimp to a duel. We learn that the German who will duel has been drawn from the officers' corps.

In the time the young diplomat goes out the two (Secretary and Military Attaché) discuss the prospects. If it comes out that Blimp came to Germany to make trouble, this would make things worse. Somebody has the idea: Blimp came to Germany because of the girl.

The Military Attaché: no officers of the Army can duel. The diplomat means: it will be a scandal in Germany, they would play it up as an act of cowardice. Anyway, one would discuss this when Blimp and the girl arrive.

As they do, there is a conference going on in the Embassy. The young diplomat leads them [in] to sit down.

The curious situation has arisen that they have to sit still [while] it is decided: should Blimp duel or not and should Edith be regarded as his fiancée or not?

The conference is over. Blimp should duel and Edith is his fiancée. The only way to keep things secret, if there's no scandal. Duelling is forbidden also in the German Army and it can be kept secret. Blimp thinks this is a nonsense. He has never seen the man he is supposed to fight. Answer: High diplomacy.

The girl protests. Why can't everything be said as it happened? What about the truth?

Both are silenced. High decisions, these are now the fine points of high diplomacy and they must leave things to those who understand matters like this.

They should be happy, after having behaved like they have, to be able to count on such men as the men from the Embassy.

Gymnasium of the Uhlan Barracks.
All the ceremony of the duel. The German officer is Lieut. Theobald (Theo) Kretschmar-Schuldorff.

The duel with all the ceremonies in the huge echoing Gymn. It is night.

Both are wounded.

An ambulance car takes both of them with highburning torches out of the courtyard.

Idyllic Country Hospital.
The two officers are lying with bandaged heads in different rooms. Both have visitors.

Edith and the Military Attaché with Blimp. A bunch of German officers to visit Theo.

The girl learns that she has to stay for two weeks because that's how long it takes for Blimp to recover and to be able to travel. As his fiancée, she might stay nearby in a little inn and visit Blimp every day.

After visitors go, Blimp enquires about Theo. He learns from Nurse that the German has also enquired about him. He asks whether they could meet? Nurse enquires and as German's reaction very favourable, she pushes Blimp's bed to Theo's room.

Theo's room. This is their first meeting.
From this [point] on, in the next three months, they meet every day. Sometimes in their bedrooms, sometimes on the balcony of the hospital to enjoy the first sunrays of the year.

They learn many things about each other.

Theo tells him he is against duelling. But what could he do? What choice did he have?

Of course the girl meets Theo too.

What are the three talking about?

The two men talk about soldiering. The German comes from a soldier family. But Germany had no wars for a generation. Good for the English! They have the whole world for their fighting. He, Theo, has a hobby of studying explosives.

We see the differences between the two soldiers. The English takes things easily. The German on the heavy side. For Blimp war is adventure, like hunting. For the German [it is] serious, to kill or be killed.

Theo has a chance (first in Blimp's presence, then alone) to speak to Edith and to hear her speaking. She is shy at first but she talks about herself more and more freely.

What Blimp thinks is silly, Theo admires. What a marvellous thing to have a wife like her. German girls are only silly geese. But Blimp doesn't understand this.

In the meantime the Prince of Wales arrives. Political aspects.

So a certain link develops between Theo and Edith. One day by chance they are alone. Theo has developed a very warm feeling towards her. And so did she. He tells her about this and she admits: she is not Blimp's fiancée at all.

This happens on the day before she and Blimp are supposed to return home.

Blimp takes the news that she stays with Theo very lightly. But when he is alone he suddenly realises that he is missing her.

He arrives in London, has a difficult time with the War Office. He shouldn't do such a thing – never again. He should leave initiative to others who understand it more.

He sees the girl all the time and his heart becomes heavier and heavier.

He puts an advertisement in *The Times* to find a girl with whom he can exchange letters from South Africa. Without knowing it he describes the girl he wants to write to as Edith.

Then another blow comes for him. He can't return to South Africa. He is going to Egypt.

(He finds Hoppy has married the girl from the theatre.)

The links between episodes should be Blimp's collection of things from the countries [where] he has been.

From Berlin, he brings a beer mug. From Egypt an old Egyptian statuette. From Burma, Burmese silk; from India a little Buddha.

From France, a German pike helmet.

We start the second sequence with terrific rain, somewhere on the battlefield in France. It is during the great advance of the Allies in 1918. Evening.

Blimp's forces reoccupy a little French inn on the roadside. They also take 17 prisoners from an Uhlan regiment. The French innkeeper and his family reappear from their hiding but have to wait because Blimp is questioning the prisoners.

He does this in accordance with the military code. Of course he can't get any results. A young officer is waiting to take over from Blimp, who goes on leave.

The army officer questions the innkeeper, who tells that 3 British soldiers have been tortured to death 3 weeks ago when the Boche occupied this place, to get information out of them. Finally they got what they wanted.

Blimp asks at the end of the fruitless questioning a personal question. What has happened to Kapitan Theo? The Uhlan officer knows, but doesn't say a word.

The car arrives and Blimp goes, saying goodbye to the young officer.

The young officer (Richard Bentley) at once, as soon as Blimp's car starts, makes short work of the Uhlans. He asks them: Are you going to talk? No? Right. A firing squad will be formed. Six of the Uhlans will be shot. The other eleven hear the shots. Their nerves crack.

The questions are asked again. Sweat on the Germans' faces? Six more are led away. Shots again. Again the questions. Now they answer any question.

In the meantime, Blimp arrives at a village school, where he should pick up another car which will bring him to the station.

The school is full of nurses. They have just come over from England. Eighty of them. But the hospitals they should start working in have been systematically bombed. This is a kind of clearing station. Now it is evening. They all sit around huge tables.

It has been emphasised that the car can only travel at night, as [the] Germans can fire at [the] road. The trick is that the Brits (Blimp's invention) have electric bulbs on a wire about 500 yards higher up and pull them across the hills. The Germans adjust their range and then one can travel.

a) 1918. Outpost in France. Blimp goes on leave tonight.

b) He arrives at post in the middle of night where he would like train in the morning. Place enormously crowded. Every building full. Blimp has theory that one man can be accommodated anywhere. He simply goes to the next house. Full with nurses, who have just arrived from England. Some 80 of them. He talks to one of them, who is like Edith was. He only learns that she is from Yorkshire. He goes. He mentions the remarkable likeness to an officer.

   At office he learns that he can't be accommodated tomorrow on train. He [had] better go down to Serpentin [where] he might have more chance. Blimp drives back to his own outpost as it is in the other direction.

c) He meets the young officer who is still questioning the Germans. He is startled that he got everything from the prisoners. He asks them how this happened. German officer explains the firing squads. Blimp raises hell. The officer tells [of] his trick. He also knows the Uhlan. He says he would have been surprised that it would be necessary.

   Blimp doesn't like this. Against the code of warfare. He is woken up. Some Germans are approaching, without arms.

As the first comes within shouting distance, we hear them calling: The war is over.

d) In a Yorkshire cloth factory. The last khaki cloth comes from the weaving machines. It means the end of the war.

Barbara's parents own the factory. Barbara shows Blimp around. The first cloth to be woven is going to be her wedding dress.

A beautiful estate. Far away a voice is calling: 'Barbaraaaaaaa! –'

B. and Blimp are walking in the distance. They call back. A priest is there to talk to Blimp. He is rather reluctant to talk to him.

e) Drawing room. The priest is thanking Blimp for arranging the concert for the Red Cross. Blimp admits his personal reasons. He wanted to find a girl who was a nurse in the war and about whom he only knew that she was from Yorkshire. So he arranged the concert on condition that former nurses should help. So he met her, Barbara Wynn [sic].

f) Prison camp. Both Barbara and Blimp are there to visit Theo. The German doesn't want to talk to them. They have a permit, but Theo doesn't come to the room where civilians meet prisoners. The commander of the camp says Blimp may go in, but no woman.

Blimp meets Theo. Very painful scene. Theo is the German officer for whom the war has not finished yet. Friendship is forgotten.

g) In Prison Commander's dining room. He invites both for lunch. They talk about the German character. Commander is an old officer. Blimp and he don't understand the Germans. Of the three, Barbara is the only one who does.

h) The glass cupboard is emptied of relics. There are now wedding presents in it. Blimp's house is full of people. The wedding took place at Barbara's home; this is an additional party before they leave for British Columbia. A funny scene with servants who are back in civilian jobs.

In the middle of the party, a telephone call for Blimp comes from Theo. He is at Victoria. They go back to Germany and train leaves tomorrow morning.

i) Blimp and two generals from the party manage to get Theo for the night.

j) In Blimp's house. In the study of the house. Blimp brings his wife to show her to Theo. He insists that she is exactly like Edith was. Theo thinks there is a lot in that. Edith is well, they have two children.

Theo is very unhappy about Germany's losing the war. He doesn't think that this is the end. Hearing that the English are forgetting straight away what criminals [?] the Germans were, he sees that is the chance for Germany to make propaganda in England and America about the 'victim Germany'. He is sure Germany has not been beaten. He shows [photographs of] his two children.

Barbara and Blimp talk about their future. They'll go to India and live there.

New trophies in cupboard.

Third episode: 1940 or 1939

Tribunal. Waiting room. All sorts of Germans, mostly refugees. One comes out, is interviewed. Theo's twin. He seems to be waiting for somebody.

Before the judges (?) Theo says he has expected his only friend living in this country to plead for him, General Wynn-Candy, but he is in France.

– How do you know that? (etc.)

An orderly comes in and whispers something into the judge's ear.

Blimp is here. In he comes. General greeting. Blimp has two days' leave. He is very martial. He gets Theo free. But in between we hear Theo's story. Edith has killed herself because she, an Englishwoman, was hindering Theo's career. That was five years ago.

Night. Blimp's house. The butler. Blimp and Theo have dinner. They talk about their own countries. Theo tells about his sons who are poisoned and have given him up. About him loving his country but agreeing that it has to be beaten so that it won't forget. He will offer his services to England: he is an expert in explosives which he has studied for decades.

We hear Blimp's views about the war. How sure he is that the Germans will be easily beaten because right is on our side. He is going to France tomorrow. It is late. Theo must go home before curfew starts, but Blimp takes responsibility for him.

Then they talk about Blimp's private life. We learn that Barbara has died fifteen years ago of some tropical disease. The whole fortune which was left from Barbara's estates Blimp has given to research into the same disease.

They speak also of Blimp's never forgetting Edith. His looking always for the same type of girl. When finally Theo goes, Blimp has a car to take him home. It is a car driven by an ATS. She is very efficient. We don't see her face.

The car in Blackout. Theo talks to the girl. Her name is Angela. She explains that she was chosen by the General from 5,000 ATS. She doesn't know why. She is sorry to lose the job as the General leaves tomorrow.

A car is coming towards them. Theo sees her face. He understands why she was chosen.

August 1940. War Office.
Blimp goes down the corridor of the War Office as he did in the first part in 1902. But it is a different Blimp.

It is an investigation of the campaign in France and Belgium.

We hear the investigations. We hear Blimp's ideas about the sporting war. He was outmanoeuvred all right, but he was happier being on the losing side than on the victorious. The victors have disgraced themselves.

He has arrived yesterday.

Blimp's home. Blimp with Theo. Blimp very bitter. The country doesn't need him anymore. They want him to retire. Theo tells him about his experiences. Nobody trusts him. He wants to help England, but he has no chance whatever. But he doesn't give up.

Blimp decides not to give up either. He has friends in the War Office. Very influential friends too.

September 1940.
Angela arrives at Blimp's house with her Army car. She reports to Blimp and hears that he has a new job and doesn't like it. Organise the Home Guard in this sector. Anyway, he asked for her. He hates to command spare-time soldiers. She excuses herself but she starts to explain the importance of the Home Guard.

1941, September. Inspection of the Home Guard by Blimp. Angela is driving him. Blimp takes great pleasure in the Home Guard. Everything is going all right.

On the way home, he asks the girl a few private questions about her private life. She tells him that she has a boyfriend in the Army.

1942. Big H.G. exercise. Blimp busy. He has headquarters. The whole machinery is organised. HQ of HG at country house in London suburb. Blimp very busy. Staff officers excited. They have a big invasion exercise. They are going to show [what they can do] to the Army. All plans ready. Attack at midnight. Every detail worked out.

General Blimp is going home but will be back at 9 pm.

Angela is driving again. He is very satisfied with himself. He invites Angela to a theatre one of these days. She is a little bit silent. What's the matter with her? He knows it is her free day. Is the fact that he asked her to drive today the reason? Has she any trouble with her boyfriend? Never mind! He invites her for lunch. But she has an appointment if the General doesn't mind.

Blimp's home. Blimp finds a message from Theo. He 'phones the number on the message. It is a High Explosive Experimental Station. First Blimp thinks it is a mistake. But when he mentions Theo's name, to his surprise they say he is working there.

We see Theo coming to the 'phone and telling the great news. Angela's boyfriend has got him the job through some friend of his – 'these young men are terrific!'

Pub outside London. Angela and her boyfriend, the young officer we saw in prologue.* She is pleading for Blimp, who has put everything into the HG exercise. But the young man says 'out of the question'.

'All right', she says, 'then I am going to warn him.' She runs out and jumps in the car and off she goes. The armoured car follows her.

She arrives at Blimp's house. Enquires. Hears Blimp at Club, hears noise of armoured car. She escapes. We hear butler answering doorbell and being taken prisoner.

She arrives at Club. Hears Blimp in Turkish Bath. Hears armoured car arriving and escapes again.

In Turkish Bath. She is not allowed in to men's. She tries everything. Finally the armoured car arrives, she is taken prisoner (we saw that in prologue).

Turkish Bath. The 'raiders' find the code and give order to let the Army march in. It is a trick they say.

We see the Army marching in. The HG smiles at them as they pass.

---

* This is the first mention in the outline of a prologue, such as appears in the film. A further reference on the next page confirms that its 'overlap' structure was already envisaged.

Blimp and young officer on a balcony see the Army. A telephone rings, a HG answers.

Young officer: Nuts, the war is over!

The Army marches and salutes up to the balcony. Young officer is trying to persuade Blimp to see that the young Army is here, ready to fight anything.

Finally Blimp gives in and salutes too.

LETTER TO WENDY HILLER*

Dear Wendy,

We have decided on 'The Life and Death of Colonel Blimp' and I am going to try to explain how we arrived at the decision so that you can share our thoughts and plans as directly as you would if you were here to contribute to them.

I must, first of all, because we still don't know one another well, reaffirm our responsibility as independent film makers.

One, we owe allegiance to nobody except the financial interests which provide our money; and, to them, the sole responsibility of ensuring them a profit, not a loss.

Two, every single foot in our films is our own responsibility and nobody else's. We refuse to be guided or coerced by any influence but our own judgement.

Three, when we start work on a new idea we must be a year ahead, not only of competitors, but also of the times. A real film, from idea to universal release, takes a year. Or more.

Four, no artist believes in escapism. And we secretly believe that no audience does. We have proved, at any rate, that they will pay to see truth, for other reasons than her nakedness.

Five, at any time, and particularly at the present, the self-respect of all collaborators, from star to prop-man, is sustained,

---

* An undated manuscript draft among the Powell papers. Wendy Hiller eventually starred in *I Know Where I'm Going* for The Archers in 1945.

or diminished, by the theme and purpose of the film they are working on. They will fight or intrigue to work on a subject they feel is urgent and contemporary, and fight equally hard to avoid working on a trivial or pointless subject. And we agree with them and want the best workmen with us; and get them. These are the main things we believe in. They have brought us an unbroken record of success and a unique position. Without the one, of course, we should not enjoy the other very long. We are under no illusions. We know we are surrounded by hungry sharks. But you have no idea what fun it is surf-bathing, if you have only paddled, with a nurse holding on to the back of your rompers. We hope you will come on in, the water's fine.

Emeric first had the idea of 'Colonel Blimp' last September. It sprang from a scene in our current film [*One of Our Aircraft is Missing*], a scene no longer in the final edition. Let us show, he said, that Blimps are made, not born. Let us show that their aversion to any form of change springs from the very qualities which have made them invaluable in action; that their lives, so full of activity, are equally full of frustration. We will show his youth and his youthful dreams; and we will show, through his eyes, the youth of today: the changing world of the last forty years through the eyes of one unchanging man; a man who has fought in three wars with honour and distinction and has not the slightest idea what any of them were really about; a man who, in his youth, fumblingly puts one woman, quite against her will or inclination, on a pedestal; and when she jumps off into another man's arms, is always trying to fill the vacant niche with women of the same size and shape. A comic, a pathetic, a controversial character. We went to see Low, his godfather and biographer. At first puzzled, then amused, finally enthusiastic, he promised his support.

So far, so good. 'Blimp' advanced from 'Possibles' to 'Probables'. You know the other 'Probables'. About a month later we had a meeting – we believe in letting things simmer a bit. Before the meeting, we had talks with Lord Hailey, the Adviser to the

Colonial Office. Also with Lord Cranbourne, the Dominions Minister, with Vincent Massey [High Commissioner for Canada]; with Brendan Bracken; and with the films division of the MoI [Ministry of Information]. Each discussion took the idea a stage further forward. At that meeting we definitely decided on 'Blimp' as our next subject. Possible Blimps were suggested: Donat, Olivier, Richardson, Portman. As you know, we prefer Olivier.

About this time I burst in upon Christopher Mann with an exciting description of Emeric's development of the three women in Blimp's life (which had only just taken shape) and the statement that you were the ideal actress for such a splendid part (for although they are three totally different women they must, of course, be conceived by one actress as a complete piece of work). He countered briskly with the information that you were in Wales, that he was your manager, and that you were coming to London, heavily disguised, in a week's time. We met you and your husband, we were very impressed, to the extent finally of inviting you to share all our plans, as outlined in my last letter.

[*Two paragraphs about Wendy Hiller's preferred project 'Granite' and The Archers' counter-suggestion of 'Boule de Suif' are omitted.*]

This excitement and suspense, plus the other subjects which we were considering, had pushed 'Blimp' into the background, but it wasn't by any means on the shelf. The proof of a good subject is when your mind goes on working independently on it; and when every other thing that you read or hear has some contribution to make to its development. At one time I tried to push 'Blimp' out altogether, saying that with the state of the world today any location work, such as we had first envisaged, was impossible. But he came back again, more firmly established than ever, by a remark of Emeric's that if he was to write a play of 'Blimp', it would be in one set: the home to which he returns

18

from his various campaigns. Once seen in this way, the real importance of the subject begins to emerge: it was to be much more a picture of London in three wars, of the home to which he returns, of his club, his friends, his relations, than a picture of sahibs at work and play. The idea took roots and grew rapidly. A difficult location trip – another of your obstacles – vanished and was replaced by a small unit for certain essential shots. The development of the characters became the important thing, the love-story of the three women, the completion of their circle of development (Emeric has a beautiful scheme for this), the relation of the young officer at the beginning of the film to events at the end, his relation to the third of the women, and a dozen fascinating problems which are rapidly being solved. Meanwhile the march of events, the Washington declaration, the Irish developments* – everything strengthened our conviction that by the time this film is ready the whole world will be ready for it. I was away, staying with my mother, for Christmas and I had plenty of leisure to read and think and wait for enlightenment. I came back convinced that we had the right subject and I found Emeric equally convinced. I enclose one of the many 'signs' which helped to strengthen my conviction (the 'Forum' article†).

So here I am back at my opening paragraph. We have decided on 'Blimp' and we hope and believe that you will share our belief and enthusiasm for the subject. It is a really wonderful part for you and I think that, even from these stray notes, you will begin to see incidents and characters emerge. In a week or two we will have filled in much of the development; you will be able to imagine scenes, to glimpse character, to start building up the creation of the whole. Don't be afraid,

---

* Presumably a reference to the signing of the Atlantic Charter by representatives of 26 countries in Washington on 1 January 1942; and possibly to the arrival of the first American troops in Northern Ireland on 26 January, which provoked a protest by the Irish Republic.
† See 'Playing the Game', p.000 below.

don't think it is too ambitious, trust us, we have unlimited confidence in ourselves and in you.

Now for the Colonel himself. The four actors already named are still the 'Possibles'. Olivier and Donat are still the 'Probables'. We have talked to both of them. With both there are obstacles to overcome: with Donat the cooperation of M.G.M.; with Olivier, the Admiralty. Both of them *can* be overcome. We are proceeding with our work and our plans. Influence, finance and public opinion are being massed on our side. Publicity is being organised. Then, when it comes to the point, you will see, obstacles will vanish, difficulties will be overcome. I speak from the experience of *49th Parallel* which was a veritable Grand National.

This letter has gone on long enough.

The best of wishes to you both. May we be as much in your thoughts as you are in ours.

LETTER FROM DAVID LOW*

Golders Green NW11
May 12th, 1942

Dear Powell,

Thank you for sending me the scheme of the film. I have thought it over carefully and have nothing but approval at this stage. The whole thing reads to me like the makings of a very good movie. After having chewed over our conversation I conclude that there are no fundamental differences of opinion

---

* David Low (1891–1963) was the creator of 'Colonel Blimp', who appeared in the *Evening Standard* throughout the 30s and remained a thorn in the side of officialdom during World War II. The fact that his immensely popular satirical character gave the film its title was enough to alert all Whitehall to its subversive potential – and doubtless helped create the climate of official hostility which persisted. See references in the letters that follow, including Grigg, 22 May, p. 27. Although not directly involved in its production, Low clearly approved The Archers' incarnation of his legendary character.

between Pressburger, yourself and myself.

Looking forward to the next development,

Yours sincerely,

David Low

LETTER FROM LAURENCE OLIVIER*

Royal Naval Air Station

Worthy Down, Winchester

May 28th, 1942

My dear Micky,

I have so little time for writing – so I will cut out all but essentials – I know you will understand.

The *idea* is unquestionably *masterly*. And the way you have written it and explained the intentions in the lay-out is most awfully attractive. But I do feel most strongly that your whole point about Blimps being made – not born is entirely missed unless you show a good bit more *how* this is done.

As it is, you declare your case, and tell a story or rather a history, but your point isn't shown. You don't say *what* makes him a blimp. Don't feel please that I'm underestimating the delightful entertainment of your story or the clever and original ways in which it is told. But as I told you I must stick to essentials and I'm presuming that criticism (constructive – I hope) is what you're after at the moment. It seems to me after studying it for quite a bit that the character just Blimpifies himself – all by himself. He starts as a keen fine young man, dissolves through a passage of time to 1918 when he appears as

---

* Olivier had already played in *49th Parallel* for The Archers (as 'Johnnie', a French-Canadian trapper) and would appear fleetingly in *The Volunteer*, their Fleet Air Arm recruiting short of 1943. But despite being their first choice to play Blimp – which he was keen to do, as this letter reveals – official disapproval of the project meant that he was not released from service (see MoI 25.6.42, p. 40 below).

half a Blimp, to emerge in 1940 a complete one. What *makes* him one? The disappointed lover isn't enough. Surely it should be previously pointed out *how* the English constitutional complacence has re-set the English nature time and time again simply by various attitudes of good taste, etc. ever since Drake and his bloody bowls.

The Elizabethans were quite a different sort of people. It must have been industrial success coupled with the smug knowledge that we had never abandoned our aristocracy (like the French) that made 'the Thing' our religion and the old school tie, our gonfalon.

I believe our national carelessly flung public school and family clichés have been far more potent in moulding our character, than the most forceful slogans in the totalitarian states. Right from 'an Oxford man never fills a sherry glass to the brim' down to 'the French Army is the finest in the world'. As Fougasse has discovered, you could trace our (possible) ruin to these very things. And we ought to have *masses* of them in the picture – and invent new ones, with of course *all* of Low's for the final sequence.

I feel there is an opportunity right at the beginning to show the mollifying effect of 'Rewards of a grateful nation' on the average man (as indeed these are designed to).

Keen, as you say, bitterly antagonistic to his superiors, go ahead, rebellious – he gets the V.C. Has that *ever* been an incentive to pursue a progressive, de-bunking, revolutionary career? – 'after all, dear old boy, aren't you being a little ungrateful? Have another drink and forget about it – here's to the jolly best V.C. yet!' (cheers) Etc.

What is the effect of a peerage on a labour M.P.?

I already suggested a scene with some uncle or other (after his disappointment in love) being jollied along with a glass of port – 'more fish in the sea than ever came out' – 'You can't keep a good man down' – after all what's 'a rag, a bone and a hank of hair?'

Through all his life he shows himself to be lulled into feeling everything's alright. There is something in the atmosphere of our whole national heritage that makes this wantonly easy.

Perhaps shortly after his first disappointment, you might see him striding down the Mall – ticking off a soldier for not saluting properly – and doing it very well, and striding off through the sunny morning, feeling much better. 'After all there's nothing so jolly fine as being a jolly fine soldier'.

I don't find much significance in the Flanders sequence beyond an attractive and possibly very amusing narration of history (and your story of course). Don't you think that perhaps after he's made such a balls up – *he* should get the credit for the information received, though of course stoutly refusing the credit, this would be found just another tribute to his sportsmanship – and at home he *just* allows it to be told (tho' a little guiltily) because it would naturally please his fiancée to believe it, until of course much later, he really believes himself and actually tells it as an anecdote at some time?

After all you are expounding *what makes blimps*! And there ought not to be a line wasted in the telling of your story that does not help, no matter how subtly, to do this. Hark at *me*!

But to go back again – Ever since Drake. It has been 'we'll muddle through' – 'we'll lost [sic] all the battles but the last', etc. ad infinitum. And when, every quarter of a century or so, some Nelson or other by sheer genius has saved our bacon for us, all it has really done has been to justify our attitude – to us.

In the earlier part of the story, all these sort of things should surround Blimp, and we should see them influence him: in the later part, he should hand them out. (His line to the German on the station 'we'll put you on your feet', etc. is perfect and comes *just* right.)

I think a good idea might be for him to be seen to un-Blimp himself quite definitely under his wife's influence, but the effect of her death would revert him completely and a hundred-fold.

Dear boy – I do hope you won't find these suggestions very

irritating. I thought the first sequence was beautifully laid out and written – though I think the statement of Spud's case in the Turkish Baths ought to be a bit better done – I don't mean Spud ought to be any cleverer – but it's a damned important bit, and there shouldn't be any reservations of opinion about it. After all it does advocate hitting below the belt – I don't mean it should be sugar-coated exactly. I mean the audience shouldn't feel it's a pity at all if possible. (*insufferable!*)

Goodbye for the time being, dear boy – I really can't write another word!

Ever as ever,

Larry

Love to Emeric

Official

Office of the High Commissioner for Canada
London SW1
5th May 1942

My dear Powell,

I read the scheme of 'Colonel Blimp' with much interest and I like it. I am writing to Sir James Grigg at the War Office and telling him that he will receive from you in due course a copy of the scheme and that after that you would like to see him. I am sure you will find him sympathetic to the ideas you have in mind.

I return the cuttings about '49th Parallel' in the USA. I am so glad it is having such a great success.

Yours sincerely
Vincent Massey

[*handwritten*] P.S. This was written before our telephone conversation this morning.

---

* Vincent Massey (1887–1964), brother of the actor Raymond (who had already appeared briefly in *49th Parallel*) was High Commissioner for Canada from 1935 to 1946 and one of Powell's valued men of influence whom he hoped would secure approval for the project.

LETTER FROM LORD VANSITTART[*]

Denham Place, Bucks
25th May 1942

My dear Powell,

   Thank you for sending me the script of Colonel Blimp which I am returning herewith. I think that the idea is excellent. It is a good story with both humour and pathos in it and is, of course, all the stronger for not being in the least unkind to Colonel Blimp, while at the same time putting your finger on his real shortcomings. These are, I think, most effectively handled. I hardly think you can improve on the form or the outline. I wish you every success with it and I am sure that you will indeed be successful.

   I should like to see it done very soon.

   Yours sincerely,
   Vansittart

LETTER FROM JACK BEDDINGTON[†]

Ministry of Information
26th May 1942

Dear Mr Powell,

'LIFE AND DEATH OF COLONEL BLIMP'

   I regret that I have not replied to your letter of May 12th before.

---

[*] Sir Robert Vansittart (1881–1957) was Permanent Under-Secretary at the Foreign Office from 1930 to 1938 and shared Churchill's view of the German threat. Powell had met him through Korda, when invited to direct a script by Vansittart, who was also an occasional poet and playwright. He was created a peer on his retirement in 1941.

[†] Jack Beddington, who had worked in advertising and created the popular Shell Guides before the war, was Head of the Film Division of the MoI and highly regarded by most filmmakers who had dealings with him.

Before we go any further, I shall be very grateful if we can see a full shooting script. We all feel that it is impossible to pass judgment on the scheme as it is before us at present. You know, none better, what a difference dialogue can make, quite apart from direction.*

Yours sincerely,

Jack Beddington

LETTER FROM SIR JAMES GRIGG†

War Office

22 May, 1942

Dear Mr Powell,

I have now had an opportunity of reading the narrative of 'The Life and Death of Colonel Blimp' and I have been considering very carefully whether it is the sort of film to which the War Office could give its support.

I am bound to say that I don't think it is. Its chief weakness seems to me that it revolves round a character that is more fictitious than real. I suppose it may be possible, if you look far enough, to find an officer who bears some resemblance to Major-General Candy, but I must confess that after three years in the War Office I have still to meet him. I cannot help thinking that at a time when public confidence in the Army and its leaders is justifiably increasing, it would be a pity to divert attention to a caricature. And after all Colonel Blimp *is* only a caricature!

---

* The 'scheme' in question is probably the 'Narrative', a 27-page synopsis produced in May 1942 ('to be regarded strictly on its practical merits for the purpose of preparation until the complete script is available'), or possibly the shorter 'Scheme', reproduced here at the end of the book ('Analysis of the Idea behind the Story of "Blimp"').

† Sir James Grigg (1890–1964) had been Permanent Secretary at the War Office before, in an unusual move, he was made Secretary of State in 1942 and found a Commons seat. A longstanding friend of Churchill's and renowned for his brusqueness, he remained at the War Office until 1945, then moved into industry.

I am sorry not to be more forthcoming, but, if you are really anxious to make a film about the modern Army, I think the best thing you can do is to get in touch with Kimberley and Lawson, the Directors of Army Kinematography and Public Relations respectively at the War Office, and discuss a suitable story with them. I know they will be very glad to help and, if you can find the right kind of story, they will see that you get the necessary facilities.

Yours sincerely,

P. J. Grigg

DRAFT LETTER FROM MICHAEL POWELL*

Dear Sir James Grigg,

I have already taken up a good deal of your time and I am sufficiently conscious of it to apologise for writing once more. I am very much obliged for your last letter but you have misstated the theme, which is as follows: 'Englishmen are by nature conservative, insular, unsuspicious, believers in good sportsmanship and anxious to believe the best of other people. These attractive virtues, which are, we hope, unchanging, can become absolute vices unless allied to a realistic acceptance of things as they are, in modern Europe and in Total War.'

If that isn't something worth saying I'd like to know what is!

This will be what the audience learns from the finished film, this is what we shall emphasise and I give you my word of honour that if you don't agree with me when you see the rough edition of the finished film then I will re-edit it and re-shoot it until you do.

We respect and understand your views about 'Colonel Blimp' and we shall change the title.

Yours sincerely,

MP

---

* Undated draft from Powell papers, which may be a reply to Grigg's letter of 22 May, or may refer to the other intervening communications.

War Office
June, 1942

Dear Mr Powell,

There is no question of your having bungled your approach. The trouble is that I find myself in complete disagreement with the basic idea underlying 'The Life and Death of Colonel Blimp.'

The theme, as I understand it, is in essence the struggle of the junior officer against the obstructiveness of the Blimps at the top and his subsequent metamorphosis into a Blimp himself. My objection to this conception of the Army is simply that it doesn't correspond to the facts. As a matter of fact the age limits for retirement in the Army are much lower than those obtaining in, for example, the Civil Service or the business world, and, if Colonel Blimp is to be found anywhere, it is not in the higher ranks of the Army but among officers who have been retired for thirty years or more.

I gather from your letter that one of your chief aims is to improve the reputation of the Army in America and Dominions. Can it be seriously suggested that the best way of achieving this is to make a film that revolves round a character like Colonel Blimp? To be quite frank I am getting rather tired of the theory that we can best enhance our reputation in the eyes either of our own people or the rest of the world by drawing attention to the faults which the critics attribute to us, especially when, as in the present case, the criticism no longer has any substance. In this case particularly it seems to me this policy will have an effect exactly contrary to what was intended and give the Blimp conception a new lease of life at a time when it is already dying from inanition.

I have not ventured to criticize the narrative of the film in detail because I gather that the synopsis you sent me is only intended to serve as a basis for discussion, but I must point out that it appears to me to contain a great many things which just couldn't happen in the Army. I daresay some of these could be omitted or rewritten without much difficulty, – although I'm not sure that some of the most improbable episodes aren't essential to your story – but I don't think it's any use going into questions of this kind because the real point of difference between us is the whole idea underlying the film. So long as this remains, I don't see what I can do to help.

Yours sincerely,
   P. J. Grigg

DRAFT LETTER FROM MICHAEL POWELL*

Dear Sir James Grigg,

In view of your letter of June 1, a copy of which was sent to the Ministry of Information, the Films Division have informed me that they cannot support my application for Laurence Olivier to play the leading part in the film. As the part has been written for Olivier and the production planned on a scale equal to his status as the most important English actor to-day this is a considerable blow to us. Apart from the financial loss involved there has been a great deal of initial work and preparation and a number of people have already been contracted and have refused other positions. In view of all this and of the reputation of Mr Pressburger and myself may I refer you to my letter of yesterday and ask you whether you will withdraw your objection to the film on the clear understanding that we shall revise the script and prepare the production in collaboration with a Technical Adviser who will be approved by you and that we shall submit the completed film first to the War Office for

* Undated draft from the Powell papers, sometime after 1 June and presumably before 25 June, when the MoI wrote refusing to release Olivier for the film (see below). This may in fact be the draft of Powell's letter of 3 June mentioned in the Ministry of Information report (p. 33 below).

approval or criticism. This was the procedure we adopted on 'One of our aircraft is missing' with the Air Ministry, who were not dissatisfied. May I ask you to give us an immediate decision as I owe it to my financial partners to involve them in as little loss as possible.

I am ready to refer you to any number of character witnesses if you should feel that you need them, but I hope that you will agree that this is a practical solution of the difficulty and the only fair one, may I say it, to men as eminent in our own work as we are.

MINISTRY OF INFORMATION

THE LIFE AND DEATH OF SUGAR CANDY

REPORT

1. This film script raises a great many points some of which are controversial. Although this does not prevent the Ministry from supporting the film the very fact that controversy is aroused suggests that the support is bound to be more limited than if the film was cast iron for all markets and in all circumstances. We should certainly hesitate to prevent the expression of opinion even if this opinion appeared ambiguous to a minority, but we must be very careful not to appear to stand behind and support a film which can be taken in the wrong way by a fair proportion of people. The response to '49th Parallel' is interesting in this connection. It stimulated in two issues of *Variety* correspondence showing that in America there is the same controversial attitude as there was here. I think on the whole those who considered '49th Parallel' deleterious underestimated the innate good sense of both the British and American public: but it may well be true that there are certain people in certain places and in certain

31

conditions who are influenced the wrong way by such a film, whereas it is very difficult to imagine an audience which could take 'Target For Tonight' in any other way but that intended – although even here we understand that in the Near East the film was criticised for not showing a thousand bombers.

2. There are two points at issue in considering General Candy. One is the Blimp theme and two is the 'German' theme.

3. Before analysing these it may be useful to classify this type of picture. It is, I take it, a drama of ideas rather than of characters. It has a certain element of satire and though it has not the special originality of a Bernard Shaw play it is not at all unlike one. In a drama of ideas it is legitimate to put forward what one might call minority ideas – to be devil's advocate – and then in the end to direct the audience towards the 'correct' idea which the author wishes them to hold. If the author is not very clear as to what this is and if he is not passionately convinced about it there is danger of the moral purpose of the story and its audience-holding power being submerged in ambiguous quicksands.

4. The superficial story of the film is about an elderly man with conservative ideas who in a flash of self-revelation sees how this came about and acknowledges that the future is with the youthful rebel. This is a simple and satisfactory point of departure which need raise no objections. In spite of the fact that the word blimp has been used the character of Clive Candy is only very mildly blimpish. He is handled, especially towards the end, with very considerable sympathy and at no point is there any serious attack upon him. Characteristics of blimpery are not analysed very deeply, in fact the *particular* Clive Candy has weakened the authors' message about blimpery. With regard to his age and the verisimilitude of his actions I think there will be no difficulty in meeting the

objections of the Secretary of State for War, and my advice would be that we should try to interpret the story to him and take notice of his specific objections and thus overcome or temper his disapproval. His letter to Mr Powell makes the point that it is bad propaganda policy to draw attention to a national failing which has now been corrected. This may sometimes be the case, but in this particular instance I see no harm and in fact positive good in a film made in this country which says that we have had our fair share of blimpism but that we are self-critical and, as the film shows, have already relegated it to the scrapheap. Of course this can be done without showing the blimp in action but it is a quite valid method to set up an Aunt Sally and then knock it down.

5. The over complication of ideas is much more dangerous. The authors attack the British outlook on life as expressed in the terms of sportsmanship and fair play. They show this in contrast to German (not Nazi) efficiency and ruthlessness. They suggest in the end that Germans can only be defeated with their own weapons. Powell's letter of June 3rd reveals that he had not seriously analysed the full implications of the obviously dialectical position in which efficiency in waging war must be combined with the civilised qualities which are part of our tradition. The script exaggerates the fair play idea to the point of ridicule and does not show those ways in which it has a constructive value. For instance, in the 1917 sequence, Candy fails to get information from the German prisoners: the tougher personality is more successful. It would have been equally 'true' if an instance had been selected in which humanity in dealing with individuals had in fact been more efficient than threats. For instance, Candy as a growing Blimp might have used threats which failed while a younger British officer working on more intelligent lines might have been successful. This is one of the scenes which suggests confusion of mind on the part of the authors, unless

they merely wished to say that we must become like Germans before we can win the war. If this is what they wished to say – and I don't think it is – then it is a film we can only deplore. It is more likely that their own minds are in conflict and they have rather wantonly played with ideas – some of which are a trifle 'daring' – in order to stimulate people to think or (a less generous interpretation) inject sensational elements for Box Office purposes.

6. There are a great number of scenes which directly or indirectly are critical of the British attitude to life and sympathetic to the German. One cannot say that the judgment is given for Germany, but undoubtedly there is an indirect sympathy. This might well be a legitimate thing to do as a contribution to our understanding of the enemy, both now and after the war. In the absence of a simply defined official policy we cannot say that this film is wrong, but at the same time as it stands at the moment our publicly known support of the film might cause misapprehension.

7. Let me take some examples:

1) THEO. Theo is the most fully realised character in the story. Owing to his sufferings and his contrast to Candy he appears to have a wisdom and a sensitivity denied to any other of the characters except Edith – and it is significant that Edith marries him and that throughout the film the German has this superiority over the Englishman – he won the woman while the Englishman continually foozled his approach. Admittedly Theo is anti-Nazi, but in his speech to the Tribunal he appears only very weakly anti-Nazi. This is no doubt all in the interests of 'truth'. Whereas the final superior truth is used for Theo, exaggeration is used for Clive.

2) PRO-BOER PROPAGANDA. In order to justify Candy's journey to Berlin the story of British atrocities in South Africa is brought to light. The authors undoubtedly want to

34

impress on the public the fact that forty years ago the Germans believed these stories. In the middle of the war and making a film which may be shown to world opinion I think this is a very dangerous thing to do. From the story point of view there is no need to describe in detail what we are supposed to have done to Boer women.

3) DUELLING. An ambiguous attitude is taken here. The Germans are shown over-serious about duelling but at the same time certain thoughts are thrown out, such as the following: 'One of the advantages of possessing duelling scars was that the natives of Africa look with more respect upon white men who bear them than upon those who don't.' It is true that the speaker is ironical, but the danger is that the context may be forgotten a week after seeing the film and this little germ of doubt retained.

4) BRITISH IN BERLIN. On page 51 the British people who have lost their jobs in Germany are seen cluttering the British Embassy 'they are a lost looking bunch of people'. This is the kind of visual impression which tends to put the Germans on top.

5) COLENSO. Edith, who is for the purposes of this film the spokesman of the authors, suggests that good manners cost us the defeats of the South African war whereas a little common sense and bad manners would have prevented a war. This strikes one of the major themes which is never really developed beyond this over simplification. The theme is followed up in the speeches of Theo when he returns to Germany and at many other points: there is never any suggestion that there is a special efficiency which arises out of the British tradition.

6) GERMANS THE MUSIC. The scenes at the prisoners of war camp no doubt show our kindliness in handling Germans but very subtly put them in the superior psychological position – their love of music and their refusal to fraternise with the British.

All these things total up into a film which asks for sympathy for the German (if not the Nazi) ideal. There is no serious distinction between Germanity and Nazidom and although the total tone of the picture is not anti-British nor Pro-German it is to a certain extent wantonly provocative. This will not harm the British public, but may give ammunition to the critics of this country in America and Russia.

Only if the writers have a passionate dynamic belief in our cause and character can they avoid falling into the traps which paradox and the drama of ideas often set. Whether these writers can do this at this late stage I don't know, but if they can see this point and are willing to clarify their intentions and weigh their words we should do all in our power to help them, as the greater part of the film is of very high quality and capable of containing an important message.

(signed) R. B. 8th June 1942
I agree   (signed) J[ack] B[eddington] 9th June 1942

MEMORANDUM FROM THE ARCHERS

16th June 1942

From: Michael Powell and Emeric Pressburger
To: Films' Division, Ministry of Information
Subject: Report on the screenplay of 'The Life and Death of Sugar Candy'.

1. Everyone must, of course, agree with the opening remarks: the majority of films made in Britain and America are self-admiring ones and they are easy to make. Their purpose can be seen and their effect can be judged. But it is also possible to make films for future audiences and for future occasions. It is true that, two years ago, anyone who made a film of 'There Shall be no Night', an anti-Russian subject, would

have been applauded, although a year later the film would have been suppressed. But it is equally true that '49th Parallel' which took two years to get on to American screens, is even more timely now than at any other period. This film, 'The Life and Death of Sugar Candy', will be finished by Christmas and distributed by the Spring: its purpose is to tell people what happened after the last war was won, and our reason is that we think that the winning of this war will be in sight by then.

The recent public discussions in America, mostly conducted in the columns of 'Variety' have shown a growing opinion that the Germans are not to be ridiculed. We would like to add to this our point that, if we make films in which Germans are taken seriously, it does not mean that we wish to make them heroes. It has never been the policy of this country to pretend that Germany would be finally defeated by our superior intelligence and our ability to make fools of the Germans but only by our 'blood and sweat and tears'.

2. It is stated that there are two distinct themes in our story: the Blimp 'theme', and the German 'theme'; but if Blimpery were not a danger, in prosecuting and in winning the war with Germany, we would not be interested in it at the present time.

3. We are challenged to state clearly the ideas towards which the audiences are to be directed.

What are the chief qualities of Clive Candy? They are the qualities of the average Englishman: an anxiety to believe the best of other people: Fairness in fighting, based upon games: Fairness after the fight is over: A natural naïveté engendered by class, insularity and the permeability of the English language.

We think these are splendid virtues: so splendid that, in order to preserve them, it is worth while shelving them until we have won the war.

37

4. The next section of the Report is helpful and positive; and we are grateful for it.

5. We hold the British way of life in such esteem that we show a German, who has only briefly been brought into contact with it, become homesick for England because he met with sportsmanship and fair play there.

   We don't say that Germans can only be defeated by their own weapons, but that they only understand their own language.

   Regarding 'efficiency' in waging war combined with the civilised qualities which are part of our tradition, this is exactly how Major Van Zijl behaves in the sequence in question: the Germans would have shot the prisoners. (We shall underline this point)

6. We resent intensely any suggestion that we are sympathetic to the German way of life.
   a) In the Germany of 1902 we show the idiotic public behaviour of officers, students and civilians in a Berlin Café;
   b) We show the solemn German pride in a barbaric duelling code of honour, incomprehensible to any civilised person; and we show very plainly how the English in Berlin at that period regarded this nonsense.
   c) We provide the Germans with a hero to their taste in the shape of Kaunitz, who would have been gladly shot by both the British and the Boers;
   d) We provide a sardonic comment on the morbidity of the whole nation by showing typical, thick-necked, brutalised, scarred German officers listening raptly to the music of Beethoven and Schubert;
   e) We show a German officer refusing to shake hands after the fight is over;
   f) We show German officers repaying the trust of the English by starting to plan another war, as their train pulls

out for Germany in 1919.

g) And finally we show an old and disillusioned German officer who prefers being a refugee in this country to being a General in his own. (We shall make this even stronger in the script)

7. We would like to answer the examples quoted:

1) We admit, of course, that Theo is a sympathetic character. So is Kurt in 'The Watch on the Rhine', and Vogel in '49th Parallel';

We agree that his character is too complex in the first episode: for example his disapproval of duelling clashes with his later behaviour, so we shall cut it. He has the obviously superior romantic attraction over Clive of being a foreigner: and Theo asks her and Clive doesn't.

2) We agree that the Boer atrocities need handling with care, but in view of present German propaganda in South Africa it would be foolish to ignore the stories altogether; and good counter-propaganda to show the reactions of a typical British officer who has been there.

3) We shall take care to make our opinion of duelling very plain.

4) It is debatable whether to show, say, Polish refugees is to belittle Poland; *but we will cut the scene.* *

5) We shall cut this speech;

6) We have indicated above how we shall treat the symphony concert plainly enough to show that the intention is not pro-German.

We hope these answers have helped to clarify our intentions: they have certainly helped us further to clarify our own thoughts: our beliefs and our loyalty to our common cause cannot be questioned after the work we have already done.

---

* These words in italics were handwritten.

PERSONAL LETTER FROM S. G. GATES

Ministry of Information
25th June 1942

Dear Mr Powell,

I am sending you herewith an official letter about 'Sugar Candy'. I am very sorry to have to administer this blow because I know something of the amount of time and thought which you and Mr Pressburger have given to this film and I recognise that from an entertainment point of view it would have proved very effective.

Although I can hold out no hope of our altering our decision, I should be only too pleased to discuss with you, if you wish, the reasons which have led us to it.

Yours sincerely,
S. G. Gates

LETTER FROM MINISTRY OF INFORMATION

Ministry of Information
25th June 1942

Dear Mr Powell,

Since your conversation with General Lawson concerning 'Sugar Candy' we have again given most careful and sympathetic consideration to all the questions arising in connection with this film and have consulted with General Lawson concerning them.

Much as I regret having to say this, I am afraid that we cannot bring ourselves to feel that the public interest would be served by the production of the film as it stands, nor do we see how it could be rendered of positive value from the point of view of national propaganda, by alterations in the dialogue or in the treatment of individual sequences.

The Ministry cannot, therefore, see its way to recommend the temporary release from the Fleet Air Arm of Laurence Olivier to enable him to play in the film; nor would it be able to recommend the provision of Service facilities.

Yours sincerely,

S. G. Gates

LETTER FROM BRENDAN BRACKEN*

Ministry of Information

7 July 1942

Dear Powell,

The pressure of work in preparation for Tuesday's debate on propaganda has prevented my giving as much time to your script as I should have liked. But I have read enough to know first that it would make an amusing and very entertaining film, and second that it would not make the sort of film which this Ministry could properly support. I fear that I must confirm the view already taken by Mr Gates and the Director-General.

I see no prospect of our being able to help you out over Laurence Olivier. I do not think that there is anybody in the Admiralty who would be ready to authorise his release for this film without a very clear assurance from us that it is in the national interest.

I realise that this is a great disappointment to you personally but I am sure it will not diminish your boundless enthusiasm. There is still a lot of work which you and the Films Division of this Ministry can do together.

Yours sincerely,

Brendan Bracken

---

* Brendan Bracken (1901–58), often regarded as Churchill's protégé, became his fourth and last Minister of Information of the war in 1941. He worked closely with the Director-General, Cyril Radcliffe, to help foster the war aims as laid down by Churchill. This letter to Powell implies that he was perhaps better disposed to *Blimp* than 'the old man'. See also Bracken's memoranda in the next section.

Secret

The following memoranda and extracts from Cabinet Minutes (held in file Premier 4 14/15 in the Public Records Office) were not available for consultation until 1972. Churchill's personal opposition to *Blimp* had long been known, but this was the first concrete evidence of his efforts to prevent it from being made, shown and finally exported.

8.9.42

PRIME MINISTER

I attach, as directed, a note on the Blimp film which is in course of being produced and which I think it of the utmost importance to get stopped.

PJG [Grigg]

THE LIFE AND DEATH OF COLONEL BLIMP

1. The theme of the film is, according to the producer, the struggle of the junior officer in the Army against the obstructiveness of the Blimps at the top and his subsequent metamorphosis into a Blimp himself. The film begins with a collision between a young officer of today and Major-General Clive Candy, aged 66. The occasion is a Home Guard exercise for the defence of London. The young man starts his attack several hours before the exercise is due to begin and surprises the opposing general while the latter is still in his Turkish bath. This is supposed to be an example of

ruthless initiative. The film then goes back to 1902 when the General himself was a subaltern with a similar intolerance of his elders and impetuous enough to embarrass the British Embassy in Germany by fighting a duel with a German officer. Then it traces his progress across the years in various parts of the British Empire, and so to the war of 1914–18 and the post-war years. In the war of 1914–18 Candy's playing the game according to the rules is contrasted with the greater realism of a South-African officer. Candy's attitude between the wars is a lack of comprehension as to why the Germans cannot realise that they were fairly and squarely beaten and there is no reason why they should not make and remain friends. A confused love interest (with three different women) also complicates the story at various intervals.

2. The producer claims that the film is intended as a tribute to the toughness and keenness of the new Army in Britain and shows how far they have progressed from the Blimpery of the pre-war Army. From this point of view he urges that it would be valuable propaganda for the U.S.A. and the Dominions because in showing that we are conscious of any faults which we may possess, we are telling the rest of the world that the faults are being eliminated.

3. The War Office have refused to give their support to the film in any way on the ground that it would give the Blimp conception of the Army officer a new lease of life at a time when it is already dying from inanition. Whatever the film makes of the spirit of the young soldier of today, the fact remains that it focuses attention on an imaginary type of Army officer which has become an object of ridicule to the general public. In the opening scheme [sic] Candy is shown as Blimp himself complete with towel and everything. Whatever it may do elsewhere the film has made a character built up by twenty years of brilliant cartooning into a figure of fun, and there is the inescapable suggestion that such a man is a type

or at any rate an example of those who have risen to high command in the Army in the period preceding this war.

4. There is the further objection that the Germans in the film are depicted as stiff and over-regimented in peace and as little more than very intense realists in war. The thug element in the make-up of the German soldier is ignored and indeed the suggestion is that if we were exactly like the Germans we should be better soldiers.

5. As stated above, the War Office have refused all facilities for the film, but production is still going on at Denham and the Minister of Information knows of no way in which it can be stopped. Steps have been taken, however, to bring home to the person financing the film the fact that it is viewed with disfavour by the War Office and that no Army facilities will be available. Whether anything will come of this indirect approach is at present uncertain.

(PRIME MINISTER'S PERSONAL MINUTE M.357/2)

MINISTER OF INFORMATION

Pray propose to me the measures necessary to stop this foolish production* before it gets any further. I am not prepared to allow propaganda detrimental to the morale of the Army, and I am sure the Cabinet will take all necessary action. Who are the people behind it?

W.S.C.

10.9.42

[handwritten] * The Blimp Film.

Ministry of Information
Malet St w.c.1

The Colonel Blimp Film

Your minute No. M.357/2

This film is being produced by Archer Films Ltd, a company entirely owned by Mr Michael Powell and Mr Emmerich Pressburger. I understand that the production is financed by General Film Distributors Ltd, the head of which is Mr Joseph [*sic*] Rank.

The Ministry of Information has no power to suppress the film. We have been unsuccessful in discouraging it by the only means open to us: that is, by withholding Government facilities for its production.

I am advised that in order to stop it the Government would need to assume powers of a very far-reaching kind. They could hardly be less than powers to suppress all films, even those based on imaginary stories, on grounds not of their revealing information to the enemy but of their expressing harmful or misguided opinions. Moreover it would be illogical for the Government to insist on a degree of control over films which it does not exercise over other means of expression, such as books or newspaper articles. Nothing less, therefore, than the imposition of a compulsory censorship of opinion upon all means of expression would meet the case, and I am certain that this could not be done without provoking infinite protest.

If you or the War Office were to let it be known to Mr Rank that it is your wish that the film should be dropped, I feel sure that it would be dropped. But I do not think that any approach of this kind should come from the Ministry of Information. As the Department responsible for Censorship, the Ministry is liable to be suspected of abusing its Censorship powers and requests from us frequently meet with a resistance which they

45

would not encounter if made by a Department that has no connexion with Censorship.

B[rendan] B[racken]
15 September 1942

(PRIME MINISTER'S PERSONAL MINUTE M.381/2)

MINISTER OF INFORMATION

We should act not on the grounds of 'expressing harmful or misguided opinions' but on the perfectly precise point of 'undermining the discipline of the Army'. You and the Secretary of State should bring the matter before the Cabinet on Monday, [*marginal note:* This was done] when I have no doubt any special authority you may require will be given you. The Ministry of Information is the seat of the Censorship, and consequently you are the channel for any Cabinet decision on the subject.

W.S.C.
17.9.42

[*handwritten*] S of S for War to see both minutes.

WAR CABINET 126 (42)
Monday 21st September 1942, 5.30 pm

[*marginal note:* Film of 'Colonel Blimp']

7. The Secretary of State for War said that a film about 'Colonel Blimp' was being made. Facilities had been asked for from the War Office. These had been refused, on the ground that the film was likely to bring ridicule upon the Army. The producers had, nevertheless, proceeded with the making of the film, which was now at an advanced stage.

There was no existing Defence Regulation under which the film could be suppressed. He understood that the Minister of

46

Information was averse from taking the very wide powers which would be necessary to stop this film.

More recently, however, an approach had been made to the financier who was backing the film, who had agreed that, when the film had reached the 'rough cut stage' it should be seen by representatives of the War Office and the Ministry of Information; and if they took the view that the film was undesirable he would arrange for it to be withdrawn.

General agreement was expressed with the view that it was impossible to allow a film to be produced which was liable to undermine the discipline of the Army; and satisfaction was expressed that this could be achieved by the friendly arrangement outlined by the Secretary of State for War.

WAR CABINET 67 (43)
10 May 1943, 5.30 pm

Film of 'Colonel Blimp' Prev ref . . .

4. The Sec of State for War said that the film had now been seen by representatives of the WO and the MoI, who took the view that it was unlikely to attract much attention or to have any undesirable consequences on the discipline of the Army. In the circumstances, he had reached the conclusion that the right plan was to allow the film to be shown.

The War Cabinet –
Endorsed this view.

INTERLUDE:
FROM THE *EVENING STANDARD* DIARY

This Diary item in the Evening Standard *on 28 June suggests that government departments reported their views on* Blimp *after its Odeon Leicester Square première on 10 June, when the*

Secretary of State for War had already told the Cabinet that it was 'cleared' after a screening before 10 May. See the Low cartoon which mocked this vetting process (p. 1).

Whitehall has decided – whether officially or unofficially is not quite clear, but the decision will be effective – that the film of Colonel Blimp is not for the present to be exported for exhibition abroad. I am able to give what I am assured is the inside story of the ban.

Mr Churchill was at the first night of the film and seems to have formed some pretty definite opinions about it. He talked to his colleagues in the Cabinet and to Whitehall officials. Then almost every Government department sent delegations to view the film and gave their own impressions.

When all the reports were in, they were solemnly collated and examined. Then some highup made the decision that it would not be advisable to let the film go out as representing the British Army.

Public attention had mainly been focused on the picture of the British officer drawn in the film, and of his extreme conservatism. But the veto decision was not made on this point at all. It was made on a point that few people would have thought of.

In the film a young army officer wins a victory over Home Guard Colonel Blimp by fighting a 'battle' some hours before the appointed zero hour. This, says Whitehall, would advertise abroad that we countenance the ethics of the Japs at Pearl Harbour!

Thus are great decisions made.

MoI
PRIME MINISTER

Mr Arthur Rank, who is the Chairman of Gaumont British, is asking if this Ministry can give him a definite decision about the export of the film 'Colonel Blimp'. So far we have been with-holding the facilities for export by air which would normally be accorded to any British film of standing.

Is it still your wish that this film should not go abroad? We have no legal power to stop it, and indeed the statements appearing in the newspapers saying that it has been banned probably only serve to advertise it.

My advice is that the film should be allowed to go. At a time when the prestige of the British higher Command and of the British fighting man stands higher in the world than it has ever done, I think the circulation of this evident fantasy presents no dangers at all. But if you still feel strongly that it should not go abroad, I will try to find means of continuing our illegal ban.

B.B.

9 July 1943

(PRIME MINISTER'S PERSONAL MINUTE M.459/3)

MINISTER OF INFORMATION

I think you should certainly stop it going abroad as long as you possibly can.

W.S.C.

11.7.43

MoI

PRIME MINISTER

You asked in your Minute No. M.459/3 that this Ministry should stop the film 'Colonel Blimp' from going abroad as long as we possibly could.

This we have so far managed to do by the unorthodox expedient of refusing the normal facilities for transport abroad by air. But even if we were able to persist in this expedient, we could not either by legal or illegal action prevent the film from going abroad by other means.

We have now had an official letter from Mr Rank, the producer of the film, informing us that he would like to show it in America and in the Empire. As the film is so boring I cannot believe that it will do any harm abroad to anyone except the company which made it. [And as this Ministry has no reason to protect the company from the consequences of its follies, I should propose to tell Mr Rank that he may make his own arrangements accordingly.]*

B.B.

23 July 1943

(PRIME MINISTER'S PERSONAL MINUTE M.523/3)

MINISTER OF INFORMATION

I do not agree with this surrender. Will you please discuss the matter with me. If necessary we must take more powers.

W.S.C.

25.7.43

MoI

PRIME MINISTER

Your minute No. M.523/3 of 25 July.

The word 'surrender' is not in our vocabulary! As a result of our illegal ban on this wretched film, 'Colonel Blimp' has received a wonderful advertisement from the Government. It is now enjoying an extensive run in the suburbs and in all sorts of places there are notices – 'See the banned film!'

If we had left that dull film alone it would probably have

---

* The section in square brackets was marked 'A' on the original, and is referred to in the handwritten note below.

proved an unprofitable undertaking, but by the time the Government have finished with it there is no knowing what profits it will have earned.

B.B.

5 August 1943

[*Slip headed by PM's seal, handwritten, n.d.*]

Mr Rowan
Please see 'A'. A reply to Mr Rank from Mr Bracken is now outstanding; Mr Bracken however is in no hurry and told me not to telegraph about it.

J.P.

[*in another hand (possibly Churchill's):* Leave it for the time being.]

PRIME MINISTER

I am not clear about your minute 'Leave it for the time being'. As you will see from Flag A, Mr Bracken has received an official letter from Mr Rank informing him that Mr Rank would like to show 'Colonel Blimp' in America and the Empire. On this Mr Bracken minuted:

'And as the Ministry has no reason for trying to protect the company from the consequences of its follies, I should propose to tell Mr Rank that he may make his own arrangements accordingly.'

May I now be informed that you approve this?

TLR

15.8.43

[*handwritten:* No. I am obstructing. Leave it till Mr B arrives.]

MOST SECRET CYPHER TELEGRAM/From: Air Ministry. To: Quadrant, 19 Aug 1943

Following for Sendall from Hodge.
We have had a further letter from Mr Rank requesting facilities for the export of the film 'Colonel Blimp'. He says it has broken all previous box-office records for the Odeon Circuit of cinemas. In view of this it is becoming practically impossible to maintain our illegal ban. May we have directions?

MOST SECRET CYPHER TELEGRAM/From: Quadrant. To: War Cabinet Offices London.
WELFARE No. 413 25 August 1943

Following for Hodge, Ministry of Information from Sendall.
Your CONCRETE 368.
Approval to release 'Blimp' has now been secured.

MINUTE OF THE EXECUTIVE BOARD OF
THE MINISTRY OF INFORMATION

FILM: THE LIFE AND DEATH OF COLONEL BLIMP

Mr Gates reported that the general objections which had been raised to the export of this film, with which Mr Rank had courteously complied, had now been withdrawn. He inquired whether any special objections now remained. Mr Grubb recalled that exception had been taken to one or two sequences in the film by certain regional specialists; and Mr Gates was invited to consider whether these should be represented to Mr Rank.

MoI 21 Sept 1943
[To: 10 Downing St, T. L. Rowan]

Dear Rowan,

I am returning your file about the release of 'Colonel Blimp' which somehow or other came into my hands while we were in America.

As you know, the Prime Minister finally authorised Mr Bracken to withdraw his ban on the export of this film.

Yours sincerely,
B C Sendall

[*handwritten:* I didn't; but P.A. TLR 22.9]

Press

The following selection of newspaper reviews, dating from the film's original release in 1943 and its reissue in restored form in 1985, give some impression of the main lines of critical response.

SUNDAY TIMES, 17 SEPT 1943

The Life and Death of Colonel Blimp, a film in Technicolor, written, produced and directed by Michael Powell and Emeric Pressburger, is like the conversation of a clever and plausible talker with the gift of the gab; that is to say, it holds the attention, it is interlarded with excellent jokes, it has patches of feeling and patches of making do, and it goes on for a long time. In another respect, too, it resembles the wily talker: it persuades its audience by appearing to advance one argument while edging in the direction of another.

The Powell–Pressburger piece is, on the face of it, about a character long dear (in the economic sense) to us all. The Blimp with whom a great comic talent has familiarised us is not an amiable but a ferocious force. He is a man in whom the sluggish or reactionary cliché is, not the symbol of fidelity to a tradition once estimable, but the natural expression of belief in a policy of death. Blimp creates the circumstances favourable to a war and then refuses to fight it. But the Blimp of this intellectually humane film is an honourable man, an incurable dreamer, a soldier holding in the midst of a totalitarian war to the rules of a game which to his romantic, if imperceptive, mind was never

54

deplorable. The story is thus not an attack on an old enemy, but a defence, reasoned and often touching, of an old friend.

Its hero (for we have no cause to refuse him the title) begins as a likeable young V.C. with enough enterprise to nose beyond the business of soldiering, but not enough wit to succeed in his adventure. He grows into a middle-aged general still honour-bound, but pursuing the shade of the romance which earlier eluded him; he ends as a charming old stranded walrus, pathetically humiliated by his inability to understand or accept the new all-in techniques. The moral of his career is left uncertain: with one voice the film censures his beliefs, with another protests that they are the beliefs of all upright men. The portrait presented, in fact, is the portrait of almost any decent, slow-witted, romantic Englishman, with this difference, that not all decent slow-witted Englishmen would show the humanity towards a German refugee shown by this Colonel Blimp.

These doubts expressed, the film is to be recommended for its study of a curious and endearing English phenomenon. Sometimes the dialogue is presented by a technique unnecessarily static, but more often, particularly in the early Berlin scenes, there are passages of enchanting satire; and the acting is generally first-rate. Roger Livesey, whose make-up in the late sequences is brilliant, gives the hero exactly the right air of devil-may-care rigidity; Deborah Kerr plays three parts with vivacity and discretion; and Anton Walbrook, as the German, acts better than ever before on the screen.

Dilys Powell

OBSERVER, 13 JUNE 1943

The Life and Death of Colonel Blimp, by which, we are solemnly assured in an advertisement, 'All entertainment, past, present and future, will be judged,' doesn't really deserve such a tough ordeal. It isn't as mediocre as all that. In fact, compared with most of the entertainment we get today, its standard is remarkably high. From the craftsman's point of view, it is a crisp, clean, workmanlike job. The dialogue is sensible; the Technicolor is unobtrusive; there are moments of acute imaginative perception; and the acting by Roger Livesey, Anton Walbrook and Deborah Kerr is good. You may not like it, but you must respect it as a work of quality.

'Blimp's' worst fault – apart from its title and its length, which is two-and-three-quarter hours and quite absurd – is an unclarity of purpose. It is a handsome piece. It is frequently a moving piece. But what is it *about*? Oh, I know what it is ostensibly about. During a Home Guard exercise a zealous young N.C.O., anticipating the scheduled war by six hours, captures the opposing brigadier in his Turkish bath. He insults the brigadier, his stomach, and his moustache. The brigadier promptly replies by pushing him into the swimming-pool. During the time they remain under water (2½ hours) the brigadier's lifestory is recalled. You see him as a young V.C., a Guards officer of the '90s. You see his impetuous journey to Berlin, to scotch rumours of British atrocities against the Boers. You see his duel with a young Uhlan officer, who wins his sweetheart but becomes his friend. You see their friendship broken and restored after the first World War. You see it renewed in the present war, when the Uhlan is a fugitive from the Nazi regime and the brigadier is retired for his reactionary views. You see the old man widowed, bombed out, and left alone, save for his M.T.C. driver and his Uhlan friend: he makes, it is true, the cover of *Picture Post*, but his BBC Postscript is cancelled in favour of Mr Priestley.

As the story of a forty years' friendship, as the case history of two men who love the same feminine type wherever she appears (for Miss Deborah Kerr trebles the parts of the M.T.C. driver, Mr Walbrook's and Mr Livesey's wife), *Blimp* is cleancut, sympathetic and true. But what is it *really* about? Don't tell me this colossal, considered affair is just a lovely romance. The enormous care taken with the film indicates that it has something much bigger to say, something it is burning to say. Three theories present themselves. *Blimp* indicates (*a*) that dear old sentimental Britain will always muddle through; (*b*) that an ex-Prussian officer advocating the bombing of hospitals, the ruthless destruction of women and children, is the right man to teach us how to wage modern war; and (*c*) that the experience of age and the functionalism of youth can be sensibly combined. 'A' has nothing to support it except Roger Livesey's winning acting. 'B' seems to have the script on its side. 'C' is my own idea, and I'm still all for 'C'. But A, B, C, or X, Y, Z, clarity is surely the thing. *The Life and Death of Colonel Blimp* will have to profess itself much more openly before it becomes a measuring stick for Shakespeare.

C. A. Lejeune

EVENING STANDARD, 12 JUNE 1943

He is not called Colonel Blimp in the film, and he is evidently a rather distant relative of David Low's cartoon character (a cadet branch of the family, perhaps). Thus, the title of the picture is misleading.

The hero is Clive Candy, an old Harrovian who has won the Victoria Cross in the Boer War. We see him spending his leave in Berlin in an unauthorised attempt to counteract anti-British propaganda. In an amusing café scene, Clive insults the German army. A duel is arranged. In the selection of an opponent, the lot falls on Theo Kretschmar-Schuldorff, a mild, pleasant Uhlan officer. The preliminaries to the sabre match make a witty and dramatic sequence.

Meanwhile, British diplomacy has found an official pretext for the duel in the startled person of Edith Hunter, an attractive English governess, who was with Clive in the café. Edith is officially requested to visit the nursing home where both Clive and Theo are recovering from sabre cuts. The duellists become friends for life. Theo marries Edith, Clive returns to England, realising too late that he also is in love with her.

Instead of a possession, Edith becomes an obsession. Twice afterwards Clive is attracted by girls who remind him of Edith.

Clive loses Theo's friendship in 1918 when the Uhlan officer becomes a prisoner of war in England, but regains it when Theo returns to this country as an anti-Hitlerite refugee. It is Theo who comforts Clive when General Candy, V.C., is no longer considered of use to his country.

Two weaknesses must be noted at this point. First, Clive Candy's supposed Blimpishness resides in the fact that he is 'captured' in a Turkish bath several hours before the time arranged for a Home Guard exercise. Now there is more than one good reason why such exercises must begin at the official zero hour if they are to have any value. Nothing would be easier or more pointless than to 'capture' a Home Guard before he left his office.

Second, the Turkish bath sequence is shown at the beginning of the picture as well as at the end. This device is unjustified, especially in a picture that runs for 2¾ hours.

There is much on the credit side, however. Roger Livesey is thoroughly likeable as Clive Candy. He 'ages' astonishingly well. Anton Walbrook is at his best as the German. Deborah Kerr is delightful in the three roles of Edith Hunter and the girls who resembled her.

Michael Powell and Emeric Pressburger, who made the film, have maintained their high standard of dialogue and direction. Technicolor is used with excellent effect. This is not a great picture, but it is exceptionally good entertainment.

Paul Trench

The Life and Death of Col. Blimp made me feel like a character from 'Itma'. I go – I come back! – I like it – I don't like it . . . First, then, the ha'pence of praise before the kicks of criticism.

It is the best Technicolor yet turned out by a British firm. Michael Powell and Emeric Pressburger have done a good job of work, and Hollywood will have to look to its laurels if this goes on. Many of the shots had the quality of beautiful paintings, one, particularly, of a café in Berlin, might have come from the brush of Renoir. It was full of sparkling light and gay atmosphere.

It is excellent entertainment, despite its long-drawn-out story of the Colonel's indiscretions in Berlin as a young officer fresh from the Boer War, right down through the trench warfare in the last war to his War Office appointment in this war. Roger Livesey's performance, as Blimp, is as good, and better, than anything we have seen on the screen for a long time. It can, without exaggeration, be called a classic piece of acting, on either stage or screen. No one could have been better, and everyone concerned owes him gratitude, for if he had been a flop no Technicolor, nor patriotic intentions could have saved the piece. Anton Walbrook, too, was excellent as an Uhlan officer. It was not his fault, but that of the author of the story, when he turned into a refugee intellectual at the end of the film, and cluttered up the place with long meanderings. Deborah Kerr as the three women in the Colonel's life knocks spots off all the glamour girls that ever came from Hollywood. It would have to be a bad film, indeed, that obscured her shining brilliance and her sure knowledge of what she is doing. She has been an asset to the British screen ever since she stepped on to her first set.

Now for the kicks. It is too long, and I don't care if it did cost twenty-five million pounds (or something like that), that's nothing to do with the point. A short film costing tuppence might knock it sideways. It is too long, moreover, because no

one decided *exactly* what they wanted to say with it! I don't
know now, and I have thought about it hard, whether the point
was that Old Blimp was a jolly good sort and ought to have been
given a good job in *this* war, or that he was a feeble old buffer
but SWEET, and good enough for the Home Guard. After all,
the H.G. is not a dustbin. Or even whether David Low needs
counteracting, and we can now realise that Old Blimp is a
DAMN GOOD SORT and feudal England is not so bad. Or
Tories are really gentlemen and sound at bottom! You can pay
your money and take your choice. And all that is a grave fault in
a propaganda picture, which is what 'Blimp' is, or supposed to
be.

Worth seeing though, if only those advertising blokes would
stop screaming their heads off – '*All* entertainment will be
judged by it,' they sob hysterically, till we long to choke them or
determine NEVER to see it.

[Unattributed]

THE TIMES, 19 JULY 1985

For the first time in over 40 years the complete version of *The
Life and Death of Colonel Blimp* may be seen in a glittering new
colour print restored by the National Film Archive, with the
assistance of the Rank Organisation and the Sainsbury Charitable Trust. Had Churchill had his way the film would never
have seen the light of day at all. 'Pray propose to me the
measures necessary to stop this foolish production', he minuted
Brendan Bracken, Minister of Information, in 1943. 'I am not
prepared to allow propaganda detrimental to the morale of the
Army . . . Who are the people behind it?'

They were in fact Michael Powell and Emeric Pressburger,
whose intention was not at all detrimental to national morale.
The life story of the grand old soldier was a celebration of
British life and character, but also an exhortation to follow

Blimp's example and throw off tradition and hierarchy where they stood in the way of the new strategies demanded by the Second World War.

The film stands up magnificently. The moods and the sentiments have lost none of their integrity; and technically it is a marvel. More and more as time goes on it is clear how far apart Michael Powell stood from his British contemporaries, in his invention, visual flair and comprehension of the magical and musical element in cinema. Nor have the performances of Roger Livesey, Anton Walbrook and a solemn, enchanting, 22-year-old Deborah Kerr dated one whit.

David Robinson

GUARDIAN, 18 JULY 1985

The magnificent new complete colour print of Powell and Pressburger's 1943 *The Life and Death of Colonel Blimp* arrives at the Screen at the Electric tomorrow, trailing its history of controversy and its reputation as one of the best films ever made in this country.

But it is impossible to look at this 165-minute epic now without admiring the way Powell's romantic imagination and power of expression makes what would otherwise look fairly innocuous so provocatively modern. Like Makavejev – a filmmaker with whom he otherwise has no possible connection – Powell takes risks, and has both the artifice and craftsmanship to bring them off triumphantly.

Essentially, his version of the life of Low's famous cartoon figure (Roger Livesey) is a love story between the film-maker and his leading character who, though absurd, still embodies everything Powell held valuable about the English character. And it is also a love story between that character and Deborah Kerr's three women – the impossible objects of desire in his life.

Perhaps only Max Ophuls could have traversed this episodic

treatise on English values with a greater sense of unity and style. But then he might have missed its almost wilful eccentricity and unruly, sometimes spiteful sense of humour. There are longueurs, but this is still a great film, and looking greater by the decade.

Derek Malcolm

FINANCIAL TIMES, 19 JULY 1985

'What is it *really* about?' queried reviewer C. A. Lejeune of Michael Powell and Emeric Pressburger's magnificently enigmatic epic, *The Life and Death of Colonel Blimp*, back in 1943. The question – posed at a time when both Churchill's government and Britain's cultural guardians treated with suspicion any departure from the reductionist tenets of realism – now seems, or should seem, quaint. The film, re-launched after painstaking archival reconstruction in a stunning new Technicolor print, seems anything but.

Blimp offers no mere nostalgic complement to the bloated yarns of Empire and period-pretty country-house sagas that have predictably clogged much of British Film Year. Pointedly re-presented as one of the key works of its unique writer/producer/ director team (and therefore of the similarly underrated native cinema of wonder), it fronts a demand that questions like Ms Lejeune's be unpacked of their basic assumptions about what British Cinema may permissibly be.

The fantasy of *Blimp* is less about escapism than about essence. Its narrative encompasses 40 years of the life and soldiering times of Major General Clive Wynne-Candy VC (Roger Livesey), in flashback from his symbolic 'death' in 1943 – the moment of apparent defeat for his defining values, and the one point in the film where the character is visually 'matched' to the David Low cartoon figure of the title. Its progress is marked by three historical moments when the gentlemanly complacency of both Candy and his country is challenged by conflict:

moments brought into productively allusive and allegorical focus by Candy's enduring friendship with German officer-cum-refugee Kretschmar-Schuldorff (Anton Walbrook) and his elusive relationships with three women (each played by Deborah Kerr).

Any isolated sequence could serve to exemplify the audacious plenitude of *Blimp*, but the very first static image from the opening titles might suffice: a heraldic tapestry of an eccentric figure on a horse, at once aptly evoking Bayeux, St George, Quixote and Blimp. Two-and-three-quarter hours of similar, seriously playful structuring of ideas and images ensues, all of it, in the strictest sense of the word, wonderful. Really.

Paul Taylor

THE LIFE AND DEATH OF
COLONEL BLIMP

"WE ARE PRESENT AT THE END OF COLONEL BLIMP" — *SAYS CRIPPS*

(Copyright in All Countries.

The Resurrection of 'Blimp'

A NOTE ON THE SCRIPT AND FILM

Michael Powell believed that 'Emeric's screenplay for *Colonel Blimp* should be in every film archive, in every film library.'* The question is, however, in what form? The text printed here attempts something that is still rare in the publication of screenplays and scripts. Usually these are transcripts of what finally appeared on screen, based either on the approved release script or simply on a description of the dialogue and action. Occasionally an 'original' script is published, although this is more common in cases where that script has not been filmed and is therefore offered as 'literature'.

The inevitable differences between script and finished film are due to many factors, some creative, others practical and circumstantial. A comparison of the original and the result would therefore often be of little interest, without a lengthy commentary on the production itself. In a few cases, however, script and film remain relatively close and the reasons for variation are interesting and comprehensible. *The Life and Death of Colonel Blimp* is one such case.

There is only one known 'full script' version, entitled 'The Life and Death of Sugar Candy' (clearly dating from some time in June 1942 when it was hoped this concession would win War Office approval). Subsequent memos identifying scenes that were to be cut, changed and added indicate that this remained

* *A Life in Movies*, p. 409.

the basis of the film's production (and its indications of sequences already cut have been retained). What makes it specially valuable is that it goes well beyond mere dialogue and action, often describing location, character and atmosphere in a highly suggestive way. Hence the decision to present this script as written, *together with* a notation of the film as it appears today. The system used is similar to that devised by Bambi Ballard for her edition of Abel Gance's script of *Napoléon*. This involves using double square brackets [[ ]] to enclose original script material which *does not* appear in the final film, and single square brackets [ ] for material added during production. This means that in some cases two variants of essentially the same speech appear consecutively, which is not ideal, but hopefully the chance to compare versions and trace shifts will compensate for any local irritation. Names and titles which were changed in production (such as Mullins to Murdoch, Colonel to General, *Die Walküre* to *Mignon*) are given in their final form after the first indication of a change.

What of the film 'text' itself? This was originally released in July 1943, running for 163 minutes. By the early 70s, the only known versions of comparable length were two original nitrate copies held by the British Film Institute Deposit Print Collection and screened occasionally at the National Film Theatre.* All other copies appeared to be, at most, between 130 and 140 minutes. The *Radio Times*, billing the first UK television transmission on Boxing Day 1972, quoted BBC sources: 'this is the longest version we could find. But rumour hath it the original ran over three hours!' The slot allocated indicates an anticipated length of about 130 minutes.

When, how often, and by how much was *Blimp* cut? These

---

* One of these was donated by Powell and the other by Rank, apparently in the late 50s. I am grateful for this and other information about versions to David Meeker, Keeper of Feature Films at the National Film and Television Archive.

are the questions which still lack definitive answers, but some reliable evidence and explanation can now be given. The US *Motion Picture Almanac* lists *Blimp* for three consecutive years, from 1944-5 to 1946-7, as belonging to 'Archers-General' and at its original length of 163 minutes.*

Correspondence in the Powell papers indicates that there was considerable speculation about how to release it in the United States; but despite the pleas of specialist independent distributors, it was eventually assigned to United Artists under Rank's overall deal with that company, and released by it in May 1945. The running time listed in the *Motion Picture Herald* review of 24 March 1945 was 148 minutes and the title is given as *Colonel Blimp*. Four years later, *Blimp* resurfaced in the trade press with a report that Rank had initiated action by the Federal Trade Commission to restrain UA from showing a version of 91 minutes, cut from the 'original' of 143 minutes.† The outcome, it was stressed, was academic, since the film 'had been out of circulation for over a year'.

By the early 50s, it appears that either the US version had become the only one available in Britain, or that the film had been further shortened – possibly in order to fit into a double-bill. Running times of 140 and 120 minutes have been quoted by various sources. All of these shortened versions (if there was more than one) seem to have had the Prologue removed, so that the action started in 1902 and moved forward to the Turkish Bath in 1942-3. This, at any rate, was the version that I first saw in a nitrate print in 1971, but unfortunately did not time.

In 1976, the BFI Deposit Collection was handed over to the

* Rank's original distributor, General, still existed in the US; and The Archers seem also to have been active in trying to place their film. Hence this 'holding' designation.

† *Motion Picture Herald*, 15 January 1949; *Kinematograph Weekly*, 13 January 1949, p. 22. Geoffrey Macnab refers to these reports, but claims in his *J. Arthur Rank and the British Film Industry* (London, 1933) that the film was reduced 'to only a little over a tidy hour', thereby adding further confusion to an already tangled tale.

National Film Archive, which took the opportunity to 'cannibalize' the three prints it now held, making a nitrate viewing copy of some 160 minutes. This was first seen publicly in 1978 at the FIAF Congress in Brighton and at the National Film Theatre's Powell–Pressburger retrospective in October–November 1978. A first phase of restoration then started, with support from the BBC, to make a printable safety negative, based on the original Technicolor separations. The result was unsatisfactory technically, but capable of being enhanced electronically for a TV transmission on 11 October 1980, billed as allowing the film to be 'seen tonight on television for the first time in its full original version'.

Work continued at the NFA, supervised by Paul de Burgh and with help from the Rank Film Laboratories and a grant from the Sainsbury Charitable Trust, which resulted in a new safety negative. This provided the basis of a reissue of the film by BFI Distribution in 1985, after a Gala Screening at the Screen on the Hill on 18 July, attended by Powell and Pressburger. It has been used as the basis for annotating the original script.

Cast and credits

Credits not enclosed in square brackets are those which appear on the original film. Uncredited contributors have been identified from a variety of sources.

SPUD WILSON	James McKechnie
STUFFY GRAVES	Neville Mapp
CLUB PORTER, 1942	Vincent Holman
CLIVE CANDY	Roger Livesey
HOPPY	David Hutcheson
PERIOD BLIMP	Spencer Trevor
COLONEL BETTERIDGE	Roland Culver
CLUB PORTER, 1902	James Knight
EDITH HUNTER	Deborah Kerr
CAFÉ ORCHESTRA LEADER	Dennis Arundell
KAUNITZ	David Ward
INDIGNANT CITIZEN	Jan van Loewen
VON SCHÖNBORN	Valentine Dyall
VON REUMANN	Carl Jaffe
VON RITTER	Albert Lieven
COLONEL GOODHEAD	Eric Maturin
'BABY-FACE' FITZROY	Frith Banbury
EMBASSY SECRETARY	Robert Harris
EMBASSY COUNSELLOR	Arthur Wontner
COLONEL BORG	Count Zichy
THEO KRETSCHMAR-SCHULDORFF	Anton Walbrook
NURSE ERNA	Jane Millican
FRAU VON KALTENECK	Ursula Jeans
PEBBLE	Phyllis Morris
AUNT MARGARET HAMILTON	Muriel Aked
JOHN MONTGOMERY MURDOCH	John Laurie

VAN ZIJL	Reginald Tate
THE TEXAN	Capt. W. H. Barrett, US Army
SERGEANT	Cpl. Thomas Palmer, US Army
NUN	Yvonne Andree
MATRON	Marjorie Greasley
BARBARA WYNNE	Deborah Kerr
BISHOP	Felix Aylmer
MRS WYNNE	Helen Debroy
MR WYNNE	Norman Pierce
MAJOR JOHN E. DAVIES	Harry Welchman
PRESIDENT OF TRIBUNAL	A. E. Matthews
ANGELA 'JOHNNY' CANNON	Deborah Kerr
BBC OFFICIAL	Edward Cooper
SECRETARY	Joan Swinstead
[SYBIL	Diana Marshall]
[SERGEANT CLEARING DEBRIS	Wally Patch]
[PRUSSIAN STUDENT	Ferdy Mayne]
[SOLDIER	John Boxer]
	[John Varley, Patrick Macnee]

Directed, produced, written by	Michael Powell
	Emeric Pressburger*
Production Manager	Sydney S. Streeter
	Alec Saville [Tom White]
Assistant Producer	Richard Vernon
Floor Manager	Arthur Lawson
Assistant Director	Ken Horne
	Tom Payne
[*Production Runner*	Roger Cherrill]
Photography	Georges Perinal
Colour control	Natalie Kalmus

* ('with acknowledgement to David Low, creator of the immortal Colonel')

Chief Electrician	Bill Wall
Camera Operator	Jack Cardiff
	Geoffrey Unsworth
	Harold Haysom
Special photographic effects	W. Percy Day
Editor	John Seabourne
Assistant Editor	Thelma Myers
	Peter Seabourne
Production Designer	Alfred Junge
Music	Allan Gray
Music Conductor	Charles Williams
Sound	C. C. Stevens
	Desmond Dew
Costume	Joseph Bato
	Matilda Etches
Make-up	George Blackler
	Dorrie Hamilton
Military Adviser	Lt.-Gen. Sir Douglas Brownrigg
Period Advisers	E. F. E. Schoen
	Dr C. Beard

The Life and Death of
Colonel Blimp

[[LAURENCE OLIVIER]] [ROGER LIVESEY]
as
Clive ('Sugar') Candy, V.C.

Served South African War 1899–1902; European War
1914–18; Major-General 1935; Retired half-pay 1941

ANTON WALBROOK
as
Theo Kretschmar-Schuldorff

Oberleutnant, Regt. of Ulans, Potsdam 1902; Unwilling
visitor to England 1918; Refugee to England 1942

DEBORAH KERR
as
The Governess 1902
The Nurse 1918
The A.T.S. Driver 1942

and
Lieutenant 'Spud' Wilson
who
believes in winning
the
FIRST BATTLE

[[THIS FILM IS DEDICATED

to the New Army of Britain,
to the new spirit in warfare,
to the new toughness in battle,
and to the men and women who
know what they are fighting
for and are fighting this war
to win it.]]

Fade in field message:
[[FROM: CORPS COMMANDER
TO: ALL UNITS
16.00 HOURS
MESSAGE BEGINS
EXERCISE BEER-MUG
TIME CAFÉ DE PARIS
MESSAGE ENDS
10 JUNE
(*Added in pencil at the bottom: 'Make it like the real thing' and
initialled by the C.O.*)]]
[4BDE BMI DATE:
BEER MUG STOP BUTTERFLY
23.59 HOURS]
(*Dissolve to:*)

SEQUENCE I

*A series of shots, composed and edited, to produce the
maximum effect of speed, efficiency and modern equipment.
Locations must be chosen roughly between Staines and Elstree,
along line of the Green Belt and the arterial roads, giving
composite impression of the approaches to West London. Some
air-shots will be necessary.*
*The intention is to create, as simply as possible, an impression of
the mechanization and resources of the modern British Army.*

EXTERIORS: DESPATCH RIDERS
*A small army of motorcycle despatch riders, several hundred of
them, are tearing along an arterial road at full speed.*

At a roundabout they divide into three columns, one going right, another left, the third straight on. We follow the third column.

The by-pass ends at a T-road. The column divides again, one column west, the other east. We follow the eastbound column. The eastbound column divides again, one half going south. We plunge, with the southbound column, into a country road. The riders are now about twenty in number.

The column dashes through a water-splash and divides again into two parties. We follow the smaller group of riders.

Three are left as they race into a picturesque village occupied by troops. One of the riders stops at a strong-point where an eager officer grabs the message.

Now there are only two riders.

At a farm, one of the two riders turns off the lane through a farmyard. [[We follow him, through the farm and down a bumpy cart-track which leads to the Headquarters in the field of 'B' Company, the 2nd Battalion, the 4th Brigade, the 2nd Division of the 6th Army Corps.]]

SEQUENCE 2
Exteriors: H.Q. 'B' Company

'B' Company is a rifle company. [[Headquarters is a field, well situated strategically but damnably uncomfortable. The Company has been dug in by itself for four days. It is in touch by runner with Battalion H.Q.

It is a fine evening now but for the past three days it has rained, which has made enthusiasm difficult, and living, cooking and sleeping impossible. They have done all the proper things, camouflaged their vehicles, and taken advantage of the surrounding terrain, what there is of it.]]

[They have made their headquarters in a farm.]

The men are half-starved, trained to a hair, ready for anything and bored stiff. That goes for the officers too.

COMMANDING OFFICER'S BILLET
LIEUTENANT 'SPUD' WILSON *is shaving under difficulties* [[*and a hawthorn hedge*]] [*in a barn*]. *He is a very large, tough, rude, young officer. But he has a manner. He gets away with murder. He is popular with his Company and stands well with his Colonel.*
He has one creed in war: he believes in winning the FIRST BATTLE.
The DESPATCH RIDER *rides up and* [[*starts to open his wallet*]] [*is toppled from his motorcycle by a rope stretched across the yard*].
[[D.R.: Message from Corps, sir.]]

Spud's company learn that 'war starts at midnight'.

79

[('STUFFY' GRAVES, *a platoon commander, is keeping watch from high in the barn.*)
STUFFY: Message has just arrived, Spud.
   (*The ambushed* DESPATCH RIDER *picks himself up.*)
RIDER: What's the ruddy idea?
SOLDIER: It's total war, isn't it? What do you want?
RIDER: Message from H.Q. Where's the C.O.?
SOLDIER: In the barn. Follow me.
   (*The* DESPATCH RIDER *continues on his bike through the farm.*
   Inside the barn, SPUD *is still shaving. The* SERGEANT-MAJOR *enters.*)
S.M.: Message from H.Q., sir.]
SPUD: Read it, [Sgt. Hawkins].
S.M.: [It's in code, sir.] (*He reads.*) 'Message begins: Exercise Invasion of London Area by Regular Army, Home Guard defending. War starts at midnight. Message ends.' The C.O.'s put in pencil [here], sir, 'Make it like the real thing.'
SPUD: [[Platoon Commanders!]] [Oh, he has, has he? Section commanders!]
   (SERGEANT-MAJOR *puts fingers in mouth and gives special whistle.*
   Sound of men coming from different directions. SPUD *continues shaving, communing with himself.*
   By now the platoon commanders are before him: 'STUFFY' GRAVES, 'ROBIN' HOOD, 'TOMMY' TUCKER *and the* SERGEANT-MAJOR.
   SPUD *addresses them sardonically.*)
SPUD: [[Gentlemen!]] [Message from H.Q.] War starts at midnight. You have your orders. Tell the men!
TOMMY: Ay, ay, sir.
SPUD: And tell them to make it like the real thing.
STUFFY: What do you mean by 'like the real thing', Spud?
SPUD: (*Savagely*) [Well,] obviously [[prisoners must be bayoneted to death, women must be raped,]] our losses

80

divided by ten and the enemy's multiplied by twenty!
[[STUFFY: Yessir.]]
[S.M.: Anything else for me, sir?
SPUD: No.]
   (*He and the others see that* SPUD *is in no good humour and they turn to go.* SPUD *goes on shaving, still communing:*)
SPUD: 'War starts at midnight'. We know.
[STUFFY: (*Joining in the chorus rhythm*) *They* know.]
SPUD: *We* attack.
STUFFY: *They* counter-attack.
SPUD: Like the real thing – my Aunt Fanny! Like the real thing –
   (*Suddenly a great idea strikes him, his voice changes, he rises from his seat transfigured.*) LIKE THE REAL THING! Sergeant Hawkins! [[Stuffy, Robin, Tommy]] [Section commanders!]
   (*By this time they are all around him again. He starts to wipe the soap off his face as he speaks.*)
SPUD: So War starts at midnight, does it? [[Sergeant-Major!]]
S.M.: Sir!
SPUD: We attack at six! [[We'll]] take all the [tommy-guns and] [[Brens and three – no,]] four [no, three] trucks. Section leaders with tommy-guns. Arm the men with [bombs,] rifles, bayonets, [[fifty rounds of spare, pick handles. I'll need all the officers]].
S.M.: Yessir.
SPUD: Tommy, [from your section] – Rice, Unsworth, [yes] the Owens, Nobby, Toots and Cochrane?
[TOMMY: Not Cochrane, sir.
SPUD: All right, I leave it to you.] Stuffy, who are the biggest toughs in your lot?
STUFFY: Bill Wall, Wimpey, Popeye, Wizard . . .
SPUD: Yours Robin?
ROBIN: Frank, Skeets and Duggie Stuart [Taffy, Geordie and Dai Evans.]
SPUD: [(*In mock Welsh accent*) We must have him, look you.

All right. Get going!] [[We'll make it real for them.]]
[S.M.: Excuse me, sir.
SPUD: Yes.
S.M.: Did you say that we attack *before* war is declared?
SPUD: Yes, like Pearl Harbour. Now get going. Oh, by the way,
   there's just one stop, at the Bull. I've got a date there with
   Mata Hari.
STUFFY: Careless talk . . .
SPUD: Yeah. Now scram.]

SEQUENCE 3 OUT

SEQUENCES 4, 5, 6, 7
Exteriors and Interiors of Spud's Commando

*Dashing down Western Avenue towards London and passing
through a barricade.*
[*The Trucks pull in at the Bull.* SPUD *goes towards the building
alone.*
SPUD: Five minutes easy, Sergeant. (*Calls to another truck.*) Five
   minutes easy, Stuffy.
   (*Rapid fade to black.*
   Soldiers waiting outside as before.)
TOMMY: I wonder what's keeping Spud?
   (ANGELA CANNON ('JOHNNY') *appears at the door,
   unnoticed by the soldiers, and moves stealthily towards her
   car. They see her.*)
JOHNNY: Afternoon, Sergeant.
S.M.: (*Puzzled*) Afternoon, miss. (*Realization dawns.*) Hey!
   (JOHNNY *quickly drives off as the soldiers rush towards
   her.*)
S.M.: Back in the trucks!]

INTERIOR: SECOND TRUCK

SPUD *points ahead.*

SPUD: See that barricade, my [[hearties]] [boys. Well] at
midnight it's going to be closed.

STUFFY: And [[none of the wicked enemy can pass]] [of course
the enemy can't get] through before because – [why?]

WHOLE TRUCK: (*With relish*) – WAR STARTS AT
MIDNIGHT!
(SPUD *grins and waves to the Home Guard on the
barricade.*)

EXTERIOR. BARRICADE: WESTERN AVENUE

The Home Guard waves to SPUD*'s commando, who all wave
back.*
Dissolve to:

EXTERIOR: WESTERN AVENUE

*The commando dashes by. Three Bren Carriers form a screen;
then the four 15-cwt trucks at careful intervals of about
100 yards, all travelling at full speed.*

INTERIOR: FIRST TRUCK

TOMMY TUCKER *sits by the* DRIVER *as Officer-Navigator to the
raid. He has maps of London but he knows the streets by heart.
The men crowded in the truck behind him with their weapons
all ready are as keen as mustard.*

DRIVER: What's the objective, sir?

TOMMY: [[Boodles Club, 28 St James's Street]] [Royal Bathers'
Club, Piccadilly]. You all know your stuff?

CHORUS: Yessir!

VOICE: What about Mata Hari?

VOICE: We'll beat her to it.

VOICE: I know a couple of short cuts after Marble Arch.

[[TOMMY: Are the other trucks O.K.?

VOICE: Right behind us, sir.]]

[[INTERIOR: SECOND TRUCK
SPUD, *the* SERGEANT-MAJOR *and* STUFFY. *His runner, his driver and his batman, three other men armed with rifles. All look grim and full of suppressed excitement.* SPUD *has a bandage round his head and looks very cross.*
S.M.: Barricade ahead, sir.
    (*Tense pause.*)
S.M.: It's open!

EXTERIOR. BARRICADE: WESTERN AVENUE
It is manned and defended but not yet closed as it is only six o'clock. SPUD's *commando is approaching. The Bren Carriers rattle through, their crews waving. The defending forces wave back, innocently.*]]

SEQUENCES 8 & 9 OUT

[INTERIOR: TRUCK
They see ANGELA's *car ahead in the London traffic.*
VOICE: There she is! Get the other truck to close up. See if you can pass her.
    (*A taxi cuts in between the truck and the car.*)
VOICE: Blast that taxi! Steady, keep right on his tail. Second left. We've got her!

EXTERIOR: SANDBAGGED ENTRANCE OF
ROYAL BATHERS' CLUB
ANGELA *pauses for an instant at the club entrance, then rushes in.*]

Exterior and Interiors: Royal Bathers' Club

[[EXTERIOR: STREET SIGN

Impressive building. Street sign on frontage: 'St James's Street,
s w 1'.
Sound of violently applied brakes, off, as SPUD's *commando*
arrives.]]
[SPUD *stands at the club entrance, directing his men.*
SPUD: Come on, Section No. 2.
CHORUS: Yessir!
SPUD: No. 3.
CHORUS: Yessir!
SPUD: You have your orders.]

INTERIOR: CLUB

The HALL PORTER *glances up.* [ANGELA *is with him, on the*
telephone. She dives beneath his desk when –]
SPUD *enters from the street, followed by* STUFFY GRAVES, *who*
stays in the door where he can command exterior and interior.
SPUD *comes up to* PORTER *with the urgent manner of one who*
carries an important message.
SPUD: (*To* PORTER) Is [[Major-]]General Wynne-Candy in the
    Club?
PORTER: No, sir. The General left an hour ago with Brigadier-
    General Caldicott and Air Vice-Marshal Lloyd-Hughes.
SPUD: Did he say where he was going?
PORTER: Excuse me, sir, what is your business with the
    General?
SPUD: I have a message for him – an urgent message.
PORTER: If you will give me the message, sir, I will see that the
    General gets it.
SPUD: But dammit all, man – ! (*Suddenly changes tone.*) Are
    you [in the] Home Guard?

85

Angela lies low and tries to warn General Candy that the Club is under attack.

PORTER: [[Are you]] [Why], sir?
SPUD: (*Low voice*) The password is 'Veuve Cliquot 1911'!
PORTER: (*Salutes*) The General and his staff [[have gone to]] [are in] the Turkish Baths, sir.
SPUD: [[(*Signs to* STUFFY, *who signals to street*)]] [(*Blows whistle*)] Right!

[[EXTERIOR: ST JAMES'S STREET
From STUFFY's *angle we see two of the trucks and the men all ready for action.* STUFFY *holds up two fingers. Two men jump down and come running up.*]]

INTERIOR: CLUB
The [[two]] *men come in, carrying rifles and bayonets and go up*

86

to SPUD *and the* PORTER.

SPUD: [(*To* SERGEANT) You're in charge up here.] Stay with
    him. (*To* PORTER) Don't leave your [[cubby-hole]] [desk]
    or [[answer]] [use] the 'phone. You're a prisoner of war.

[PORTER: But war starts at midnight.

SPUD: Ah ha, that's what you think. Sergeant, that girl under
    the desk: she's a prisoner too.

SGT.: Sir!

SPUD: Corporal, follow me. Brute force and ruddy ignorance.

CPL.: (*To men*) Come on, after him – and double up.
    (*Dissolve to:*)]

[[SEQUENCE 12
Exterior: His Majesty's Theatre

SPUD's *commando dashes up and passes the Theatre.*
Dissolve to:

SEQUENCE 13
Exterior: Turkish Baths

A GIRL *in A.T.S. uniform is telephoning from a public box near
the entrance.*
SPUD's *commando sweeps up. This is the final objective. They
attack in strength, the trucks emptying like magic, the Bren
Carriers facing three ways along the street, their crews ready.*
SPUD *is the first out. His quick eye spots the* GIRL.

SPUD: Sergeant-Major!

S.M.: Sir?

SPUD: See that girl in the phone-box?

S.M.: Yessir.

SPUD: Nail her in!

S.M.: Yessir. Owen!

> (SPUD, *without waiting to see his orders carried out, runs up the steps of the Turkish Baths, where he stops and turns.*)

SPUD: Rice! Wimpey! Stand guard!

RICE: ⎫
WIMPEY: ⎬ Sir.

SPUD: (*To others*) This is it, boys! Follow me! Brute force and bloody ignorance!

> (*He crashes in, followed by his men.*
> WIMPEY *and* RICE *exchange disgusted glances.*)

WIMPEY: Pipped at the ruddy post!

RICE: Last chance we'll have to see a General in the nood!

SEQUENCES 14 & 15
Interior: Turkish Baths

THE HOTTEST ROOM
Through clouds of steam, half a dozen nude pink figures, scantily draped in towels, sit or recline at ease.]]

ATTENDANT'S DESK (OUTSIDE)
SPUD *and his men crowd the entrance. The* ATTENDANT *stares horrified at them. The telephone bell is ringing like mad.*

SPUD: (*To* ATTENDANT) [[You're a prisoner of war!]] [Don't argue!] Wizard! Guard this man. (*He moves off.*) And answer that dam' phone!

> (WIZARD *takes the receiver off, grimly covering the* ATTENDANT *with his tommy-gun meanwhile. Over the receiver we hear an excited* GIRL's *voice.* WIZARD *plays up.*)

WIZARD: [Yes, miss.] Warn who, miss? General Wynne-Candy, miss? Can't do that, miss. (*Holds receiver away from his ear as girl's voice screams.*)

[[GIRL'S VOICE: What do you mean? I *must* speak to him! (*Camera tracks swiftly into close shot of receiver. We can hear plainly the* GIRL'S *voice and sound of hammering.*)

GIRL'S VOICE: (*Evidently to* SERGEANT-MAJOR) What are you doing? Stop it! How dare you! (*She evidently kicks the door of the booth.*) Help! Police! (*Then back to the telephone*) Porter! Hullo! Hullo!

(WIZARD *is enjoying himself.*)

WIZARD: Yes, miss. (*He listens.*) Sorry, miss,]] the General's a prisoner of war. (*Listens.*) [[Yes, miss. You're a prisoner of war too.]] [And so are you.] (*Listens, then suddenly gets impatient.*) You're NUTS! The War's over! (*He rings off.*)

THE HOTTEST ROOM

SPUD *and his merry men invade the room, guns and other weapons in their hands.*

They look strange and alarming in their battledress in the incongruous setting.

SPUD *peers through the steam.* [[*He sees his Final Objective.*

SPUD: All right, boys! Surround 'em!]]

(*The commando at once invests the whole room. Some cover the waking figures. Others guard the approaches, their backs to the scene. Still others are seen through the glass partition rounding up the attendants and some other bathers.*)

[SPUD: Qu-i-e-t! Quiet, please. You're all prisoners. Now stay where you are. (*To* ATTENDANT) Where's General Wynne-Candy?

ATTENDANT: Who, sir?

SPUD: You heard. Now show me the way. Come on.]

(SPUD, *almost frightened now that he has reached his objective, advances with an obvious effort on the Final*

89

Objective: MAJOR-GENERAL SIR CLIVE WYNNE-CANDY,
V.C., D.S.O.
GENERAL WYNNE-CANDY *is so like Colonel Blimp in*
appearance that he must certainly have been the model who
inspired David Low.
He IS Blimp.
Here is the great face, the sweeping moustaches, the ivory-
domed head, the noble belly, even the little crease on his fat
chest.
In BLACK AND WHITE, Colonel Blimp is an awe-
inspiring figure; but in TECHNICOLOR!
No wonder SPUD *hesitates. He is sweating, not only from*
the heat.
He stands a moment looking down at his sleeping prize.
Then he gently taps him on the shoulder.)
SPUD: [(*To himself*) This is it.] Sir! (*Pause.*) SIR!
[GENERAL: (*Eyes still closed*) Go away.
SPUD: General Wynne-Candy!]
(*Do you remember in Kipling's 'The White Seal', when the*
diminutive Kotick by his barking, wakes Sea-Catch, the
great Walrus; how Sea-Catch starts awake, banging his
neighbour with his flipper and coughing and spluttering
'Eh? How? What?'
Even so wakes General Clive Wynne-Candy.)
GENERAL: Hm – What – Who is it?
SPUD: Lieutenant Wilson, sir. 2nd Battalion, the
    [[Devonshires]] [Loamshires], sir.
GENERAL: Hm! (*He is still half asleep.*) What[['s the matter]]
    [do you want], eh?
SPUD: Well, sir . . . I'm afraid, sir . . . ('*After all, he is a*
    General.')
GENERAL: Well? – Say it, man! I've no time to waste!
SPUD: (*Relaxes and although very hot begins at last to enjoy*
    himself) Oh, yes, you have, sir!
GENERAL: I beg your pardon, sir?

SPUD: You've got all night, sir.

(*All round them the other members of the staff are waking. They see the armed, clothed figures. The* GENERAL *stares at* SPUD *as if he were a dangerous lunatic. He looks around for help.*)

GENERAL: Attendant!

SPUD: I'm afraid he can't come.

GENERAL: [[Can't come! Can't – attendant!]] (*Pause.*) Why?

SPUD: He's a prisoner of war.

GENERAL: (*Slowly*) What's going on here?

SPUD: Invasion[, sir].

[[GENERAL: (*Slowly*) And may I ask who is invading who?

SPUD: I am invading this Turkish Bath.

GENERAL: Do – you – know – who – you – are – talking to, sir?

SPUD: Yes, sir. I am addressing Major-General Clive Wynne-Candy, General Officer Commanding the Home Guard, Exercise Beer-mug, sir. You and your staff are my prisoners.

ANOTHER GENERAL: (*To* CANDY) I say, Suggie, this is a devil of a mess!]]

GENERAL: (*To* SPUD) But you damned young idiot, war starts at midnight! Haven't you been told!

SPUD: (*Inwardly trembling, outwardly brazen*) Yes, sir. That's why we're here.

GENERAL: And may I ask [[again]], on – what – authority?

SPUD: On the authority of these guns and these men [,sir].

(*The* GENERAL *looks around him and takes in the whole outrageous scene suddenly. He nearly has a fit. He gasps:*)

GENERAL: Authority – authority – how dare you, sir – how dare you [[– I'll have you broke for this – I'll –]] GET OUT OF HERE SIR YOU AND YOUR GANG OF AWFUL MILITIA GANGSTERS [[I'LL HAVE YOU]] [GET OUT!] – (*He suddenly stops a little helplessly.*)

SPUD: (*He gets things moving*) [[STUFFY!]] [Popeye, guard these men.]

[[STUFFY]] [POPEYE]: YESSIR!

SPUD: [Stuffy.] Go to the cubicles. Find which is General
    Wynne-Candy's. [[There'll be]] [You'll find] a brown
    pigskin case there. Bring it.

STUFFY: Yessir. (*Goes.*)

GENERAL: But you can't do that! The code is in that case! The
    whole Exercise will be a farce if you have that code!

SPUD: [[(*Furious; his men have been insulted*) It's a farce
    already!]] [Oh no, sir. This is going to be the real thing, sir.

GENERAL: But war starts at midnight.

SPUD: Oh yes.] You say, 'War starts at midnight' – how do you
    know the enemy says so too?

GENERAL: (*Stares; then quite mildly*) But my dear fellow, that
    was agreed, wasn't it?

SPUD: (*By now the sweat is streaming off him from heat and
    fury*) Agreed, my – foot! [[What's agreement got to do with
    it?]] How many agreements have been kept by the enemy
    since this War started? [[Why do we believe again and
    again what they are telling us? Why have we always waited
    for him at the front of the house while he steals in through
    the back door and kicks us in the pants? Tell me why, sir.
    (SPUD *reckless now, his uniform a sponge, dashes a
    bucketful of sweat off his face and sweeps on.*) I'll tell you,
    sir! Because]] we agree to keep the Rules of the Game,
    [[that's why]] [and they keep kicking us in the seat of the
    pants]! [[Don't forget another agreement!]] When [[we]] [I]
    joined the Army, [[we agreed to defend our country by
    every means at our disposal]] [the only agreement I entered
    into was to defend my country by any means at my
    disposal], not only by National Sporting Club Rules but by
    every means that has existed since Cain slugged Abel!

[GENERAL: Stop . . .]

SPUD: Don't we know they're counting on us to keep to the
    Rules. Don't we know it's a standing joke with them, that
    they boast about it, that they –

92

GENERAL: STOP [[IT]]! (*His parade voice has so much authority that he actually brings* SPUD *to a dead stop.*) Lieutenant Watson – or whatever your name is – you are not [[on a platform]] in Hyde Park with an audience of [[tarts and]] loafers. I am Major-General Wynne-Candy. [[This is General Wyndham Cook.]] These other gentlemen have all seen service, distinguished service, with the British Army!

SPUD: (*Undaunted*) Well, all I can say is, sir, that when Napoleon said an army marches on its stomach [[he must have been thinking of old gentlemen like]] – I'd better stop, sir!

GENERAL: (*He is very angry, but he sees that the grand manner won't help him*) You're an extremely impudent young officer, sir. But let me tell you that in forty years [time] you'll be an old gentleman, too. And if your belly keeps pace with your head, you'll have a bigger one than any of us!

SPUD: Maybe I shall. In forty years. But [[I'll bet that you were the same in the last war. And forty years ago!]] [I doubt it. And I doubt if I'll have time to grow a moustache like yours, sir. But at least in 1983 I'll be able to say I was a fellow of enterprise.]
(*This is too much for the* GENERAL *who drops forty years of authority and experience like a cloak and goes for his impudent young antagonist with his bare fists.*
SPUD, *devastated by heat, emotion and a wild desire to laugh, weakly defends himself, moving hastily backwards before the windmill attack of the* GENERAL, *who all the time is bellowing:*)

GENERAL: I'll punch your head for that, young fellow! I'll punch your head! Put 'em up! D'you hear me? (*Grunt.*) Think you can say what you like to an old 'un, do you? [[I'll teach you!]] Do you know how many wars – I've been in? I was fighting for my country when your father was still in bum-freezers! (*Smack – thud – grunt.*) [[*You* set up to teach *me* what a soldier should or shouldn't do – (*He gets a bit tangled up with the sibilants here, but emerges from the foam like Venus.*) – Pah!]] Puppy! Gangster! [[I repeat! Gangster!]]

(*At this point,* SPUD'*s retreating feet find air beneath them and he falls backwards into the plunge-bath. Without hesitation the* GENERAL *leaps in on top of him. The battle continues in three and a half feet of cold water.*
Clouds of steam ascend, hiding the combatants as it thickens. Through the gathering clouds the voice of the GENERAL *continues to boom, but as the clouds thicken, the voice gets fainter.*)

GENERAL: (*Booming through the steam*) [[What do you know about me?]] You laugh at my big belly, but you don't know how I got it – ! You laugh at my moustache, but you don't know why I grew it! – (*His voice grows fainter.*) How do you know what sort of man I was – when I was as young as you are – forty years ago – forty years ago –
(*Blimp's – beg pardon –* CANDY'*s last words sound hollow and faint. Already they are no longer real.*
The words hang in the air, like the thick clouds of steam.
[[*For a moment there is silence.*
Then a full orchestra plays the opening chords of Brünhilde's great and difficult soprano solo in Wagner's 'Walkury' [sic].
The music breaks off.
Then a very real, ordinary young man's voice starts to sing (very flat) the Aria, from somewhere nearby.
This voice belongs to 2ND LIEUTENANT HOPWELL.
Then another young man's voice with a familiar note in it joins in the Aria from the plunge-bath.]] *The clouds of steam thin and clear away.*
YOUNG CLIVE CANDY *emerges from the pool.*)

(*top*) Alfred Junge's original design for the Steam Room.
(*bottom*) General Candy resists the young idea: 'In forty years time you'll
be an old gentleman too.'

Interior: Turkish Baths (1902)

THE HOTTEST ROOM

YOUNG CLIVE CANDY *heaves himself out of the pool in one movement. He is 26, very fit, full of impatience and enthusiasm.*
[ATTENDANT: Everything you want, Mr Candy, sir?
CLIVE: Yes, thank you.]
> (*He knows every twist and turn in the* [[Brünhilde]] [Mignon] *Aria which he declaims with great vigour.* [*An answering voice takes up the Aria. The curtains of a cubicle part to reveal* 2ND LIEUTENANT HOPWELL, *in a turban, singing at the top of his voice. They strike a pose together.*]
> A BLIMP OF THE PERIOD *wakes up furious.*)

PERIOD BLIMP: Quiet! People are trying to sleep!
> [[(2ND LIEUTENANT HOPWELL *stops singing and sits bolt upright on the slab where he was being pummelled by the attendant.*)

HOPPY: Suggie!
> (CLIVE CANDY *breaks off the Aria abruptly.*)]]

CLIVE: Hoppy! My old horse [[my antique stallion]]! Since when are you in London?
> (*By this time they have met.*)

HOPPY: Got back yesterday. Sick leave. I've been chasing you all over town. (*Awkwardly.*) I say, old chap, I was awfully sorry to hear about your leg – (*He has been avoiding looking down but now he does. His sympathetic expression changes.*) Jumping Jehosaphat! They're both there!
CLIVE: What the hell did you think I was standing on?
HOPPY: I thought you had a wooden leg.
CLIVE: Why should I have a wooden leg?
HOPPY: They told me in Bloemfontein that they cut off your left leg.

Young Clive and Hoppy disturb a sleeping Period Blimp with their rendition of 'I am Titania'.

(*They both examine attentively Clive's left leg.*
CLIVE *shakes his head.*)
CLIVE: Can't have, old boy. I'd have known about it.
(*They both roar with laughter.*
[[*The two young men lower their voices but soon forget again.*)
CLIVE: I got it in the shoulder.
HOPPY: (*Peers*) Can't see a thing. Now whose leg do you suppose they really cut off?
CLIVE: It's the other one. (*He means the other shoulder.*)
HOPPY: (*Looking at the leg*) What do you mean?
CLIVE: (*Turning, showing angry scar*) Here.
HOPPY: Oh, I see. So it is. (*Professionally.*) Stop you playing polo?

CLIVE: Not much. Where are you putting up?
(*They have both raised their voices again.*)
HOPPY: Stayed at Horsey Loudon's last night – you know he
married little Nancy Thingumabob?
CLIVE: No!
HOPPY: Fact! But I found out this morning that they sport a
phonograph. So I said to Horsey – by the way, the old boy's
putting on weight – 'Sorry, old man, thanks for the doss
down but phonographs are barred!'
CLIVE: (*Nods solemnly*) Don't blame you. Serious matter –
phonographs.
HOPPY: (*Grins*) I'd hate it to burst out one morning with –
(*He sweeps once more into the Mignon Aria, at the top of
his lungs which are good.*
CLIVE *joins in enthusiastically. His lungs are also not
negligible.*)
HOPPY: (*During bar rest*) Mouldy pipes, you've got.
CLIVE: Mouldy? My pipes? (*He pulls out all the stops.*)

INTERIOR: CUBICLES
PERIOD BLIMP *tears open his curtain.*
PERIOD BLIMP: (*Yells*) Attendant! Attendant! Confound it! I'll
never get to sleep again. Stop that confounded Covent
Garden CATERWAULING!!
CLIVE: (*Very pleased*) See! *My* pipes!
PERIOD BLIMP'S VOICE: My shoes!
CLIVE: (*Shouts*) Don't go, sir! We're evacuating! (*Breaks into
song.*)
'Cherries so red!
Strawberries ripe!
(HOPPY *joins in.*)
At home of course they'll be storming.
(*Linking arms.*)
Never mind the abuse!
(*Marching off.*)

You've had the excuse!
You've BEEN TO COVENT GARDEN IN THE
    MORNING!'
PERIOD BLIMP'S VOICE: My shoes!
2ND BLIMP: Quiet!
3RD BLIMP: Stop that noise! Attendant!
PERIOD BLIMP: (*fff*) MY SHOES!!]]
    (*Dissolve to:*)

SEQUENCE 18
Interior: Royal Bathers' Club

ENTRANCE HALL
*The inner doors open and the two friends come marching out in
the same tempo, very pleased with themselves, in colourful
smart uniforms, their great-coats over their shoulders, their caps
and swords at a dashing angle, looking as if they had just
stepped out of a bandbox. They adjust their gloves.*
CLIVE: Call a cabby, porter!
PORTER: Yes, sir. [(*Signals to* DOORMAN.)]
HOPPY: Hansom, mind! Growlers barred.
PORTER: [[Of course]] [He knows], sir.
    ([[PORTER]] [DOORMAN] *runs out and we hear him blow
    his whistle. There is a blast of cold wind as the door swings.
    It is a wintry day in January.*)
CLIVE: (*Yawns*) Could have done with a nap myself.
HOPPY: You've got all night, haven't you?
CLIVE: [[Must go]] [Going] to the theatre tonight.
HOPPY: Can't you sleep there?
CLIVE: Invited. Two ladies.
HOPPY: Can I come along?
CLIVE: One is the mother.
    (HOPPY *understands.*

Meanwhile sound of clop-clopping, 'Whoa!' etc. The
[[PORTER]] [DOORMAN] *reappears, shivering and blowing*
on his hands to warm them.)

[[PORTER: Hansom, gentlemen.]]

[DOORMAN: Your cab, sir.]

(*But before they can move, the inner doors are flung open*
again and out storms the PERIOD BLIMP, *in the uniform of*
a Major-General, which at that time was even more
gorgeous than at present. The two young officers click
heels, and give him a terrific salute. He acknowledges and is
about to pass when he recognizes them. They remain stiffly
at attention. He has them on toast.)

PERIOD BLIMP: Ha! The opera-singers, eh? No wonder
civilians are grumbling about the Army! Ought to be
ashamed of yourselves – yelling and screaming like some
damned foreigner! A nice state of things! Officers and men
losing their lives in South Africa while young officers are
roaring about public places like drunkards – (*A sudden idea*
strikes him.) Perhaps you are drunk. (*Goes closer, sniffing.*)
[[Let me smell your breath! (*Sniffs.*)

(*As he speaks, someone comes in from outside. The wind*
blows CLIVE's *coat aside, where it hangs over his chest,*]]
[CLIVE *adjusts his helmet, causing his cloak to fall back,*]
revealing a scarlet ribbon, ornamented with the Maltese
Cross.

The MAJOR-GENERAL [*i.e.* PERIOD BLIMP] *stares. The*
young officers stand like ramrods.)

PERIOD BLIMP: Eh? What's this?

CLIVE: V[[ictoria]] C[[ross]], sir.

PERIOD BLIMP: Where d'you get it, eh?

CLIVE: South Africa [Jordaan Siding], sir. [[Windhoek.]]

PERIOD BLIMP: [[Hm!]] You're [Candy,] 'Sugar' Candy?

CLIVE: Yes, sir.

PERIOD BLIMP: Hm! [[Heard of you!]] (*Pause.*) Good show,
Candy.

(*He holds out his hand. They shake hands.*)

CLIVE: Thank you, sir.

    (*He looks at* HOPPY.)

HOPPY: [[2nd Lieutenant]] Hopwell, sir.

PERIOD BLIMP: Hopwell – Hopwell! [What,] Son of Barney Hopwell of the 66th?

HOPPY: Yes, sir.

PERIOD BLIMP: (*Shakes hands*) Glad to know you, my boy. (*Surveys them.*) You're very musical [[,you two]]?

HOPPY: No, sir.

[PERIOD BLIMP: (*To* CLIVE) And so are you.]

CLIVE: [[You mean the Brünhilde Aria, sir?]] [D'you mean *Mignon*, sir, 'I am Titania'?]

PERIOD BLIMP: [[Whathilde?]] [You're what?]

CLIVE: [[Brünhilde]] [Titania], sir. We two were shut up with her in a blockhouse for seven months near Jordaan Siding –

PERIOD BLIMP: (*Fogged*) [[With Matilda?]] [I beg your pardon?]

CLIVE: [[Brünhilde, sir. Character in opera by Wagner.]] [It's an aria, sir.] We had a phonograph and we broke every record but this one. We know it by heart.

PERIOD BLIMP: Hahahaha! [[Dashed good.]] [(*Moves to the door.*) Well, are you boys going to the (*inaudible word*)?

CLIVE: Yes, sir.

PERIOD BLIMP: That's where I'm lying.

EXTERIOR: CLUB STEPS

[PERIOD BLIMP: Can I give you a lift?

    (CLIVE *opens the hansom door for him.*)

CLIVE: No thank you, sir. We have a cab.

    (*The* GENERAL *gets into their cab.*)

GENERAL: (*To* CAB DRIVER) St James's Palace.

CAB DRIVER: Right, sir.]

PERIOD BLIMP: Well, I hope you two [[lads]] [boys] enjoy your leave: you've earned it.

CLIVE: Thank you, sir. [Mind yourself on the door, sir.]
   ([[*They give another terrific salute as the* GENERAL *rolls out.
   They prepare to follow. Sound of cab driving away.*]] *They*
   [[*look out*]] [*look at one another*].)
HOPPY: The old horse thief!
CLIVE: [[Porter]] [Boy]! Another hansom!
   ([[*Outside, the* PORTER]] [*The* DOORMAN] *blows his
   whistle.* [[*Dissolve to:*]])

SEQUENCE 19
[[*Interior: Hansom Cab*]] [*Exterior: In Front of Club*]

[[*The complete change of atmosphere and period is conveyed by
the leisurely progress and the absence of the internal combustion
engine. All around one hears only the clop-clopping of
innumerable hoofs, with occasional snatches of sound, such as a
barrel-organ playing 'You are my Honey, Honeysuckle'.*
CLIVE *sits, muffled up, contentedly looking at the pageant of the
town.* HOPPY *is apparently looking for something in his
pockets.*]]
[CLIVE *and* HOPPY *cross the road to a* HOT POTATO SELLER'S
cart.
HOT POT SELLER: Hot potatoes, sir?
HOPPY: No, we've just come over for a warm.
   (*An early automobile passes.*)
CLIVE: (*To* HOPPY) You ever ridden in one?
HOPPY: Rather. All the way to Epsom.
CLIVE: Lovely lines, hasn't she?
HOPPY: Topping.]
CLIVE: (*Deep breath*) Same beastly [[raw]] drizzle! Same [[old
   slush]] [fog] and soot! Good old London!
HOPPY: [(*Looks for something in his pockets*)] Now listen,
   Suggie! Remember that interview you gave *The Times*?

CLIVE: You don't mean to say you read it?

HOPPY: Me? No! But I have a niece[[. She]] [who] has a governess [[and the governess]] [who] has a sister.

CLIVE: Pretty?

HOPPY: [[I don't know her from Adam.]] [Never laid eyes on her.] But *she* read it.

CLIVE: (*Frowns*) Who?

HOPPY: My niece's governess's sister. In Berlin. So she wrote to her sister here, who gave the letter to my niece to give to me to give to you. [[See?]]

CLIVE: (*Concentrates*) Who do I give it to?

HOPPY: Nobody. It's for you. Here it is.

CLIVE: (*Takes it gingerly*) Why [[me]]?

HOPPY: [Well,] Read it [,you big ape]. You'll [[see]] [find out]. It's interesting.

(*Dissolve to:* [*Text of* EDITH'*s letter:*
'. . . tales of atrocities by our soldiers against the Boers are being printed by these <u>odious</u> newspapers and encouraged by <u>certain</u> <u>high</u> <u>personages</u> who are <u>determined</u> to foment trouble between Germany and England. There is one agent, in particular, named KAUNITZ who is a <u>LIAR</u> and SCOUNDREL! Now this Lieut. Candy sounds a splendid fellow and he is just returned from South Africa. If only he would come to Berlin and TELL THE TRUTH! That would do more good than a hundred interviews! Do you not think, my dear Martha, that Mr. Hopwell would be likely to know this young officer. I seem to remember that he noted the same name in one of his . . .'*])

[[SEQUENCE 20
Exterior: Hansom, Her Majesty's Theatre

Effect shot of the façade of Her Majesty's Theatre. The hansom

bowls by with the two young officers in it.
Dissolve to:

SEQUENCES 21, 22, 23
The War Office

The War Office has been finished the year before and, besides being brand new, was regarded as the tops in official architecture.

STAIRCASE
One of the great staircases surrounding the cage where the latest thing in lifts had just been installed.
CLIVE and HOPPY run up the staircase, three steps at a time.
Dissolve to:

CORRIDOR
One of the interminable corridors. CLIVE *and* HOPPY *arrive at the door of an office.* HOPPY *gives* CLIVE *an encouraging gesture.* CLIVE *knocks and goes in.*
Dissolve to:]]

COLONEL BETTERIDGE'S OFFICE [HIS NAME ON THE DOOR]
The COLONEL *is about fifty, pleasant but very uncompromising on questions of army etiquette. He detests pauses in conversation. [Another officer,* MAJOR PLUMLEY, *shares his office and says little.]*
CLIVE *stands before his desk.*
BETTERIDGE: Sit down!
CLIVE: (*Sits*) Thank you, sir.
BETTERIDGE: Fire away!
CLIVE: Well, sir, I have a friend —

104

BETTERIDGE: Good. Not everybody can say that. Continue!

CLIVE: This friend of mine, sir, has a niece –

BETTERIDGE: (*Examines* CLIVE's *application for appointment*)
Cut it short, my boy, you say here it's about a letter. One,
who wrote it? Two, what's in it? Three, what's the War
Office got to do with it? Four, I'll tell you. Five, Out! (*He
gestures towards door, fixes* CLIVE, *barks:*) One!

CLIVE: (*Hurriedly*) A girl wrote it from Berlin, sir. Her name is
Edith Hunter. She's a governess there.

BETTERIDGE: [Rather an] Uncomfortable billet just now.

CLIVE: That's just it, sir. They hate us in Germany. They are
spreading propaganda all over Europe that we are killing
women and children in South Africa, that we are starving
them in concentration camps, shooting mothers, burning
babies – you wouldn't believe the things they have
invented! I spoke this afternoon to Conan Doyle. He thinks
something ought to be done about it too.

BETTERIDGE: About what? [[Where does this letter of yours
come in?]] [What's all this about a letter?] And who's
Conan Doyle?

CLIVE: The author chap, sir – writes the Sherlock Holmes
stories in the *Strand Magazine*.
(*The* COLONEL *at last shows some animation and interest.*)

BETTERIDGE: This Doyle fellow writes the Sherlock Holmes
stories?

CLIVE: Yes, sir. Conan Doyle. You must have seen his name.

BETTERIDGE: Never heard of him. But I've read every Sherlock
Holmes story since they started in July '91.

CLIVE: (*Eagerly; he also is a fan*) Are you reading *The Hound of
the Baskervilles*, sir?

BETTERIDGE: Am I not! What did you think of the end of the
last instalment?

CLIVE: Bit of a facer for poor old Watson, sir.

BETTERIDGE: (*Laughs and recites:*) 'A lovely evening, my dear
Watson. I really think you will be more comfortable outside

'I've read every Sherlock Holmes story since they started in July '91.'

than in.' (*Laughs.*) Sarcastic devil, that [fellow] Holmes. I once had a C.O. just like him. [[This Conan Doyle]] [He] must be [[a sound sort of]] [rather a good] fellow, as authors go.

CLIVE: (*Encouraged*) Well, sir, Mr Conan Doyle is collecting material about our campaign in South Africa to counter German propaganda. *The Times* printed an interview with me about seven weeks ago –

BETTERIDGE: That's bad. Good rule to keep out of the papers. Still *The Times* is a bit different.

[MAJOR PLUMLEY: (*Murmurs agreement*) Mmm, yes.]

CLIVE: Yes, sir. I mentioned in the interview the name of a place called Jordaan Siding. I spent seven months there. Now this girl writes from Berlin that the worst stories of all are being put about by a fellow called Kaunitz who says he saw with his own eyes British soldiers kill two hundred and fifty women and children at Jordaan Siding in order to save feeding them!

BETTERIDGE: Do you know this fellow Kaunitz?

CLIVE: Of course, sir. He's the most awful little [[skunk]] [rat]! He was spying for *us*, he was spying for the *Boers*, he made South Africa too hot for himself and skipped. Both sides would have shot him if they'd caught him.

BETTERIDGE: I see. Now what do you want me to do?

CLIVE: (*Enthusiastically*) My leave isn't up for four weeks, sir. Why shouldn't I go to Berlin and confront this little rat? I'll soon –

BETTERIDGE: (*Shocked*) My dear boy – first of all, it's not done. This isn't Army business, it's Embassy. Leave politics to the politicians. You wouldn't like a diplomat to come charging into the front line with your company, would you?

CLIVE: It might do him a lot of good!

BETTERIDGE: (*Standing up*) Juvenile nonsense, my lad!

CLIVE: (*At once standing also*) Sorry, sir!

[[BETTERIDGE: That's all right, Candy. Never go off at half-cock, my boy. Keep cool. Keep your mouth shut. Avoid politicians like the plague. That's the way to get on in the Army.

CLIVE: Yes, sir.]]*

BETTERIDGE: You were [[given leave]] [sent home] in order to recuperate. Your country needs you. Play golf?

CLIVE: Yes, sir.

BETTERIDGE: What's your form?

CLIVE: About ten, sir.

BETTERIDGE: (*Satisfied*) Care for a game?

CLIVE: Sorry, sir. I'm invited by Lady Gilpin to Leicestershire. Start tomorrow.

---

* This exchange is marked for cutting in the typescript, but was in fact included in the added Sequence 48A. See pp. 172–3.

BETTERIDGE: Well, enjoy yourself.
> (*Telephone rings.* MAJOR PLUMLEY *answers, but soon loses interest in the call while he listens to the following exchange.*
> *They move towards the door.*)

BETTERIDGE: By-the-way, [[this fellow –]] this author chap.
[CLIVE: Author chap?
BETTERIDGE: This fellow] who wrote *The Hound of the Baskervilles* –
CLIVE: [[Yes, sir?]] [Conan Doyle.]
BETTERIDGE: [Yes.] You didn't happen to ask him, by any chance, what happens in the next instalment?
[MAJOR PLUMLEY: (*To his caller*) Just a moment.]
CLIVE: Yes, sir. There's another murder!
BETTERIDGE: (*Very concerned*) Not the Baronet?
CLIVE: No, sir. The Baronet is safe.
BETTERIDGE: (*Relieved*) [Good,] I'm glad – (*He opens the door* [[*and* CLIVE *goes*]]. [MAJOR PLUMLEY *is equally relieved.*])

CORRIDOR

[FIRST PASSER-BY: Warm for January.
SECOND PASSER-BY: Damn cold I call it.
> (BETTERIDGE *closes the door, then opens it again to give* CLIVE *parting advice.*)

BETTERIDGE: Take my tip, my boy. You've got a damn good V.C., now keep quiet for a bit, eh?
> (*He closes the door.* CLIVE *whistles 'Titania' as he joins* HOPPY.] HOPPY *is very curious.* CLIVE *jerks his head and they walk down the corridor as they talk.*)

HOPPY: Well? What did he say?
[[CLIVE: (*Sardonically*) 'Lovely evening, my dear Watson!'
HOPPY: What?
CLIVE: (*Same tone*) 'You'll be more comfortable outside than in.'
HOPPY: You're cracked. Did he say you could go?

CLIVE: (*Scornfully*) 'Leave politics to the politicians!'
HOPPY: (*Exasperated*) Are you going or aren't you?
CLIVE: (*Stops*) Yes!
HOPPY: With or without approval?
CLIVE: Well, he didn't say I couldn't.
      (*They look at each other.*)
CLIVE: If I ask somebody else, they may forbid me to go.
      (*Pause.*)]] Look here, do you want to go to the Theatre
      tonight?
HOPPY: [[But]] [Well I like that] you said –
CLIVE: Never mind what I said. (*He shows ticket.*) Here! Box A,
      Her Majesty's Theatre. 'The Last of the Dandies'. Introduce
      yourself to Lady Gilpin – tell them I had to go on [[Secret
      Service]] [some secret mission] – make me out a mysterious
      romantic figure. The girl's [[nice]] [pretty], the mother's a
      Gorgon.
      (CLIVE *starts off again at a great pace,* HOPPY, *dazed but
      obedient, panting after him.*)
HOPPY: [[You mean you're going straight away?]] [Are you
      going on a secret mission?]
CLIVE: [[Of course.]] [Yes, to Berlin.
HOPPY: Did he send you?
CLIVE: No, it's a secret from him too.]
[[HOPPY: But – how will you go?
CLIVE: Cab, boat-train, boat, another train – they must have
      trains in Germany as well as here. Fitzroy is some sort of
      Secretary at the Berlin Embassy. I'll wire him I'm coming
      and I'll wire the girl from my hotel.
HOPPY: Hotel . . . ?
CLIVE: Well, they must have hotels in Berlin, too.]]
      (*Dissolve to:*)

Insert: a primitive coloured postcard of the Wilhelmplatz.
CLIVE's *pen makes an X where the Kaiserhof Hotel stands on
the corner of the Mohrenstrasse.*

CLIVE'S ROOM
*It is not the best room in the hotel but it is all right. The window
looks out over the railway station, from below comes the sound
of locomotives, etc. It is snowing outside.*
The room is cold and CLIVE *has his overcoat over his shoulders
and a rug round his legs. He is, of course, in mufti. The time is
9.30 in the morning.*
CLIVE *is writing picture postcards. Several are lying on the table
beside him. He is whistling: 'You are my Honey, Honeysuckle, I
am the Bee!'*
Insert: postcard. CLIVE *writes: 'Dear Hoppy, Have outspanned
at the Kaiserhof Hotel. Berlin is bigger than I thought. Have not
seen Miss You-Know-Who yet but –'*
A knock at the door.
CLIVE: (*Calls*) Come in!
    (*Nothing happens.*
    CLIVE *frowns and hunts on the table. He picks up a slip of
    paper on which he has written the most necessary phrases
    for everyday use during his stay in Germany. The German
    is written phonetically with the English translation
    opposite.*
    Insert: CLIVE's *emergency list.*)
CLIVE: (*Reading from list, in awful German, very loud*)
    Cumman zee hairin!
    (*The door opens. A* PAGE *comes in with a salver and a
    card.*)
PAGE: Das Fräulein wartet im kleinen Salon.

CLIVE: (*Understands not one word but reads card*) Fräulein –
    Edith Hunter – here?
PAGE: Jawohl – im kleinen Salon – klein! (*Gestures with hand
    to show 'klein' means 'little'.*) Klein – Salon!
    (*Cut to:*)]]

[SEQUENCE 24
Royal Bathers' Club

HOPPY *enters as the* PORTER *is putting a Berlin postcard on the
letter board.*
HOPPY: Morning, Preedy. Did you send those flowers?
PREEDY: Yes, sir. Oh, Mr Hopwell, there's a postcard for you,
    sir.
HOPPY: From Mr Candy, ha.
PREEDY: How is Mr Candy?
HOPPY: Read it for yourself. (*He rushes off.*)
    (PREEDY *reads.*
    Insert: 'My dear Watson, Have outspanned at Kaiserhof
    Hotel. Sherlock Holmes.')]

SEQUENCES 25 & 26
Kaiserhof Hotel, Berlin

LITTLE SALON
*It is a pleasant little room, decorated and furnished in rococo
style.*
EDITH HUNTER *is* [[*seated composedly on a sofa in the centre of
the room*]] [*pacing impatiently*]. *She is very neat; and well,
though not extravagantly dressed. She is what was known in
1902 as a 'New Woman': which meant that she intended to*

live her own life and knew her own mind. She has character to back it up; and brains. The sedateness of her appearance is mitigated by little crystals of snow, melting and glistening in her hair and on her furs.

STAIRCASE
At the bottom of the main staircase, outside the Little Salon. [[CLIVE *comes down at breakneck speed, halts abruptly at the foot of the stairs, glances sharply but with secret approval at his manly figure in a full-length mirror and continues with equal impetuosity into the Little Salon.*]]
PAGE: (*To* CLIVE) Das ist die Dame in dem kleinen Salon.

LITTLE SALON
CLIVE *enters and stops.* EDITH [[*rises.* EDITH *bows*]] [*standing, inclines her head*]. CLIVE *bows.*
EDITH: [[You are Lieutenant Candy]] [Mr Candy], I believe.
CLIVE: [[In England. Here I'm plain Mister. You are Miss Hunter?]] [Miss Hunter?]
EDITH: Yes. Thank you for your telegram. It came as a great surprise to me. I had no idea you were in Berlin.
CLIVE: Nor had I until now.
EDITH: I beg your pardon.
CLIVE: I only arrived yesterday.
EDITH: (*Stares*) Do you – can you possibly mean that you have come solely on account of my letter?
CLIVE: Well – naturally.
EDITH: Oh! (*She is rather overwhelmed.*)
CLIVE: (*Concerned*) You don't mind – do you?
EDITH: (*Recovering*) No. Of course not.
CLIVE: Well . . .
        (*She still stares, forgetting her manners.*)
CLIVE: Shall we sit down?
        (*They sit.*
        He waits for her to speak. Neither is a great

conversationalist.)

EDITH: Did you have a good journey?

CLIVE: Excellent. (*Pause.*) I'm sorry to bring you out in such weather. I was about to call on you.

EDITH: I have changed my address.

CLIVE: Indeed?

EDITH: Yes. My position became intolerable. I have had to leave.

CLIVE: No.

EDITH: (*Nods*) English people are not very popular in Berlin at the moment [you know].

CLIVE: Do you mean that you had to give up your job because you are English?

[EDITH: Yes.]

CLIVE: Can you get another job?

EDITH: Perhaps. In a few months' time. Not now.

CLIVE: Well, what are you going to do *now*?

EDITH: Go back.

CLIVE: To England?

EDITH: (*Nods again, very dejected*) I'm afraid so.

CLIVE: Cheer up! England isn't as bad as all that.

EDITH: (*Her eyes flash*) That is what we both want to prove, isn't it, Mr Candy?

CLIVE: (*Stirred*) Yes, Miss Hunter.

EDITH: How shall we begin?

(*There is a pause. Both frown in concentration.*)

CLIVE: You mentioned in your letter a man called Kaunitz. Do you know what he looks like?

EDITH: I've never seen him.

[[CLIVE: Because if he's the same fellow I hope he is, I'd like a word with him.]]

EDITH: I know a café where he and his friends have their Stammtisch – it means they have a table regularly reserved for them there . . . a kind of . . .

CLIVE: (*Not interested in the niceties of translation, cuts in*) Do you know any of his friends, Miss Hunter?

EDITH: (*A little put out*) Yes, one. A student, the brother of my employer – (*She smiles ruefully*) my ex-employer. He is a Burschenschafter. Do you know what 'Burschenschafts' are?

CLIVE: ('*This girl is a bit of a blue-stocking. Pity. She's pretty.*') No, Miss Hunter.

EDITH: They are Associations of Students professing Political Principles. They assert them by drinking beer and fighting duels.

CLIVE: [[I see.]] Duelling is very popular here, I believe?

EDITH: Oh, yes. It's a proud father that has a scarred son, and vice-versa. German girls find scars very attractive. (CLIVE *is a little shocked by this open reference to sex-attraction.* EDITH *is quite detached.*)

EDITH: A book was published recently on the German colonies in which it was specifically stated that one of the advantages of possessing duelling-scars was that the natives of Africa look with more respect upon white men who bear them than upon those who do not.

CLIVE: (*Gapes*) I feel like Stanley and Livingstone.

EDITH: Surely not both, Mr Candy.

CLIVE: No, of course not. You are Miss Livingstone. (*Laughs.*) I'm the missionary!

EDITH: (*Coldly*) *Livingstone* was the missionary, Mr Candy.

CLIVE: (*Rather dashed; he begins to think* EDITH *a horrid girl*) Ah – yes – of course he was. (*Pause.*) Well, what about this café? Can [[we go there]] [you take me there] tonight?

EDITH: Do you wish me to accompany you?

CLIVE: Well, of course.

EDITH: (*Rises*) Very well.

CLIVE: (*Flounders*) I mean – it's awfully kind of you – I'd obviously be absolutely lost without you.

EDITH: (*Having asserted herself is now disposed to be nice to this good-looking but over-assertive young man. She smiles*

charmingly) [[Then you *are* Livingstone after all, Mr
Candy.]] [Then, Mr Candy, you are Livingstone, I presume.]
(*She frankly holds out her hand. He shakes it firmly.
Dissolve to:*)

[[SEQUENCE 27*
Exterior: British Embassy, Berlin

A brass plate covered with snow.
*A gloved hand wipes it clean revealing the inscription.
Dissolve to:*

SEQUENCE 28
Interior: British Embassy, Berlin

OFFICE OF 'BABY-FACE' FITZROY
*It is the smallest and most inconvenient office in the Embassy. It
is a very odd shape. It connects by a multitude of doors with the
offices of other Secretaries, still minor, but far more important
than* MR FITZROY.
*This statement of fact and opinion is, needless to say, not shared
by* MR FITZROY, *who has a very great idea of his own
importance.*
As the scene opens, he is seated at his desk, impeccably and

---

* Sequences 27–30 were among a number noted as cut in a script revision memo of 19
June 1942. In this case, the reason may have been a combination of response to the
Ministry of Information's criticism (e.g. to the portrayal of the British who have lost
their jobs in Germany in 1902 as 'a lost-looking bunch of people'), and a deliberate
streamlining of the already over-long screenplay by eliminating unnecessary
exposition and atmosphere (as in the early Embassy scenes). The Berlin scenes were
also generously detailed thanks to Emeric Pressburger's first-hand knowledge of
and affection for Berlin, where he had lived from 1928 to 1933.

officially dressed (above-desk) in black coat, starched collar and cuffs, grey tie, etc. from which we can deduce the neat striped trousers and patent leather shoes (below desk).
A pile of letters lies before him which he is hastily reading and then stamping with the Embassy stamp (but not, of course, signing or initialling). He contrives to make the simple action look portentous and when he pauses and scrutinizes one of the letters and puts it aside for consideration, one feels that the unfortunate Subject involved has practically forfeited his national status.
CLIVE sits, patiently waiting, opposite BABY-FACE, who had been a very junior contemporary of his at Harrow. He is impressed, as was intended, by his host's show of importance. The door to the waiting room opens and VENNING, an old clerk, puts his head in, evidently not for the first time.
VENNING: (*Pleading*) Mr Fitzroy!
BABY-FACE: All right, Venning, I'm coming . . .
    (VENNING *fades away.* CLIVE *stands up.*)
CLIVE: Look here, old man, I'll come back another time. I didn't know you were as busy as all this.
BABY-FACE: Always on Tuesdays . . .
CLIVE: When can we get together?
BABY-FACE: What about Saturday? We could have a drink or something . . .
CLIVE: I'll be on my way back by then. Well, Baby-Face, (MR FITZROY *winces*) pity you're so busy. I wanted to have a talk with you. (*He looks round as a Secretary crosses from one door to the other, stepping over* MR FITZROY *en route.*) You must feel like Baden-Powell in Mafeking . . .
BABY-FACE: Eh?
CLIVE: . . . besieged on all sides.
BABY-FACE: Oh! You mean that crowd in the waiting room?
VENNING: (*Fading in*) Five past, Mr Fitzroy. (*Fading out.*)
BABY-FACE: All right, Venning. (*To* CLIVE) Well, they'll have to wait that's all. I'll tell Venning to take you out the back way

so that you won't be bothered by them.

CLIVE: They don't bother me. They prove I was right to come here.

BABY-FACE: Why? Are you working for Thomas Cook?

CLIVE: What the deuce d'you mean?

BABY-FACE: Well, they all want to go back to England, they? How do I know what you mean?

CLIVE: (*Patiently*) If you'll listen I'll tell you. They want to go back because they've lost their jobs. Why have they lost their jobs? Because of anti-British propaganda. Because of liars like Kaunitz.

BABY-FACE: (*Pauses, stamp in air*) Kaunitz? Who's he?

CLIVE: Don't you ever read the papers, man?

BABY-FACE: We have a Press Attaché who . . .

CLIVE: (*Getting warm*) But you ought to know about him yourself. It's his lies that are filling your waiting room. Don't you know that he's accusing us of murdering women and children in South Africa?

BABY-FACE: What do you mean 'us'? I haven't murdered anybody.

CLIVE: US! you silly ass! US, the British Army!

BABY-FACE: (*Surprised*) Are you in the Army?

CLIVE: (*Furious*) Yes, I am! And I've been in South Africa! And I know Kaunitz, if nobody else does in this place that calls itself an Embassy!

BABY-FACE: My dear Suggie, don't get so excited . . .

CLIVE: (*Parade voice*) Shut up! And STAND UP when I speak to you!

(CLIVE *has not been through a Subaltern's War for nothing.* BABY-FACE *shoots to his feet as if he'd been kicked from below, revealing that, below desk, he is wearing a pair of heavy tweed knickerbockers.* CLIVE *stares then deliberately walks round and inspects him. It is further revealed that he has thick stockings and heavy boots with skates attached to them, which makes it difficult to be impressive when standing.*)

117

CLIVE: Ye Gods and Little Fishes! Skates! What is this! The British Embassy or a Winter Sports' Club?

BABY-FACE: (*Caught bending*) I was just trying them on when you came in. (*He tries to regain his important tone.*) I have to go skating with the daughter of the Second Secretary. I'm late already . . .

(*He sits down again. But* CANDY *is still furious. He leans over the desk to within a few inches of the startled young man's face.*)

CLIVE: (*Ferociously*) I hope you break your silly neck! And the silly neck of the silly Second Secretary's silly pudding-faced daughter! And now I'm going to find Kaunitz and pull his nose for him – HARD! Goodbye.

(CLIVE *whirls round and the slam of the door almost rocks the building.*

BABY-FACE *stares after* CLIVE, *stunned.*

VENNING *re-opens the door.*)

VENNING: *Ten* past, Mr Fitzroy.

BABY-FACE: (*Blankly*) He's mad! Absolutely mad! We were at Harrow together, Venning. All this nonsense about Kaunitz.

(*Suddenly his expression changes. He has just realized the implications of* CLIVE'*s remarks about Kaunitz.*)

BABY-FACE: KAUNITZ! But I say! He must be stopped! He's going to make an awful scandal! Just now, too! Stop him, Venning! Stop him!

(BABY-FACE *rushes forward himself, forgetting his skates, which promptly catch in the carpet and trip him up. He falls.*)

BABY-FACE: (*Wails*) Oh, damn these skates!

(*Dissolve to:*)

Interior: British Embassy, Berlin

OFFICE OF SECOND SECRETARY
The time is about half an hour later. The SECOND SECRETARY
is a diplomat de carrière, cool, reasonable, about forty-five.
BABY-FACE FITZROY *sits to one side.* CLIVE *faces the*
SECRETARY *who is making a note.*

2ND SECRETARY: (*Looking up and laying down his quill pen*)
Yes – my dear Candy – I think I understand. It's not a bad
idea. Unfortunately there are complications.

CLIVE: It seemed clear enough to me.

2ND SECRETARY: (*Smiles*) Yet there are one or two things you
may not know. (*It is a charming smile.*) First there is the
'Alldeutscher Verband'.

CLIVE: Yes, sir. I've heard about them.

2ND SECRETARY: Indeed? From whom?

CLIVE: From a young lady who lost her job because of anti-
British propaganda.

2ND SECRETARY: Ah, yes, I see. Then she will have told you
that the whole propaganda against us is party-politics – a
slogan for the banner of this Alldeutscher Verband. The
German Government has officially condemned it.

CLIVE: But how about all these mass-meetings, sir – in Cologne
and Dresden – how do we know how the German People –

2ND SECRETARY: Let us leave the German People out of it,
shall we? In Germany there is only one man who counts:
the Kaiser; and the Kaiser desires only the friendliest
relations with England.

CLIVE: He's got a funny way of showing it.

2ND SECRETARY: I assure you it is true. But let me come to my
second point. I propose to make you a present of a piece of
highly confidential information. (*Impressively.*) The Prince
of Wales is coming to Berlin.

CLIVE: (*Surprised*) No! When?

2ND SECRETARY: On the 27th of January. I repeat this is strictly in confidence. The official reason is the Kaiser's birthday party. But it has been arranged that both His Royal Highness and His Imperial Majesty will make a speech; and their speeches will put the seal on the agreements of friendship between the two countries. (*He smiles winningly.*) So you see what harm your solitary exploit might do, Candy. Not that I don't admire your pluck – especially, may I say, as a soldier on active service, who certainly needs a permit to cross the Channel . . .

CLIVE: I am not on active service, sir. I am on sick leave.

2ND SECRETARY: Oh, we know all about you. There are not many Candys with the V.C.

(CLIVE *is silent.*)

2ND SECRETARY: You see, a soldier who has won the V.C. is not an ordinary soldier. His views, like his deeds, receive more attention than those of the average man. So, should trouble result from your actions here, it would be more than average trouble. (*Pause.*) Well?

CLIVE: (*Slowly*) Of course, sir, if His Royal Highness the Prince of Wales is . . .

2ND SECRETARY: Exactly. That is the correct attitude and, after all, you could hardly have known about it, could you? (*He has looked at his watch.*) You have missed the afternoon train. Pity. It's an excellent train. But you can take it tomorrow. (*To* BABY-FACE) Why don't you show Candy the town tonight, Fitzroy? You could take him to the Opera!

CLIVE: Thank you, sir, but I have an appointment tonight.

(MR FITZROY'*s face is an undiplomatic mirror. He is extremely relieved at* CLIVE'*s refusal. The* SECOND SECRETARY *stands, bringing the two young men to their feet. He shakes hands with* CLIVE.)

2ND SECRETARY: It was an idea of yours, Candy. Don't run away with the idea that I think it isn't. But, next

time, do ask the advice of some older man. (*He smiles.*)
Experientia docet, you know. Take advantage of the
experience of age. Goodbye, my boy! A pleasant crossing!
CLIVE: Thank you, sir.
(*He starts for the door.*)
2ND SECRETARY: (*To* BABY-FACE) Show Candy the way out,
Fitzroy, and then come back. I want a word with you.
BABY-FACE: Yes, sir.
CLIVE: Thank you – I know the way out.
(*He is gone, without a glance at* BABY-FACE.)

SEQUENCE 30
Interior: British Embassy, Berlin

WAITING ROOM
CLIVE *comes out of the* SECOND SECRETARY'*s office, shutting
the door behind him. He pauses at what he sees.*
*There are three rows of benches, all crowded with people,
mostly professional classes, business men, schoolteachers,
governesses, people who have been compelled to give up their
jobs because of the anti-British feeling. They are a lost-looking
bunch of people. They look up as* CLIVE *comes out.*
After a second's pause, CLIVE *crosses the room. He gives the
impression that he does not dare to look these people in the face.
Fade out.*]]

SEQUENCES 31 & 32
Café Hohenzollern, Berlin

*It is a typical big Berlin musical café. It has two floors, an upper
and a lower, connected by a very wide shallow staircase covered*

with red carpet. *The time is about 9 p.m. and people are crowding in through the wide doors from the wintry street outside. It is still snowing. The Porter outside carries a huge, open umbrella.*

The Patrons of the Café are mostly from the middle class and upwards. Students are there in their coloured caps (each student organization has a different cap), artists, officers, one or two parties of society people, ordinary townspeople with their families – all sorts. They eat and drink; glasses of hot punch and mugs of beer are the favourites and there is a great bustle everywhere.

On the upper floor, where the landing makes a big bay, there is an orchestra. Their standard of playing is quite high. The orchestra consists of a piano, a drum, a double-bass, a cello, a flute, a clarinet, two violas and four violins; and, of course, a conductor. But the more unusual feature is a wooden frame on a pole into which numbers can be inserted. Before each new piece, its number is put up, corresponding with the number in a little booklet placed on every table giving the name of the piece and its composer. There is consequently a great turning-over of leaves at every table when a new number is put up, for the café habitués are music-lovers; in fact many of the regulars know their favourite numbers by heart and applaud as soon as they are put up.

At the start of the scene, a number is just finishing. There is some applause. Then a new number is hoisted and we see the various reactions of the crowded, noisy colourful café.

At a table for two, close to the orchestra on the upper floor, sit EDITH *and* CLIVE. *They are drinking punch and eating cakes. The cake-holder is like a little silver tower with different cakes on each landing and is to be seen on many of the tables.*

EDITH is looking up the number in her book.

EDITH: [[773]] [93] . . . It is a song – all the rage just now: 'Die Mull . . .', 'The Mill Went Round and Round', Mr Candy. (*The orchestra starts to play.* EDITH *hums it.*

CLIVE, *who is looking very uncomfortable, takes the plunge.*)

CLIVE: Miss Hunter. I am afraid I have met you here under false pretences.

EDITH: Indeed! Why?

CLIVE: There are – political complications. [The Prince of Wales is coming to Berlin. He's invited to the Kaiser's birthday party. A goodwill visit, all that sort of thing, you know.

EDITH: Yes, I know. It is in the papers.

CLIVE: You see, Miss Hunter, I know a chap in our Embassy here. We were at school together. His name's Fitzroy, only we used to call him 'Baby-Face'.

EDITH: But how are the Prince of Wales and your friend Baby-Face connected?

CLIVE: Well, you see, he nearly had a fit when he knew why I'd come – Baby-Face, I mean. He dragged me in to see the First Secretary, and he nearly had a fit too. A possible scandal, you know.

EDITH: Are you coming to a point, Mr Candy?

CLIVE: The point is that] I had to promise to do nothing. [And I went bail for you too.] Apparently it's a matter for careful diplomacy. You can see what they mean.

EDITH: (*Flatly*) Yes, of course.

CLIVE: I know nothing about politics. [[I rather flew off the handle, I'm afraid . . . sticking my nose in where I'm not wanted . . .]] [I stuck my head in where I wasn't wanted] and I could get [[in all kinds of]] [into the most awful] trouble.

EDITH: (*Brightly*) Trouble, Mr Candy?

CLIVE: Well – I am a soldier – you know that, Miss Hunter.

EDITH: I thought you were a soldier this morning, Mr Candy. Or have you joined the Army since luncheon.

CLIVE: (*Dazed*) [[I beg your pardon.]] [(*Purses his lips.*)]

EDITH: (*With sudden animated interest*) [[Look! That is their table]] [Table's filling up].

123

(*Below we see a big round table, reserved for its usual regulars, the first of whom, two students in their caps, are just arriving.*

CLIVE *stares.*)

CLIVE: Whose table?

EDITH: Don't you remember the Stammtisch? That is where Kaunitz will sit.

CLIVE: You know, it's a bit staggering to see a girl take such an interest in politics.

EDITH: Politics?

CLIVE: Well, what else would you call it? German propaganda against England – counter-propaganda – the Alldeutscher Verband – that's politics, isn't it?

EDITH: Not for me – nor for a lot of people. You see, when our Embassy in Berlin reports to the Foreign Office in London that 'a slight change is visible in the attitude of the German nationals towards the Boer question', *I* have to report in my letter home that I have lost my position and am returning to the bosom of my family.

CLIVE: I suppose they will be rather sick about it.

EDITH: On the contrary, they will welcome me with open arms.

CLIVE: (*Quite at sea*) [[Oh.]] [I don't blame them either.]

EDITH: You see, Mr Candy, my family was opposed to my going to Berlin. They said that the best place for a young girl is Home.

CLIVE: (*Sententious*) Quite so!

EDITH: (*Sparkle in her eye*) Why?

CLIVE: (*Flustered*) What do you mean – 'Why?'?

EDITH: How do you know what is the best place for a girl? Are you a girl?

CLIVE: (*Embarrassed*) Well, really, Miss Hunter . . .

EDITH: (*Remorselessly*) Have you any daughters?

CLIVE: I say – really . . .

EDITH: (*Suddenly relents and smiles*) [[I know I'm not being fair on you. But]] [You see,] while you've been fighting, we

124

women have been thinking. Think [for] yourself, Mr Candy. What careers are [there] open to a woman? (CLIVE *fumbles.*)

EDITH: (*Answering herself*) She can get married.

CLIVE: (*Relieved*) I was just going to –

EDITH: But suppose she doesn't want to 'get married'? (*She pronounces the two words with delicate scorn.*) She can go and be a governess. But what does a governess know, Mr Candy? Nothing I assure you. So what can she teach the children in her charge? Very little except good manners – if she [herself] has good manners.

CLIVE: Still – good manners are important.

EDITH: Did you [[discover]] [learn] that in South Africa, Mr Candy? My brothers say good manners cost us Magerfontein, Stormberg and Colenso, six thousand men killed, twenty thousand wounded and two years of war when, with a little commonsense and bad manners, there would have been no war at all!

(*At the table below there are by now several German officers present as well as the students and a couple of ordinary citizens. A waiter has just brought beer. The students have a special gesture, making silly-looking circles with their beer-mugs before drinking.*

CLIVE *continues his conversation with this astonishing young woman who thinks marriage and good manners over-rated.*)

CLIVE: One thing I don't understand, Miss Hunter, is why you have to teach German children manners. I should have thought there were plenty of English kids who –

EDITH: I will tell you, if you promise not to laugh.

CLIVE: Promise!

EDITH: My only asset is a fluent command of English.

CLIVE: (*Greatly daring*) Hear! Hear!

EDITH: (*Frowns*) Obviously to teach English in England is to carry coals to Newcastle – and correspondingly ill-paid. I therefore decided to obtain a post in Germany, where [my] English would command a premium; and, having learnt German, to return to England where my German [[would]] –

(*She stops short, seeing* CLIVE *is not listening. His eyes are on the entrance-door.*

At the entrance, KAUNITZ *has just come in and is shaking and brushing the snow from his clothes. He crosses the crowded café to the big table immediately below* CLIVE *and* EDITH, *where he is noisily greeted by name and introduced to two of the officers who are newcomers.*

CLIVE *is still astonished at seeing* KAUNITZ *actually here in the flesh.*)

CLIVE: Well, I'll be sugared!

EDITH: That is he?

CLIVE: It's him all right, the little skunk!

EDITH: Well, shall we go? (*Gathering together her things.*)

CLIVE: Go? Oh, yes I suppose so. (*He hates to go.*)

EDITH: (*Rises*) History will remember this as the great Retreat from the Café Hohenzollern.

CLIVE: (*Pleading*) Just a second. Please.

(EDITH *sits again.* CLIVE *is rapidly turning the pages of the music catalogue. He finds what he wants.*)

CLIVE: Here we are! Can we ask the orchestra to play [[139]] [141]?

EDITH: Why – yes. Call a waiter. Herr Ober!

CLIVE: (*Commanding voice*) Herr Ober!

(*A waiter comes. Meanwhile,* EDITH *reaches for the catalogue and looks in it.*)

EDITH: Why it's [[Wagner! The Brünhilde Aria!]] [*Mignon*, 'I am Titania'.] Do you really like –

CLIVE: Please! Ask him! I'll explain later. [[One-three-nine]] [One-four-one]. And please ask for the bill.

(*The orchestra is just finishing a piece. The waiter comes up to the conductor and asks him to play [[139]] [141],*

126

indicating where the request comes from.
The leader looks across, smiles and bows.
We see CLIVE *and* EDITH *across the café. They smile.*
Below, two waiters bring a fresh load of beer to the big
table. Some people around are looking up at the orchestra.
They clap as they see the new number. Others consult their
books.
Up at the orchestra, we see [[139]] [141] *going up on the pole.*
At the table above, CLIVE *explains to* EDITH, *while*
watching KAUNITZ.)

CLIVE: Kaunitz was a prisoner in our blockhouse for seven
    weeks. This was the only record we had on our
    phonograph. I want to see if he remembers it.
    (*At this moment the orchestra plunges into the opening*
    chords of the Aria.
    KAUNITZ, *sitting with his friends, looks round with a*
    frown.
    CLIVE, *above, is delighted.*)

CLIVE: Touched him on the raw all right!
    (KAUNITZ *beckons his waiter.*)

EDITH: (*Excited*) He's calling the waiter!
    (CLIVE *is already waving a twenty-mark note to attract his*
    waiter.)

CLIVE: Herr Ober! (*To* EDITH) Is it done to bribe the orchestra?

EDITH: (*Her blood is up too*) Not with money! [Beer!] (*To the*
    waiter) Bier für das Orchester!
    (KAUNITZ, *with vigorous gestures, has told his waiter to*
    tell the conductor to change the piece of music. The waiter
    goes across and up the stairs to deliver the message.)

EDITH: (*Thrilled*) He's going to stop it.
    (*They watch in tense excitement.*
    KAUNITZ *sits frowning impatiently. His friends kid him a*
    little.
    Above, the waiter crosses from the top of the stairs to the
    orchestra, who are in the middle of the piece. The waiter

whispers in the ear of the conductor, who looks puzzled.
The waiter persists and points down to KAUNITZ's *table.*
The conductor looks down at KAUNITZ.
Below, from his angle, we see KAUNITZ *and his friends.*
The conductor smiles at these important customers, nods
and turns to his orchestra. He prepares to bring the piece to
an abrupt close.
KAUNITZ *smiles, gratified.*
EDITH *takes this to heart.* CLIVE *is watching for his own*
waiter.)
EDITH: Oh dear! He's going to stop!
CLIVE: [[Cheer up!]] [Round one to Kaunitz.] Reinforcements
are coming!
(*From* CLIVE's *angle, we see his waiter, carrying a huge tray*
piled with a dozen beer-mugs, bearing down on the
beaming orchestra. The waiter evidently explains to the
conductor that the beer has come from the [[Wagner]]
[Mignon] *fans. The conductor, who was skilfully about to*
bring the piece to a close, turns and bows in the direction of
CLIVE *and* EDITH, *turns back and changing tempo*
continues to conduct the orchestra in the Aria with greater
fire than ever.
KAUNITZ, *who has turned his back on the orchestra,*
satisfied that he has buried Titania, chokes in his beer, and
starts coughing. His friends pat him on the back. He turns
round, furious, and glares up at the orchestra.
His waiter arrives back and explains with apologies what
happened. Some of his friends start to share his annoyance.
They all look up at the table over their heads.
CLIVE *and* EDITH, *who have been looking down, hastily*
draw back just in time.
CLIVE *and* EDITH *exchange grins, safely out of sight*
above.)
[[EDITH: Now what?]]

(CLIVE *shrugs, but there is a gleam in his eye that would alarm the First Secretary.*
KAUNITZ, *with a face of thunder, pushes back his chair, crosses the café and runs up the stairs to stop it himself. His table applaud him vigorously.*)
[CLIVE: He's coming up!
EDITH: Let's go, Mr Candy.
CLIVE: (*Shrugs*) Bit late now.]
EDITH: I hope he doesn't see you!
CLIVE: (*Alas for diplomacy!*) I hope he does!
   (KAUNITZ *arrives at the top of the stairs. He pauses, throws a glance towards his impudent rivals, invisible until now, then is about to cross to the orchestra. A chord of memory vibrates. He stops, looks again.*
   CLIVE *returns his look.* KAUNITZ *can hardly believe his eyes. Then he comes towards* CLIVE, *who rises pleasantly and with great nonchalance.*)
CLIVE: Hullo, Kaunitz!
   (KAUNITZ *approaches slowly. He has had quite a shock but he controls himself. He makes no attempt at formal greeting and he ignores the girl. He stops at the table and looks at* CLIVE *with a grin.*
   People around sense that something is in the air.
   Down below the friends of KAUNITZ *all stand up and step back to see what is going on, which makes other people look up.*)
KAUNITZ: [[Das ist ja zu gut um wahr zu! ('*This is too good to be true.*')]] [Das ist ja eine schöne Überraschung, Herr Candy. ('*This is a pleasant surprise, Mr Candy.*')]
CLIVE: Come on, Kaunitz, you speak English!
KAUNITZ: I do. But I prefer German!
   (*He suddenly steps to the balcony rail and at the full pressure of his lungs addresses the crowded café:*)
KAUNITZ: Meine Damen und Herren!
   (*The orchestra stops abruptly. There is a commotion as*

people turn round, jump to their feet or ask each other who
the speaker is.
KAUNITZ, *still grinning like a fox, looks down, waiting for*
silence.
This is more than EDITH *has bargained for. She begins to*
see the possible dangers.)
[[EDITH: Let us go, Mr Candy!
CLIVE: (*Shrugs*) Bit late now!]]
(*He steps over to* KAUNITZ.)
CLIVE: (*Persuasively*) Stop it, Kaunitz, I'm with a lady.
KAUNITZ: You should have thought of that before you started
    your little joke!
CLIVE: (*Taking his arm*) Stop it, Kaunitz!
KAUNITZ: (*Furiously*) Take off your hands!
(*He tries to strike down* CLIVE's *hand from his arm. But the*
Englishman's grip at once tightens and the blow only hurts
his own hand. This makes him livid with anger. Never
ceasing to struggle in CLIVE's *iron grip* (CLIVE *now holds*
him helpless by both arms) he shouts for help.)
KAUNITZ: Kameraden!
(*His friends below, joined by others, are already surging*
towards the stairs.)
SHOUTS: Durchlassen! ('*Gangway.*') Platz machen. Zurück!
(KAUNITZ, *still held powerless by* CLIVE *who, for obvious*
reasons, is not anxious to let go, is still struggling madly on
the verge of a fit.)
KAUNITZ: (*Screaming*) Lass mich los, du Schwein! ('*Let go, you*
swine.') Kameraden! – You English swine! – You English
    murderer! – (*He spits in* CLIVE's *face.*)
(*This is too much for* CLIVE. *He suddenly lets go of*
KAUNITZ. *The man staggers, then recovers.*
CLIVE *hits him – once. It is enough. Up till now his actions*
have been purely defensive but he has been longing to hit
KAUNITZ *for days. All that longing is behind the punch*
which knocks KAUNITZ *cold. He falls on the table and*

'Stop it, Kaunitz, I'm with a lady.' Clive causes a diplomatic incident.

showers of little cakes descend upon the upturned faces
below.
CLIVE *turns to* EDITH, *who takes his arm and they start to*
go.
Four friends of KAUNITZ, *panting and indignant, bar their*
way: an Ulan officer, two students, an ordinary citizen. The
latter crosses to KAUNITZ *and, with help, gets the*
unconscious man on to a chair.)
CIVILIAN: (*To* STUDENT) Rasch! Hilf mir, Hans! ('*Quick! Give*
me a hand, Hans!')
ULAN: (*To* CLIVE) Sie werden dafür Rechenschaft geben, Sie
Flegel! ('*You will have to give satisfaction for this, you*
loafer!')
CLIVE: (*Getting the tone all right. To* EDITH) Please tell him

that it's his fault – (*he points to* KAUNITZ) – he started it!

1ST STUDENT: (*Surprised*) Engländer!

ULAN: (*Shocked*) Unerhört! ('*Unheard of!*')

(*The* CAFÉ MANAGER *tries to force his way through the crowd.*)

MANAGER: Meine Herren! Bitte keinen Skandal! Bitte, nehmen Sie Ihre Plätze ein! ('*Gentlemen! Please, no scandal! Please return to your tables!*')

2ND STUDENT: (*To* MANAGER) Eine Schande! Sie dulden englische Schweine in Ihrem Lokal! ('*Scandal yourself! Allowing English pigs into your café!*')

EDITH: (*Getting warm*) Wir haben gar nichts gemacht! ('*We haven't done anything!*')

1ST STUDENT: (*Rudely*) Wir haben nichts mit Ihnen zu tun, Fräulein! ('*We have nothing to do with you, miss.*')

CLIVE: (*Treads hard on* STUDENT's *toes*) Manners!

CIVILIAN: Ich spreche Englisch! ('*I speak English!*') (*To* CLIVE) You shall get into great trouble, my man! You are not now in England.

CLIVE: You saw very well that he asked for it!

2ND STUDENT:⎫
ULAN:⎭ Was sagt er? ('*What's he say?*')

CIVILIAN: (*Ignoring them, shaking his finger at* CLIVE) Herr Kaunitz is the friend of us! You [[shall]] [will] satisfaction give!

EDITH: Please stop shouting! You don't [[know who this gentleman is]] [understand]! He (*Points to* CLIVE) and Herr Kaunitz are old friends!

CHORUS: Was sagt er?

(CIVILIAN *translates hurriedly.*)

CLIVE: (*To* EDITH) It's going a bit far to call that skunk a friend of mine!

CIVILIAN: (*Shocked*) Herr Kaunitz is a member of der Alldeutsche Verband!

CLIVE: Then the Alldeutscher Verband ought to be ashamed of itself.

CHORUS: Was sagt er?

132

CIVILIAN: (*Translates, then to* CLIVE, *very excitedly*) Mein
    Herr! Officers of the Imperial German Army are members
    of der Alldeutsche Verband!
CLIVE: Then the officers of the Imperial German Army ought to
    be ashamed of themselves too!
CHORUS: Was sagt er?
    ([*German anger continues, untranslated.*]
    Quick dissolve to:)

SEQUENCE 33
Interior: British Embassy, Berlin

CORRIDOR
*Two pairs of jackboots, wonderfully polished, snugly fitting,
beautifully in step, marching firmly down the corridor of the
Embassy.*
They come to a door, halt, stand rigid.
*A pair of dark trousers and elastic-sided boots, which have
evidently preceded the two pairs of jackboots, vanish through
the door, preceded by an agitated knock.*
*The owners of the jackboots are two very smart officers in the
uniform of the 2nd Regiment of Ulans of the Guard. Both are
Oberleutnants.*
The owner of the elastic-sided boots reappears. It is VENNING.
He leaves the door wide open and motions towards it.
VENNING: (*In bad German*) Bitte sehr!
    (*Without a word, the two officers march in.*
    VENNING *closes the door.*)

SEQUENCE 34
Interior: British Embassy, Berlin

OFFICE OF BABY-FACE FITZROY
BABY-FACE *is standing, startled, behind his desk.*
The two officers click their heels, bow, shake hands.
1ST ULAN: von Ritter!
2ND ULAN: von Schönborn!
BABY-FACE: (*Mutters*) – er – Fitzroy –
(VON RITTER *is the elder of the two officers. He has charm.*)
VON SCHÖNBORN: Kann ich mit Ihnen Deutsch sprechen?
BABY-FACE: [[(*Haltingly*) Ich kann nicht – very sorry – No!]] [Natürlich.]
VON RITTER: (*Smiles*) [[I speak a very little English.]] [Being on British territory, shall we speak English?]
BABY-FACE: [[Oh, good!]] [Right ho.] How can I help you, gentlemen? Won't you sit down?
VON RITTER: Thank you.
(*The two officers sit.*)
VON RITTER: We wish some information about a compatriot of yours in Berlin – [[called]] [a certain] (*He consults a note*) Candy.
BABY-FACE: (*Spontaneously*) *Clive* Candy?
VON RITTER: (*Referring again to note*) Yes. Clive Candy.
BABY-FACE: (*Happily*) You've come to the right man! I know him well, we were at [[school]] [Harrow] together.
VON RITTER: Indeed?
BABY-FACE: Of course we lost touch a bit since the War. He's Army, you know.
VON RITTER: He is an officer of the British Army?
BABY-FACE: Yes. He's just come back from South Africa.
VON RITTER: (*Very pleased*) This is excellent news. (*To* VON SCHÖNBORN) Ausgezeichnet! Er ist ein Offizier!

VON SCHÖNBORN: (*Equally pleased*) Grossartig!
VON RITTER: (*To* FITZROY) You have relieved us from great
    doubts.
BABY-FACE: I don't quite understand . . .
VON RITTER: We were worried that your friend might not be
    able to give satisfaction.
BABY-FACE: Satisfaction?
VON RITTER: It is understood that an officer of the Imperial
    German Army cannot demand satisfaction from an
    opponent who is not his equal in position and honour. But
    since this Clive Candy is a British officer, he can be
    challenged.
BABY-FACE: (*Faintly*) Challenged to what?
VON RITTER: To duel, Mr Fitzroy!
BABY-FACE: Duel!

SEQUENCE 35
Interior: British Embassy, Berlin

CORRIDOR
It is empty except for VENNING *ambling down with a dispatch-
box.*
BABY-FACE *shoots out of his office across the corridor into the
office opposite. At once he reappears almost dragging* MAJOR
GOODHEAD, *the Military Attaché, whom he propels into his
own office to meet the two Ulans.*
He himself pounces on VENNING, *who is now near at hand.*
BABY-FACE: Venning! Hurry over to the Kaiserhof! Bring Mr
    Clive Candy here at once! Don't come back without him!
    Now hurry!
VENNING: Ye-yes, Mr Fitzroy.
    (BABY-FACE *at once turns and vanishes into the office of
    the* THIRD SECRETARY.

135

VENNING *stands dithering about uncertain what to do with the dispatch-box, finally knocks at a new door, the office of the* SECOND SECRETARY, *and goes in to deliver it.*
MR FITZROY *and three new gentlemen rush out of the* THIRD SECRETARY'*s office and cross to the office of the* SECOND SECRETARY, *They all crowd in.*
A moment later, VENNING *shoots out followed by* MR FITZROY *very annoyed and hectoring.*)
BABY-FACE: I told you to HURRY, Venning! Now don't argue, GO AT ONCE!
(MAJOR GOODHEAD, *with a face of thunder, hurtles out of* MR FITZROY'*s office and up the corridor.*
VENNING *really gets under way.*
Behind him the party, reinforced to the number of seven, comes sweeping out of the SECOND SECRETARY'*s office and up the corridor to the large and important door of the* FIRST SECRETARY. *On the way they are overtaken by* MAJOR GOODHEAD. *All arrive at the door together. There is a pause. The* SECOND SECRETARY *knocks. Then he and the* MILITARY ATTACHÉ *go in, beckoning to* MR FITZROY, *who meekly follows.*)

SEQUENCE 36
Interior: British Embassy, Berlin

OFFICE OF THE FIRST SECRETARY
It is a very large and splendid room with a high ceiling. A blazing fire is burning under the elaborate mantelpiece. The two gentlemen and the gallant officer enter. They stop, seeing that the FIRST SECRETARY *is engaged with a visitor. The* FIRST SECRETARY *is a very wise, very courteous elderly gentleman. His visitor is seated with his back to the door.*
[[1ST SECRETARY: Come in, gentlemen. This is Lieutenant

136

Clive Candy recently arrived from England. I gather from your expressions that you are anxious to meet him.
(CLIVE *has meanwhile stood up.*
The MILITARY ATTACHÉ *advances, bristling.*)]]
GOODHEAD: [[The Second Regiment of Ulans of the Guard are also anxious to have that privilege, sir.]] (*Glares at* CLIVE.) Mr Candy has insulted the whole German Army!
CLIVE: (*Respectfully, to* MAJOR GOODHEAD) I didn't insult anybody, sir. I only said that if Army officers were in the Alldeutscher Verband with Kaunitz –
GOODHEAD: – then the German Army ought to be ashamed of itself! Exactly! (*To* FIRST SECRETARY) Eighty-two Ulan officers want to challenge him.
1ST SECRETARY: (*Quietly*) Lieutenant Candy has told me the whole story. (*To* CLIVE) By the way, the girl you mentioned, is she trustworthy?
CLIVE: [[Unquestionably]] [Undoubtedly], sir.
1ST SECRETARY: (*Nods, then to* MAJOR GOODHEAD) Major Goodhead, surely it's not suggested that Lieutenant Candy should fight the whole Officers Corps?
GOODHEAD: (*Stiffly*) They are drawing lots, sir, to decide who is to have the honour of fighting this gentleman (*Pointedly*) who has not insulted anybody!
1ST SECRETARY: I see. Have you any suggestions, Major?
GOODHEAD: (*Pacifically*) Militarily speaking, Mr Candy has no option. He cannot fight a duel. He must run away!
2ND SECRETARY: (*Belligerently*) And politically speaking, such an action would be disastrous. Mr Candy must fight!
1ST SECRETARY: Gentlemen! One moment! Surely you are leaving Lieutenant Candy out of your calculations?
CLIVE: I'll fight if necessary, sir.
1ST SECRETARY: My dear boy, I know that. (*Pause.*) You had better go to your hotel now and stay there. Oh, and can you get in touch with Miss – ?
CLIVE: Hunter, sir? [[I think I can.]] [I believe I could.]

1ST SECRETARY: Explain to her that it is necessary to give the impression that your reason for coming to Berlin was to see her. You are probably in love with her, or something of the sort.

CLIVE: Oh, but I say, sir, I'm not!

1ST SECRETARY: My dear Lieutenant, you have caused enough trouble already. Do what I ask. Meanwhile I and these gentlemen will discuss the best way to get you out of this. *And us!*

[BABY-FACE: (*Sotto voce to* CLIVE) Well. You are a . . .]
(*Dissolve to:*)

SEQUENCE 37
Interior: British Embassy, Berlin

OFFICE OF SECOND SECRETARY
Insert: a thin brown booklet (usually known as 'The Brown Codex'). It is the famous:

EHREN – CODEX
('*Code of Honour*')
L. BARBASETTI
ÜBERSETZT UND UNSEREN GEBRAUCHEN ANGEPASST
VON
('*Translated and for our own purpose adapted by*')
GUSTAV RISTOW*

The time is later on, the afternoon of the same day. It is a Conference of Seconds. Those of the Englishman are: The SECOND SECRETARY *and the* MILITARY ATTACHÉ. *Those of the German:* VON RITTER *and* VON REUMANN. *(The latter, who is a Rittmeister (Captain), is an older officer in the same*

---

* The Powell papers include a specially commissioned translation of the *Ehren Codex*, which was closely followed in the film to ensure full authenticity for the duel scene.

Regiment of Ulans, he speaks English even better than von Ritter.) All four are seated around a big round table. It is a very serious Conference. The Englishmen are naturally ill-at-ease; the Germans are not, having done this sort of thing before: VON REUMANN *is lofty,* VON RITTER *is affable.*
[[*The Codex lies on the polished table.* VON RITTER *pushes it across to* MAJOR GOODHEAD.]]

VON RITTER: [(*To* VON REUMANN) May I have the Codex, Herr Rittmeister?] This is our famous 'Brown Codex', Major Goodhead, the 'Code of Honour' observed by all duellists. We thought you might not be familiar with it.

GOODHEAD: (*Drily*) Thank you. I shall study it with attention.

VON RITTER: We have permission to offer for the site of the duel the gymnasium at the barracks of our Regiment.
(*The* MAJOR *and the* SECRETARY *exchange glances. The* SECRETARY *nods firmly.*)

GOODHEAD: (*Gloomily*) We agree.

VON RITTER: We are now in a position to announce the name of our fellow officer, who will fight Lieutenant Candy: Oberleutnant Theodor Kretschmar-Schuldorff.

2ND SECRETARY: May I make a note of that?

VON RITTER: With the greatest pleasure.

VON REUMANN: Here is his card. (*He passes it across.*)

VON RITTER: Have you gentlemen any suggestions regarding choice of Leader for the Duel?

GOODHEAD: (*Still gloomily*) We suggest the Military Attaché [[of]] [to] the Swedish [[Embassy]] [Legation].
(*The two Germans confer solemnly in a whisper.*)

VON REUMANN: We agree. His name?

GOODHEAD: Colonel Borg.

VON REUMANN: (*Writing*) Colonel Borg.

VON RITTER: Regarding sabres, we shall, of course, supply a number to choose from.

GOODHEAD: With your permission, we shall supply a number as well.

139

VON RITTER: Certainly. The choice of sabres will be determined by lot.

2ND SECRETARY: (*Nods*) Good.

(VON REUMANN *reaches for the 'Brown Codex' and, opening it at para. 137, points to it.*)

VON REUMANN: You know, of course, that the sabre must not exceed the maximum weight of 60 Dekagrammes!

(VON REUMANN *passes the book to the* SECOND SECRETARY, *who reads it gravely.*)

GOODHEAD: (*Reading also*) We shall make a note of it. (*He does so.*)

VON RITTER: You will bring your own doctor, of course – (*The two Englishmen nod*) and we shall bring ours.

2ND SECRETARY: (*Swallowing slightly*) We agree. (*His imagination is beginning to work.*)

VON RITTER: Do you prefer to strip the upper part of the body of the combatants or do you prefer them in shirtsleeves? (SECOND SECRETARY *swallows again.*)

GOODHEAD: (*Curtly*) Shirtsleeves. (*He points to passage in book.*) I see here that Paragraph 133 says: 'It is advisable a few hours previous to the duel, to take a bath!'

VON RITTER: Only the principals. Not the seconds. (*He laughs.*) (*The others smile, even the sensitive* SECRETARY. *The ice is slightly broken.*)

2ND SECRETARY: It is a very strange sensation to be preparing a duel between two people who have never even seen each other.

VON RITTER: (*Carelessly*) It happens sometimes. Marriages also! (*He laughs again.*) By the way, has your man ever fought a duel?

GOODHEAD: No. Has yours?

(VON RITTER *stands, exchanging a glance with* VON REUMANN.)

VON RITTER: Between ourselves, Theo does not really approve of duels.

2ND SECRETARY: (*Hopefully*) Then [gentlemen] – is this fight really necessary?

VON RITTER: (*Very seriously and choosing his words*) [Sir.] There are in a soldier's life moments when his personal feelings do not count. Oberleutnant Kretschmar-Schuldorff knows his duty very well.
(*All the gentlemen stand up.*)

GOODHEAD: We have not agreed the time, gentlemen.

VON REUMANN: [[Is]] [Will] seven o'clock in the morning [be] agreeable to you?
(*The two Englishmen confer.*)

[GOODHEAD: Get it over early.]

2ND SECRETARY: (*Nods*) [We agree] Seven o'clock.

VON RITTER: It would be advisable to meet half an hour earlier.

GOODHEAD: At 6.30 a.m. in the gymnasium, at the barracks of the Second Ulans.
[[(*Far away a town clock starts to strike the hour.*
VON RITTER *picks up the 'Brown Codex'*.)

VON RITTER: The 'Code of Honour' prescribes that the watches of the Seconds should be synchronized by the town clock. It is now three o'clock precisely!
(*All four gentlemen set their watches.*]]
Dissolve to:)

SEQUENCE 38
Interior: The Gymnasium, Berlin

[[*The clock, high on the wall, stands at 6.50. Outside the glass roof it is still black night.*]]
The camera moves to show the vast, bare, brilliantly-lit place. The limits of the combat area have been marked out on the floor by the Seconds: VON REUMANN *is still supervising it with* COLONEL BORG.

CLIVE CANDY *enters, accompanied by the* FIRST SECRETARY. *Their clothes are powdered with snow.*
CLIVE's *two Seconds cross at once to meet him and his companion.*
[2ND SECRETARY: Here comes our man.]
GOODHEAD: 'Morning! (*To* CLIVE *only*) Slept well?
CLIVE: (*Cheerfully*) Very.
1ST SECRETARY: He was still sleeping when I called for him at the hotel.
CLIVE: They forgot to wake me.
2ND SECRETARY: Your nerves are all right, my boy.
 (*While talking, they cross to their end of the hall, where there are two chairs and a bench. A similar arrangement exists at the opposite end for the Germans. The English* DOCTOR *is waiting and is introduced. He is an elderly man, an ex-Army surgeon, Lancashire-born.*)
GOODHEAD: Dr Crowther – [[Lieutenant]] [Mr] Candy.
CROWTHER: How d'ye do? (*Shakes hands and shifts hand to* CLIVE's *wrist without relaxing his hold. He feels the pulse, meanwhile scrutinizing* CLIVE, *who smiles back good-humouredly.*)
CLIVE: (*Surveying his party with humour*) Why wasn't I allowed any breakfast?
GOODHEAD: (*Producing the 'Codex'*) Because the book says not.
CLIVE: It would.
 (*The* DOCTOR *shuts his watch with a snap, restores it to his pocket and grunts:*)
CROWTHER: All right! You'll do.
 (*He starts to take off his jacket.*)
GOODHEAD: I hope you have read it?
CLIVE: Miss Hunter read it. She says it's a joke good enough for *Punch*! (*Looks around.*) Where is Theo Kretschmar-Schuldorff?
GOODHEAD: He hasn't shown up yet.

1ST SECRETARY: I congratulate you on your pronunciation of his name.

CLIVE: I learnt it by heart. [[Then]] [So that] when my grandchildren ask: 'Grandpa! Have you ever cut anybody's ear off?' I shall be able to answer: 'Yes – Theo Kretschmar-Schuldorff's.' Nobody could invent a name like that. Who's this?

(*A tall* OFFICER *in a different uniform approaches.*)

GOODHEAD: Colonel Borg, the Swedish Military Attaché. He is going to lead the combat. (*Introduces.*) Colonel Borg [[Lieutenant]] [Mr] Candy.

COL. BORG: (*Bows*) I must of course use German expressions. I shall say 'Los!' for starting and 'Halt' for stop. Can you memorize these two words?

CLIVE: I'll try, sir. Anyway at the beginning I'll be pretty sure you mean 'Start'! And, during the combat you're not likely to say 'Start' again!

COL. BORG: (*Stolidly*) That is true. Excuse me. (*He bows again and goes.*)

[[(CLIVE *looks up at the clock on the wall.*)]]

CLIVE: Seven o'clock. (*Looks towards entrance.*) Theo Kretschmar-Schuldorff will forfeit his entrance fee if he isn't –

(*He breaks off.*
At the entrance, at the other end of the hall, three German officers of the 2nd Ulans have entered. The officer slightly in the lead of the other two is THEO KRETSCHMAR-SCHULDORFF. *He walks swiftly, looking neither to the right nor to the left, followed closely by the others, the only noise their boots on the hard floor of the gymnasium and the swish of their heavy greatcoats, flecked with snow. They reach the 'German' end of the hall and are greeted by the little group of their people.*
THEO *salutes smartly, clicking his heels each time before he shakes hands with his fellow officers (*VON RITTER *and*

143

VON REUMANN) *with the German Army Surgeon and with* COLONEL BORG. *He looks a tall, ominous figure in his slightly fantastic uniform, he has, as yet, no personality beyond being the chosen representative of eighty-two serious-minded indignant Ulan officers.*
Formalities done, THEO *at once starts to remove greatcoat, jacket and trappings. As yet we only see these actions through* CLIVE's *eyes, at the full length of the hall. No clear conversation can be heard, only a distant sharp mutter, sounding hollow in the rafters of the empty gymnasium.*
COLONEL BORG *leaves the German group and crosses towards the British.*
CLIVE *is in his shirtsleeves. He looks wistfully at the other group.*)

CLIVE: I wish I'd brought *my* uniform!

GOODHEAD: (*Reacts, then remarks*) How are you with a sabre?

CLIVE: [Oh, I don't know.] I know which end to hold.

GOODHEAD: We drew lots for each weapon.

CLIVE: I hope mine is a nice light one.

GOODHEAD: All sabres weigh the same.

(COLONEL BORG *joins them.*)

COL. BORG: Excuse me, please. [Would you undo your shirt?]
(*He unbuttons* CLIVE's *shirt and peers inside.* CLIVE *reacts.*)

COL. BORG: Right! (*He points to Clive's right arm.*) Do you want to roll up your sleeve or rip it off?

CLIVE: What's better?

COL. BORG: I am not permitted to give advice.

CLIVE: I think I'll rip it.

COL. BORG: (*Nods*) It is definitely better.

CLIVE: Doctor! Your scissors, please!
(*The* DOCTOR *steps forward with a fearsome pair of scissors. He cuts the sleeve, then rips it off.*
While he is doing this, CLIVE *speaks to him.*)

144

CLIVE: (*Low voice*) What did he hope to find there? (*He means inside his shirt.*)

CROWTHER: (*Same tone*) Protective bandages.

(CLIVE *nods.*)

COL. BORG: (*To* CLIVE) Now you, alone, will come with me, please.

1ST SECRETARY: Good luck.

(*The* SECOND SECRETARY *and* MAJOR GOODHEAD *keep their fingers crossed.*

CLIVE *and* COLONEL BORG *march solemnly together until he stops* CLIVE *with a gesture in his half of the chalked arena. The German is already standing in his place. The two sabres are on a bench, equidistant from both combatants.*

Both men secretly eye each other with curiosity. The German is a tall broad-shouldered man, about 30, with a fine thoughtful face.

The Ritual of German Duelling now follows:

First the Protocol.

COLONEL BORG *takes a sheet of paper from his pocket and, standing between the opponents, reads aloud, first German, then English.*)

COL. BORG: (*Reads*) Ich werde jetzt das Protokol vorlesen – I shall read now the Protocol.

a) Sie dürfen den Kampf nur auf das Commando 'Los' beginnen – You will start only at the command 'Los!'

b) Sie müssen den Kampf auf das von wem immer gegeben Commando 'Halt' unterbrechen – You must stop the combat if you hear the command 'Halt' whoever may say it.

c) Sobald Sie sich verwundet fühlen, Sie haben den Kampf sofort einzustellen und durch zurückspringen die Distanz anzunehmen, auch wenn nicht 'Halt' commandiert wird – If you feel to be wounded you must stop the combat and by leaping back you must regain position at the original distance even if no 'Halt' has been commanded.

d) Es ist verboten, die Waffe des Gegners mit der freien Hand zu ergreifen – It is forbidden to seize the weapon of the opponent with the bare hand.

(*The* COLONEL *looks interrogatively at both opponents. They nod. They have understood.*
The COLONEL *raises his voice.*)

COL. BORG: Secundanten, bitte!

(*They step forward,* VON RITTER *crosses to the bench by the wall, takes the sabres, offers one to* THEO, *hands the other to* MAJOR GOODHEAD, *who offers it to* CLIVE.
The four Seconds take up position. Each combatant has one Second on either side, remaining at such a distance that they do not interfere with the free movements of the principals. All Seconds have sabres too.
COLONEL BORG *sees that all is correct, then addresses the principals.*)

COL. BORG: Fechtstellung einnehmen! – Into fighting-position, please!

(*In the 'Fighting-Position' the sabres are extended towards the opponent at the full stretch of the arm.*
COLONEL BORG *steps forward and, standing between them, takes hold of the two sharp points, bringing them together until they are a little less then two feet apart.*
For a moment, he holds them thus with the tips of his fingers. Then suddenly he steps back, snatching his hands from the blades, and gives the command to start.)

COL. BORG: Los!

(*The fight starts. They are both strong swordsmen.*
The camera begins to move away, further and further, higher and higher.
We see CLIVE's *two Seconds. They stand with the points of their two sabres towards the floor, ready to intervene and strike up the fighters' blades if necessary.*

Honour is satisfied: the ritual of German duelling.

The clash of steel and the stamp and quick movements of the fighters' feet go steadily on.

Then we see the German Seconds, also standing motionless and watchful, with downward pointing swords.

The movement of the camera quickens. It sweeps away from the fighters and high above them. They and their Seconds are small figures in the middle of the vast brightly-lit hall. The clash of steel becomes fainter.

Above the hissing gas-chandeliers the cross-trees of the roof are in semi-darkness.

Then – without a break – the camera slips through the huge windows and we are out in the street.)

SEQUENCE 39
Exterior: Barracks, Berlin

Snow is softly falling between the camera and the brightly-lit windows of the gymnasium. There are streaks of light in the sky but the street is still dark except where the lamps throw pools of light.

The camera has travelled back so far now that we see the walls of the barracks and the sentry-box at the gates.

In the foreground appears a waiting carriage, the horses and coachmen wrapped in their blankets, both half asleep. But the two occupants of the carriage are not asleep: they are EDITH HUNTER *and* BABY-FACE FITZROY. *Both are watching the lighted windows across the street, muffled in fur coats and heavy robes. It is a hard winter, the winter of Berlin.*

In the carriage they watch the distant windows in silence.

EDITH *is very anxious.*

EDITH: (*Low voice*) They must have started by now.

BABY-FACE: (*Tactfully*) You never know. I heard of one chap whose nerve broke – absolutely went all to pieces –

EDITH: (*Same tone*) Poor fellow.

BABY-FACE: (*Running on*) He was in such a funk – this chap – that he couldn't even lift his arm. His Seconds tried to lift it for him but as soon as they let go down it dropped like a railroad signal. Rum! (*He ruminates for a moment:* EDITH *glances at him with distaste.*) I say, I hope our chap doesn't get killed, it'll create an awful stink if he does.

EDITH: (*Very angry*) Mr Fitzroy! [I think] you are the most odious man I have ever met! And if anything happens to him I – I will blow up [[the]] [your] Embassy!

BABY-FACE: I say! (*Stares.*) [[D'you know, I really believe you would!]] Are you [[an anarchist (*sic*)]] [a suffragette] Miss Hunter?

EDITH: [[Not yet!]] [Never mind!] But if anything should

happen to Mr Candy –

BABY-FACE: (*Comprehending*) Oh! You mean Suggie! I was
     talking about the German fellow. Why, Sugar Candy won
     the Shield at school two years running. Nothing can happen
     to him. Old Suggie's never – (*He suddenly stops speaking.*)
     (EDITH *is not listening. She is staring towards the gate of
     the barracks, horrorstruck.*)

EDITH: (*Almost inaudibly*) . . . Oh! [Look] . . .
     (MR FITZROY *turns sharply and follows her glance.
     The gate has just been opened.
     An ambulance-wagon comes rumbling out of the barracks,
     turns sharply and is off down the street, the Army driver
     lashing the two horses to make them gallop.
     Through the frozen snow on the sides of the wagon we see
     the great Red Crosses.
     The lights go out in the gymnasium.
     The duel is over.
     Fade out.*)

SEQUENCE 40
Interior: Nursing Home

*The Nursing Home, a very exclusive and expensive one, almost
a private hotel, is on the Stolpchensee, one of the lovely inland
lakes in the forests to the south-west of the city, covered with
skaters in winter and with boats and bathers in summer.*

THE VESTIBULE
*The vestibule, which is large and handsome, has long windows
looking out over the forest and lake. As this is only one day after
the duel, the landscape is covered with snow.
On Visitors' Day the vestibule is crowded with people going and
coming, chatting to convalescents and each other. But today*

149

is not Visitors' Day and there is only one visitor visible: EDITH
HUNTER. *She wears the same outfit as in the carriage. Several
nurses are bustling about.*

EDITH *is preoccupied but no longer violently anxious as she
was in the carriage.*

From the corridor at one side, MAJOR GOODHEAD *and the*
SECOND SECRETARY *appear and come towards her, their faces
relieved.*

GOODHEAD: You can go in now, Miss Hunter.

EDITH: How is he?

GOODHEAD: The doctor says six to eight weeks, not more.

EDITH: I'm so glad.

GOODHEAD: Permission has been granted for you to stay here
  in the building.

EDITH: (*Surprised*) Oh, but I am not staying in Germany,
  [[Major]] [Colonel] Goodhead. I go home tomorrow. I
  have already telegraphed my father.

GOODHEAD: (*To* SECOND SECRETARY) Haven't you told
  her?

2ND SECRETARY: (*Embarrassed*) ... No ...
  (EDITH *turns slowly and looks with large eyes at the*
  SECRETARY.)

2ND SECRETARY: Now you must be sensible, Miss Hunter.
  We are very fortunate that everything has [[turned out as
  it has]] [gone off so well]. Do you want to spoil
  everything? The duel was generally supposed to be about
  you. What would people think if you left him now,
  wounded and alone in a Nursing Home? [Naturally] I
  thought that you understood all this, otherwise why have
  you come here?

EDITH: To say goodbye to Mr Candy.

2ND SECRETARY: (*With fatherly patience*) Go in now, Miss
  Hunter. By the way, don't bother about the bill. They
  have orders to send it to the Embassy. Good morning.

GOODHEAD: Good morning, Miss Hunter.

Edith learns that 'The duel was generally supposed to be about you.'

EDITH: (*Rather blankly*) Good morning. (*To herself*) Well!
(*They go off. She goes down the corridor to* CLIVE'*s room.*)

SEQUENCE 41
Interior: Nursing Home

CLIVE'S ROOM
CLIVE *is in bed, propped up with pillows. His head is so ban-
daged that only his nose and eyes are visible.*
NURSE KONIG *is putting logs into the big stove.*
EDITH *knocks at the door and enters.*
[NURSE K: Bitte.]
   (*For the fraction of a second, she is considerably startled by*

sight of CLIVE. *Then she recovers and addresses the nurse.*)

EDITH: Guten Tag, Fräulein.

(NURSE KONIG *speaks English fluently and incessantly.*)

NURSE K: (*Brightly*) Good afternoon, miss, you are Miss Hunter, are you not? My name is Erna Konig and I speak really excellent English.
(*This is true but her English has the excellence of a gleaming set of false teeth.*)

EDITH: Oh, that's splendid. (*Looks at* CLIVE. *His eyes smile and he waves. She smiles. To* NURSE) How is he? (*In low voice.*)

NURSE K: (*In loud cheery voice*) He cannot hear or speak. It will be difficult for a few days until we remove the bandage. He has a fine cut, the upper lip is almost severed. Really it is almost 10 centimetres in length, a knife could not have done it better. Do let me take your coat, Miss Hunter!

EDITH: (*As she takes off coat*) Is he in pain?

NURSE K: Yes. Certainly. He is a lucky man that there are no glass splinters in the wound.

EDITH: Glass splinters? Oh! Yes.

NURSE K: It is a common accident in our winter.

EDITH: (*Playing for time*) It must be.

NURSE K: The snow freezes on the boot, the warm room melts the ice, the little piece of slippery ice lies in wait for the hurrying foot and – PFAFF!
(EDITH *nods, breathless.*)

NURSE K: But to fall right through the glass window of the British Ambassador. Ah! That is not so common!

EDITH: (*She now has all the dope*) No. Indeed.

NURSE K: And would you believe, there is another accident in the other wing! An officer! He has cut himself to the forehead. Twelve stitches!

EDITH: It is quite a coincidence.

NURSE K: I go now to tell the Head Nurse that you have

152

arrived. I am ordered to prepare your room. You are
staying here, don't you?

EDITH: Yes, Nurse Konig, I do.

NURSE K: If you talk to him, please to shout. (*She goes but
turns at the door, beams reassuringly.*) I come back.
(EDITH *turns and looks at* CLIVE. *His eyes are smiling.*
EDITH *crosses and smiles down at him. He looks
extremely funny, with his bandaged head as big as a
football. She bends close to him.*)

EDITH: (*Shouts*) I have got you into [[a nice]] [an awful] mess!
[(*Repeats loudly.*) Awful mess.]
(CLIVE *nods. He agrees.*)

EDITH: [[And you have]] [You've] got me into a [[nice]] mess too!
(CLIVE *nods again.*)

EDITH: [I forgive you.] Do you want me to write to your
people in England?
(CLIVE *nods.*)

EDITH: [[To your]] parents?
(CLIVE *shakes his head.*)

EDITH: Brother – sister?
(CLIVE *shakes his head.*)

EDITH: (*Same tone*) Fiancée?
(CLIVE, *violent shake of head. He points to a pile of
personal belongings on the table near the bed. The only
thing helpful is a wallet.*)

EDITH: [Oh, you want] Your wallet?
(CLIVE *nods.*
*She goes and gets it. He opens it, takes out letter and
shows the signature to Edith.*
*Insert: the letter. On this page there are only a few words
in a large, sprawling handwriting:*
　　　　　'Your
　　　　　　Affectionate
　　　　　　Aunt
　　　　　　Margaret Hamilton'

153

EDITH: (*Off*) [Oh, your Aunt.] What is the address?
(CLIVE's *hand turns back to the first page. This contains the address and the main body of the letter, which is short and to the point:*

33 *Cadogan Place,*

January 20th 1902   S.W.I

My dear Nephew,
    You seem to prefer the hospitality of your Club to that of my house. I therefore suggest that in future you send all your peculiar-smelling stuffed animals to your Club as well.

P.T.O.

    EDITH *incredulously turns the letter over, unable to believe that this is all. But it is. She can hardly help smiling as she hands it back to* CLIVE.)

EDITH: Your Aunt seems to like short letters. What shall I [tell her] [[write]]? The truth?
(CLIVE *shakes his head.*)

EDITH: Accident?
(CLIVE *nods.*
Insert: he takes a snapshot out of the case. It is a very bad one of a South African hunting group with dead animals. One of the group is presumably CLIVE *but they all look alike.*)

EDITH: (*Nods*) Hunting accident?
(CLIVE *nods.*)

EDITH: Do you know that Oberleutnant Kretschmar-Schuldorff is here?
(CLIVE *nods.*)

EDITH: He has a [very] bad cut on his forehead.
(CLIVE *by signs indicates he has had eight stitches. How many had the other fellow?*)

EDITH: [He has] *Twelve* stitches!
(CLIVE, *very proud, makes sign of satisfaction.*

NURSE KONIG *comes in with a tray of chocolate and cakes.*)
NURSE K: Here is refreshment, Miss Hunter. Then you must
    depart for today.
EDITH: When can he have visitors?
NURSE K: Wednesday is Visitors' Day, Miss Hunter.
EDITH: Every Wednesday?
NURSE K: Every Wednesday from 3 till 5 p.m. At five o'clock a
    bell is rung for the end of visiting hours. [[Will Mr Candy
    have many visitors besides yourself, Miss Hunter?
EDITH: I suspect, quite a number. (*She smiles.*)]]
    (*Dissolve to:*)

SEQUENCE 42
Interior: Nursing Home

THE VESTIBULE
The bell, announcing the end of visiting hours, is ringing.
*The vestibule is full of people: groups talking to patients who
are able to move or be wheeled about, visitors leaving, visitors
who have met other visitors who are acquaintances. It is an
expensive and fashionable Nursing Home, with visitors to
match.*
*Suddenly there is quite a stir. There is a sound of marching
boots. All heads turn towards a corridor which debouches on
the left of the hall: a group of officers of the 2nd Regiment of
Ulans of the Guard appears. Conscious of their fine appearance
and of the sensation they are causing, they cross the hall in a
solid body making a good deal of noise.*
A GIRL, *in the foreground, near the camera, says:*
GIRL: Ulanen! [Wunderbar!]
    (*A new commotion arises from the corridor which
    debouches on the right of the hall. All heads turn in that
    direction. A group of officers of a famous English regiment*

155

*are emerging, also in full regimentals. They are also
conscious of the stir they are creating. Their leader, a
colonel, has a magnificent bristling moustache. They cross
the hall towards the exit.*

[[*The young* GIRL *is even more excited by the English. She
turns excitedly to her escort, a middle-aged 'Berliner'.*)

GIRL: Das sind ja Ausländer! (*'They are foreigners.'*)

ESCORT: Wir müssen gehen, Elizabeth! (*'We must go,
Elizabeth!'*)]]

(*At the exit, the two parties of officers have arrived at the
same time. Each party politely waves the other on.*)

[1ST BRITISH OFFICER: After you, sir.

GERMAN OFFICER: (*Gestures*) Bitte sehr, dahin.

1ST BRITISH OFFICER: What did he say, Aubrey?

2ND BRITISH OFFICER: I think he meant you should go first.

1ST BRITISH OFFICER: Can't do that, can we? (*To* GERMAN
OFFICER) You and I, you know, together.

GERMAN OFFICER: Bitte sehr.]

(*Finally the difficulty is solved by the respective senior
officers who go out together, followed by the others in pairs
– one Englishman and one German.*

EDITH, *in a deep easy chair close by, has watched this
couple with amusement. She now stands up, her finger in
her book to keep the place.*)

GIRL: Was können sie bloss sein? (*'What can they be?'*)

[ESCORT: Keine Ahnung. (*'No idea.'*)]

EDITH: Engländer. (*'English.'*)

GIRL: Danke [[sehr]] [Fräulein]!

(*She smiles.*

EDITH *smiles back. She starts to cross the hall towards the
corridor on the right.*)

[[SEQUENCE 43
Interior: Nursing Home

CORRIDOR
EDITH *opens the door of* CLIVE's *room and goes in.*]]

SEQUENCE 44
Interior: Nursing Home

CLIVE'S ROOM
NURSE KONIG *has collected a number of ash-trays full of cigar-butts and pipe-dottels. She does not approve of smoking.*
NURSE K: I thought nobody can smoke more than a German officer. Now I see a British officer can surpass him.
(CLIVE *is sitting up, in a chair by the stove. The swathing bandages are off his head, which is now a normal size. He can speak but not move his head. He has a complicated bandage under his nose and fastened to his neck.*
He has a mirror in front of him and with a pair of tooth-brushes, he is trying out the effect of several kinds of moustaches.)
CLIVE: (*Answering*) And not only in smoking, my dear Nurse Konig!
NURSE K: (*Indignant*) And in what else also?
CLIVE: Eating – drinking – making love – growing moustaches – (*Sees* EDITH.) Miss Hunter! I'm going to grow a moustache! What is your opinion?
EDITH: Excellent! [[The Colonel]] [Our dragoons] gave you the idea!
CLIVE: (*Astonished and admiring*) You always find me out!
EDITH: I saw [[him]] [them] cross the vestibule, preceded by [[his]] [their] moustaches. [[Your supporters]] [They] nearly

157

caused a diplomatic incident at the door, they collided with
a party of Ulans coming from – (*She points up the
corridor.*)

CLIVE: (*Glancing at* NURSE KONIG) My dear Miss Hunter,
soldiers cause *military* incidents, they leave diplomacy to
the diplomats!

EDITH: Really?

(*They both enjoy having their private joke and sharing it
with each other.*)

NURSE K: A German man would shave *off* his moustache to
show he *had* a scar!

CLIVE: That's just one of the points where we differ, my dear
Nurse [[Konig]] [Erna].

(NURSE KONIG *does not mind being teased at all. Her
national and native self-esteem is too thick.*)

CLIVE: (*To* EDITH) Shall you like me with a moustache, Miss
Hunter?

EDITH: How do you know you can grow one?

CLIVE: Nurse [[Konig]] [Erna]! [[Konig]] [Erna]! Is it allowed to
insult the patients?

(NURSE KONIG, *her tray full of ash-trays, smiles
indulgently.*)

CLIVE: What view, if any, do you take of my great moustache
plan?

NURSE K: (*Examines him gravely, gives judgment*) You are of
the moustache-type.

CLIVE: (*Triumphant*) Thank you.

(*She goes out.* EDITH *sits down by* CLIVE.)

EDITH: Is the British Army enjoying itself in Berlin?

CLIVE: On the whole – yes. They had lunch yesterday in the
Regimental Mess of the First Dragoon Guards. The Kaiser
spoke – and the Prince of Wales spoke –

EDITH: [[What did they say?]] [Spoke about what?]

CLIVE: Nobody could remember.

EDITH: When do they return to London?

CLIVE: In a week. Would you care to accompany them?

EDITH: They will have a special train, surely?

CLIVE: We could always try. (*Carelessly.*) Or – you could [[wait]] [stay] another five weeks and go back with me. Great care must be taken of me.

EDITH: No doubt.

[CLIVE: No answer at all. Will you or won't you? If you stay on, you may get another job.

EDITH: We'll see.]

(NURSE KONIG *returns, bringing a folding card table and two packs of cards.* EDITH *looks surprised and turns to* CLIVE.)

[EDITH: Oh, are we going to play cards?]

CLIVE: I asked Nurse Erna to fix up a bridge-four. [[I]] [We] don't want [[you]] to get bored.

NURSE K: The Head Nurse is finding a suitable couple for you to play with [after dinner]. But you must not sit up after 10.30 at the very latest.

EDITH: I promise you, Nurse Erna.

CLIVE: (*Shuffling*) [[Do you play auction?]] [You do play?]

EDITH: [[I am afraid not.]] Only whist.

CLIVE: It's simple. [[Come on.]] Let's play a trial game of double-dummy.

[NURSE K: I will bring a lamp.]

(CLIVE *starts to deal the cards out on the green baize. Dissolve to:*)

SEQUENCE 45
Interior: Nursing Home

CLIVE'S ROOM

The end of a game in progress. It is now night. An oil-lamp shines down on the table. EDITH's *hand sweeps up the last three tricks.*

CLIVE: (*Off*) You're a good pupil, Edith.
(*There are still only the two of them.* EDITH *has changed into a dinner-dress.* CLIVE *has made himself respectable. On a little table, near, are drinks and glasses.* NURSE KONIG *hovers, ready to leave.*)
CLIVE: (*Totting up figures*) Game – and rubber! (*More figures.*) That makes £32,000 I owe you. [Toss you.] Double or quits!
EDITH: Agreed.
(CLIVE *tosses coin. It falls on the table. He covers it with his hand. Both their heads come together over it. Very solemn.*)
CLIVE: Well! Which is it?
EDITH: Heads – no, I mean TAILS!
CLIVE: (*Uncovering*) Heads it is! We're quits!
(EDITH *sighs.* CLIVE *smiles. She smiles back. They have not been so intimate before. Nor so alone.*)
NURSE K: [[There are]] [The] cigarettes [are] here but please remember that smoking is bad for you, Mr Candy.
CLIVE: (*In excruciating German*) Ich liebe Sie, Nurse Erna!
EDITH: You are an angel, Nurse Erna.
NURSE K: (*Smiles approvingly*) Good night.
(*A knock comes at the door. There are voices.*)
EDITH: Here come our bridge-players. (*To* NURSE KONIG) [[Please]] [Would you] let them in.
(NURSE KONIG *opens the door.*
A tall YOUNG WOMAN *comes in, followed by somebody in a wheelchair, pushed by the* HEAD NURSE: *somebody in the uniform of the Second Ulans.*
CLIVE *stares. It is* THEO KRETSCHMAR-SCHULDORFF.
EDITH *has never seen* THEO, *but of course she recognizes the uniform and guesses at once who it is. A glance at* CLIVE's *face confirms her guess.*
The HEAD NURSE *is quite innocent of what she has done in bringing these men together.*
Of course THEO *and the* WOMAN *with him know exactly*

whom they are going to meet: THEO *is smiling and the German* WOMAN *is charming.*

THEO *speaks no English, or at least very little. He is very good-looking and about four years older than Clive. He is an excellent officer of the more thoughtful type. If he were not a soldier he might have been an artist. In one thing he is very much a German: he is thorough in everything he undertakes. He makes many friends and is a good friend himself. It is his own decision which has led to this meeting with his former opponent. The* WOMAN *is his girl-friend. Their association is not rooted in deep feelings but on a simple physical basis. If one of them were to say one day: 'I am leaving you because I have fallen in love with somebody,' there would be no tragedy about it.*

The WOMAN *is about thirty. Extremely clever, of the best Berlin society: 'eine moderne Frau' but in a very different way from* EDITH, *who believes sincerely in the importance of her beliefs.* FRAU VON KALTENECK, *on the contrary, would be much happier if she did not have to ride or hunt or be a sportswoman. She speaks good English and from the first moment is interested in* CLIVE.)

HEAD NURSE: (*Introducing*) Oberleutnant Kretschmar-Schuldorff – Miss Hunter – Mr Candy – Frau von Kalteneck. Ich hoffe Sie werden sich amusieren! ('*I hope you will enjoy yourselves.*')

(*Everybody shakes hands, the two men very heartily.*)

FRAU V. K: How do you do?

EDITH: How do you do?

CLIVE: How d'you do?

THEO: Kretschmar-Schuldorff!

CLIVE: (*Grins*) Yes, I know!

HEAD NURSE: (*To* THEO) Ich hol' Sie ab um zehn. ('*I will call for you at ten.*')

(*Both nurses go.*

There is no awkward pause. On the contrary, they all four

*feel like children when the grown-ups have at last left them
alone.*

CLIVE *turns to* THEO *very cordially and sincerely.*)

CLIVE: I'm very glad you've come.

(THEO *smiles.*)

FRAU V. K: I promised Theo to make a little speech. He would
like to have made it himself. (*She looks at* THEO.)

THEO: Very much.

FRAU V. K: Theo knows only two English expressions: 'very
much' and 'not very much'. Right, Theo?

THEO: Very much.

FRAU V. K: He [[wanted to]] [would like to have] come before.
(*Looks at* THEO.)

THEO: Very much.

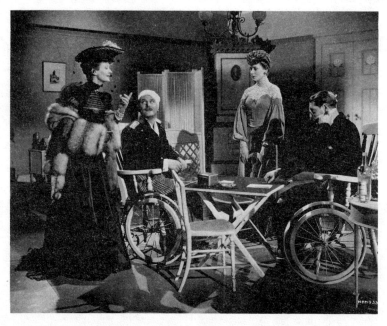

Frau von Kalteneck explains that Theo knows only two English
expressions.

FRAU V. K: But he was afraid nobody can translate to you what he says.

CLIVE: Miss Hunter speaks German. (*To* THEO) She sprecken German!

THEO: (*To* EDITH) Wirklich? ('*Really?*')

EDITH: Nicht sehr gut. ('*Not very well.*')

THEO: (*Politely*) Ich finde, ausgezeichnet! ('*I find, excellently.*')

FRAU V. K: Theo has heard that you took part in the South African campaign and that you have won a very famous [[decoration]] [medal]. (*She gestures as she speaks, so that* THEO *can follow.*)

THEO: Viktoria Kreuz.

EDITH: Victoria Cross.

FRAU V. K: He envies you because a German Officer knows about war only from the newspapers –

EDITH: (*Smiling*) And mostly wrongly.

FRAU V. K: *And* mostly wrongly.

CLIVE: Let's have a drink! Sherry?

FRAU V. K: I would love a glass of sherry.

CLIVE: (*To* THEO) Do you like sherry?

THEO: Not very much.

CLIVE: Port?

THEO: (*Politely towards* EDITH) Miss Hunter?

CLIVE: She and I, we drink Kirchwater. (*He means Kirschwasser and shows the bottle.*)

THEO: (*Corrects him*) Kirschwasser.

CLIVE: Yes – Kirchwater. Do you like it?

THEO: Very much.

(CLIVE *pours drinks.*)

FRAU V. K: Let me help you. (*She joins* CLIVE.) Do you know Berlin, Mr Candy?

CLIVE: The Hotel Kaiserhof, the British Embassy, the Café Hohenzollern, and the gymnasium of the barracks of the Second Ulans!

FRAU V. K: I hope we shall be able to show you more than that.

(*She smiles at him.*) Do you like the Opera? Concerts?

CLIVE: I prefer riding; hunting or polo.

FRAU V. K: I love riding and I adore sports.

(EDITH *offers cigarettes to* THEO. *He takes one.*)

THEO: Danke Bestens. ('*Thank you very much.*') Haben Sie Sport gerne, gnädiges Fräulein? ('*Do you like sports?*')

EDITH: (*Shakes head*) Ich bin nicht talentiert für Sports.

THEO: (*Lifting glass*) Prosit!

(*They both drink.*

CLIVE *has dealt out four cards on the table.*)

CLIVE: [[Draw]] [Cut] for partners!

(*They each turn a card face upwards on the table.*)

FRAU V. K: (*To* CLIVE) You and I. (*She smiles.*)

EDITH: (*To* THEO) Sie und ich.

THEO: Grossartig! ('*Excellent.*') Ich hoffe wir spielen jeden Abend. ('*I hope we shall play every night.*')

[CLIVE: What's he say?

THEO: Very much.]

(*Fade out.*)

SEQUENCE 46
Interior: British Embassy, Berlin

OFFICE OF THE SECOND SECRETARY
Fade in.
Insert: the bill of the ERHOLUNGSHEIM AM STOLPCHENSEE ('*Nursing Home at Stolpchensee*'). *The bill is made out in German, and the* SECRETARY's *gold-mounted pencil is ticking off the items. The pencil stops at one particular item, underlines it; the pencil is put down and the* SECRETARY's *hand presses a push-button on his desk.*
A distant bell rings.
The SECOND SECRETARY *is trying to be annoyed.*

Outside the sun is shining, it is early spring and the first leaves are appearing on the trees.

The door opens and BABY-FACE FITZROY *puts his head round it.*

BABY-FACE: [[Excuse me, sir, I –]] [I say . . .]

2ND SECRETARY: [[Ah, Mr Fitzroy, I was just about to summon you. Come in.]] [Oh, Baby-Face, I want you a moment.]

BABY-FACE: (*Apprehensively*) [[Yes, sir.]] [What is it? Those nursing home accounts?]

(*He comes in, revealing that he is beautifully dressed for tennis and even has his racket in his hand.*
The SECRETARY *has looked at the bill.*)

2ND SECRETARY: [Yes.] Will you kindly explain [[,Mr Fitzroy,]] what the deuce this item means? Forty[[-two]] packs of playing cards!! It's enough for the Casino at Monte Carlo!

BABY-FACE: [[Yes, sir]] [I know]. I spoke to Miss Hunter – she says [[the evenings were so long –]] there's nothing [[much]] [else] to do at Stolpchensee in winter –

2ND SECRETARY: (*Having made his protest, subsides*) Very well. (*He ticks the item and goes on down the list. He looks up and for the first time sees* BABY-FACE *in his spotless flannels, college scarf and Harrow blazer.*)

2ND SECRETARY: [[Well, Fitzroy, what's all this?]] [Don't you *ever* do any work?]

BABY-FACE: [[Tennis, sir.]] First time this year – if you can spare me, sir.

2ND SECRETARY: Hm! Well, don't catch cold! (*Looks at bill.*) *These nursing homes are an expensive business. Is Miss Hunter returning to England?*

BABY-FACE: As far as I know, sir.

2ND SECRETARY: But not at our expense, I hope?

BABY-FACE: [[Oh,]] [Good heavens] no, sir. She was going anyway [[you remember]].

2ND SECRETARY: (*Grunts, then suddenly*) Well, so was Candy for that matter! Eh?

BABY-FACE: Yes, sir, he had a return ticket but it's expired.

2ND SECRETARY: (*Sigh*) Very well. Buy him a new one.

[[(BABY-FACE *is going, when the* SECOND SECRETARY *stops him.*)

2ND SECRETARY: Mr Fitzroy!

BABY-FACE: Sir?]]

2ND SECRETARY: [[Have]] [And get] Candy [to] give you that [[time-expired]] [old] ticket. We'll [[try and]] claim a refund [[from]] [at] Cooks.

(*Dissolve to:*)

SEQUENCE 47
Interior: Nursing Home

CLIVE'S ROOM

CLIVE *and* EDITH *are packing.*

The window is half open to the garden. The sun is shining, but the stove is still burning for it is cold out of the rays of the sun. EDITH *is very quiet and subdued, noticeably so to anyone but* CLIVE, *who is whistling noisily. His moustache is coming on nicely although it does not yet hide the scar. Each time he comes within range of the mirror,* CLIVE *takes an approving look at the new moustache.*

EDITH *is just packing some handkerchiefs when* CLIVE *stops her and takes them.*

CLIVE: Half a mo'! Those belong to Theo. Put them with the alarm-clock. (EDITH *does so.*) How's your own packing going? (*Looks at watch.*)

EDITH: (*She finds it difficult to speak*) Not far.

CLIVE: Well, you'd better hurry up then.

EDITH: [(*Tearful*)] I'll be all right.

CLIVE: Don't be so sure. We've only got half an hour if we are going to call at the Embassy first. I can manage here. Come on, stop mooning about!

EDITH: (*Tearfully and angrily*) I'm *not* mooning about!

CLIVE: Keep your hair on! (*He stares.*) I say, old girl, what's up? (*She turns away. He revolves round her with a bewildered look, peers in her face.*
She looks back at him. She is crying.
CLIVE *is frightfully taken aback and quite helpless.*)

CLIVE: Edith! I say – Edith! What's the matter? It's not because I didn't call for you yesterday, is it? You know – Frau von Kalteneck left last night for the South.

EDITH: (*Sobbing*) Did she?

CLIVE: But you knew she was going!

EDITH: I'd forgotten . . .

CLIVE: I can't help it if you don't like horses, can I? We went to see her racing-stables – she has some fine [[horses]] [beasts] but they're too fat. Edith! do stop crying! Suppose somebody comes in.

EDITH: (*With feminine logic*) Nobody will come in . . .

CLIVE: Look! I promise to take you out the first night we're back in London! [[We'll go to]] 'Her Majesty's' [Theatre] – 'The Last of the Dandies' – they say it's [an] awfully good [show].

EDITH: (*Still sobbing*) – I saw – the paper said –

CLIVE: What paper? What do you mean? Is that what's making you cry?

EDITH: (*Shakes her head*) – the paper said – there's a new play at 'Her Majesty's Theatre' – called 'Ulysses' – !*
(*The door opens and somebody does come in:* NURSE KONIG.

---

* The Archers scrupulously researched the repertory of London theatres in early 1902, to discover what Clive *could* have seen. Among the Pressburger papers is a transcript of a *Times* review of Stephen Phillips's *Ulysses*, published on 3 February, which no doubt inspired Edith's reference.

She has an armful of books.
EDITH *quickly turns her back.*)
NURSE K: (*To* CLIVE) Oberleutnant Kretschmar-Schuldorff
returns your books, Mr Candy. He is on his way to see you.
EDITH: (*Moving at once*) I must hurry!
CLIVE: You'd better! We'll meet in the hall!
EDITH: Yes. (*She has gone.*)
(CLIVE *looks after her with a frown for a moment. Then his
face clears. Girls are strange and anyway there will be lots
of time to find out what's wrong. He looks ruefully at the
books, which are all German editions.*)
CLIVE: What am I going to do with them? I don't read German.
Miss Hunter got them for me.
NURSE K: You can present them to our library.
CLIVE: Clever Nurse Erna. (*The* [[Brünhilde]] [Mignon] *Aria is
whistled outside.*) So Clive Candy's name will always live
in a corner at Stolpchensee! (*Changes tone.*) But I must
write my name in them. (*He hears the whistle.*) Hullo,
Theo!
(THEO *appears at the window. During the first part of the
scene* CLIVE *is writing his name in the books.*)
THEO: (*He speaks a hybrid language now, like* CLIVE) Kann ich
come in?
CLIVE: Certainly, [come in] my old horse. (*As* THEO *climbs
through.*) My old steeplechaser!
(THEO's *scar is visible on his forehead. Otherwise he is all
right.* THEO *looks round.*)
THEO: Wo ist Edith?
CLIVE: Packing.
THEO: (*Surprised*) Packing?
CLIVE: Well, of course! Und Sie? How much longer Sie?
THEO: Eine week – or two. (*Makes sign with fingers.*) Clive!
CLIVE: Eh?
THEO: Edith come here! Translate for us!
NURSE K: I can translate –

THEO: (*Shakes his head*) Nicht das! Very important.

NURSE K: Shall I fetch Miss Hunter?

CLIVE: Now look here, don't disturb her, she'll never be ready! (*To* THEO) Ich mussen call at Embassy, old man – get my ticket nach London.

THEO: (*Insists, to* NURSE KONIG) [Ja.] Please!

(NURSE KONIG *leaves the room.*

CLIVE *does not understand at all. He shrugs despairingly and points to the drinks.*)

CLIVE: Drink?

THEO: [Nein.] Not now.

CLIVE: All right. What the blazes is up with everybody?

THEO: (*Very sincerely*) Clive! You and I friends. Yes or no?

CLIVE: Of course we're friends!

THEO: [[Very sorry, but you and I]] [We] must duel again!

CLIVE: (*Stares*) Where's your dictionary, old chap? You must have got two pages stuck together!

THEO: (*Smiling*) I – love – your – (*He tries to find the word 'fiancée' but can't.*) Teufel! Your – Miss Hunter –

CLIVE: (*Can't believe his ears*) Say that again!

THEO: I – love – your – Miss Hunter!

CLIVE: You're cuckoo!

THEO: (*Still smiling*) [[No]] [No, ich nein 'cuckoo'], you 'cuckoo'! Because Miss Hunter love me!

(CLIVE *stares. Gets up. Examines* THEO *again.*

THEO *nods.* CLIVE *suddenly smiles.*)

CLIVE: Congratulations! (*He grabs* THEO'*s hand.*) When did it happen? Why don't I know about it?

THEO: (*Still smiling*) No duel?

CLIVE: Duel? I – (*Thumps chest.*) Ich! fight anyone who tries to stop it! *Now* will you have a drink?

THEO: Double drink!

CLIVE: (*Pouring*) But you know, old man, Edith was never my fiancée.

THEO: Fiancée! The word I not find!

169

CLIVE: (*Handing drink*) Not my fiancée! (*Chinks glasses.*)
   Lovely girl! Sweet girl! (*They drink.*) But not my fiancée!
THEO: [[(*Thoughtfully*) So?]] [Bottoms up!]
   (*The door opens.* NURSE KONIG *comes in. She evidently
   knows or has guessed the whole situation.*)
CLIVE: Have a drink, Nurse Konig! Where's the fiancée? (*He
   bows to* THEO, *who bows back.*)
NURSE K: She can't come down –
CLIVE: Then we go up. Come on, Theo!
   (*They start for the door. Stop with the same idea. Look at
   each other, turn, pick up bottles and glasses and hurry out.*)

SEQUENCE 48
Interior: Nursing Home

EDITH'S ROOM
EDITH *looks like a young woman waiting to have her mind
made up for her. She is not packing.*
[CLIVE: (*Off*) Edith!
EDITH: Come in.]
   (*The door flies open and she starts round as* THEO *and*
   CLIVE *invade the room, beaming and carrying bottles and
   glasses.*
   *One glance at their faces shows her that the ice has been
   broken.*)
CLIVE: Edith, my child! I feel like a proud father!
EDITH: (*Rather faintly*) Do you, Clive? Why?
CLIVE: I have to give you away, don't I?
EDITH: How did you find out?
CLIVE: Theo told me in fluent Double Dutch.
THEO: (*Proudly*) I told. (*To* EDITH) Das einzige Wort ich
   konnte nicht finden war 'fiancée'.
   (*They all dissolve in laughter.*

170

CLIVE *hands round drinks.*)

CLIVE: A toast! This to the happiness of my fiancée who was
never my fiancée and of the man who tried to kill me before
he was introduced to me. Prosit!
(*They all drink.*)

CLIVE: (*Puts down glass*) May I kiss the bride?

THEO: Why ask? I have [did] not ask!
(EDITH *looks at* CLIVE. *He steps swiftly forward and takes
her in his arms for the first and last time.*
*They kiss each other. It is an important moment. It is a
brotherly and sisterly kiss; but for a fraction of a second
both close their eyes.*
When CLIVE's *eyes are open his whole expression has
changed. Suddenly he has realized the truth.*)

EDITH: (*Low voice*) Goodbye, Clive.

CLIVE: Goodbye, Edith – old girl. I hope we'll meet again
sometime –

EDITH: I'm sure we shall –
(CLIVE *turns to* THEO *and takes his hand. He still holds*
EDITH's. *He is just a little drunk.*)

CLIVE: Now look here, you son of a gun! You won't understand
a word of what I'm going to say – but I came to Berlin to
find a rat and found two of the grandest people I ever met.
[[I'm a little bit drunk.]] I leave to you, you Prussian stiff-
neck, this girl in trust; and if you don't take care of her I'll
raise the whole of England against you! The Navy will
steam up your stinking Stolpchensee! I shall lead the Army
down Unter den Linden! and we'll –

[[EDITH: (*Laughing*) Stop! Kamerad!]]
(CLIVE *stops, stares, finishes his drink and pours out
another one for himself and* THEO.
THEO *has an inkling of how the land lies. He looks gaily
and tenderly at them both before he speaks.*)

THEO: (*To* CLIVE) [Clive,] my English is not very much. But my
friendship for you is very much.

[[EDITH: And I'm sorry that I have to refuse your invitation to
     go to 'Her Majesty's Theatre'.]]
   (*Fade out.*)

[SEQUENCE 48A
Interior: War Office, Colonel Betteridge's Office

Door of Betteridge's office as in Sequences 21–23
BETTERIDGE: (*Off*) I hope it's taught you a damn good lesson,
     Candy. (*Now inside the office.*) Trouble with you young
     fellows is you always want to go changing everything. And
     what's the result? You spend all your leave in a nursing
     home full of foreigners. You cost the Treasury a lot of
     money. You make the Foreign Office very cross, yes very
     cross. And what do you get for it? Your beauty's spoilt.
     You weren't any fashion plate before. I'd be surprised if any
     woman would look twice at you now.
CLIVE: So would I, sir.
BETTERIDGE: When you were here in January, I told you very
     clearly it was not your concern. It was an Embassy job.
CLIVE: Well, sir, I suppose I thought I'd take a chance.
BETTERIDGE: A chance? A chance? You can't afford to take a
     chance with your career, my boy. You *are* in the Army as a
     career, aren't you, not for five minutes? You were putting
     up a pretty good show. You go barging in on this nonsense
     and you come pretty near to getting yourself kicked out.
     You don't want to get yourself kicked out, do you?
CLIVE: No, sir.
BETTERIDGE: Well, let me tell you one thing. Don't bother your
     head with things you don't understand and you won't go
     far wrong. Don't go off at half-cock. Keep cool. Keep your
     mouth shut. And avoid politicians like the plague. That's
     the way to get on in the Army.

CLIVE: Thank you, sir.

BETTERIDGE: (*Moving round the desk*) Care to dine at my club tonight?

CLIVE: Sorry, sir, I'm taking someone to the theatre.

BETTERIDGE: Pretty?

CLIVE: I haven't met her yet, sir.

BETTERIDGE: You're still a bit cracked, my boy. Well, I hope you improve as you get older. And cheer up, my boy.

CLIVE: Yes, sir.

(*Dissolve to:*)]

SEQUENCE 49
Interior: Her Majesty's Theatre

The new musical play Ulysses *by Stephen Phillips is being performed.*
*The scene is Olympus, the Council of the Gods. Zeus despatches Hermes to earth with orders to Calypso to free the ship of Ulysses. Background of thunder, etc. The curtain descends with a crashing climax from the orchestra and the effects man.**

[ATHENE: Father, whose oath in hollow Hell is heard;
   Whose act is lightning after thunder-word;
   A boon! a boon! – that I compassion find
   For one, the most unhappy of mankind.

ZEUS: How is he named?

ATHENE: Ulysses. He who planned
   To take the towered city of Troy-land.

ZEUS: What wouldst thou?

ATHENE: This! That he at the last may view

---

* This sequence was originally planned to start after the curtain had fallen, with no dialogue from the play included, and with Hoppy and Clive and their partners in facing boxes. It was then altered to overlap with a scene from *Ulysses*; and the Hoppy/Sybil and Clive/Miss Hunter exchanges were reversed.

The warrior's return: Clive attends a performance of *Ulysses*.

    The smoke of his own fire curling blue.

ZEUS: Where bides the man?

ATHENE: Calypso this long while
    Detains him in her languorous ocean-isle.

POSEIDON: Father of gods, this man has stricken blind
    My dear son Polyphemus, and with wind,
    With roaring waves, by me let him be hurled
    From sea to sea and dashed about the world.

ZEUS: Peace, children, and from your shrill reviling cease!
    Hermes, command Calypso to release
    Ulysses and to waft him over seas.
    Ulysses shall return.

POSEIDON: Cloud-gatherer, stay!

ZEUS: Yet canst you work in mischief on the way
    Yet ere he touch at last his native shore,

Ulysses must abide one labour more.
(HOPPY *and* SYBIL *arrive late in their box at this point*.)]
HOPPY: (*In a box*) Where's the bar?
SYBIL: Darling, do control yourself.
HOPPY: I say, there's old Suggie.
SYBIL: Really, darling? Where?
HOPPY: Suggie . . . Suggie . . . Suggie. (*Getting louder, until he attracts a scowl from one of the actors*.)
(CLIVE, *at last, responds*.)
SYBIL: (*Whispers*) Who is the girl with Clive, darling? Do you know her?
HOPPY: (*He seems to be enjoying a secret joke*) As a matter of fact I do.
SYBIL: Well, darling [who is she]?
HOPPY: (*Still enjoying his joke*) I believe he met her sister in Berlin –
SYBIL: Darling, why all this mystery? Who is she?
HOPPY: My niece's governess – a Miss Hunter.
CLIVE: (*Whispers to his companion*) [[What is the world coming to?]] [Wonders will never cease.]
[[GIRL: What, Lieutenant Candy?]]
CLIVE: (*Indicating girl with Hoppy*) Sybil Gilpin out without her mother! [And with Hoppy too.]
GIRL: Oh, didn't you know [,Mr Candy]? They are married!
CLIVE: Hoppy! Sybil!
GIRL: Over a month [ago. The family were quite taken by surprise. It was very romantic and sudden. They met here in this very theatre.]
CLIVE: [[And to think that I sent Hoppy to take my place –]] [I know,] I seem to be a born matchmaker.
(*Dissolve to:*)

SEQUENCE 50*
Interior: 33 Cadogan Place

HALL

A brisk tattoo with the front door knocker is bringing PEBBLE
to the door with dignified haste. PEBBLE *is the Head
Parlourmaid of Lady Margaret Hamilton's exclusively female
establishment.*

PEBBLE *opens the door on the chain.*

CLIVE *is outside.*

CLIVE: [[Good evening]] [Hello], Pebble!

PEBBLE: Master Clive!
> (*She half closes the door, slips the chain and opens it wide.*
> CLIVE *steps in. They talk in low tones as she closes the door
> and takes his things.*)

PEBBLE: Your Aunt is asleep.

CLIVE: [[Never mind, Pebble. Don't wake her.]] [All right, don't
disturb her.] I didn't feel like going to the Club tonight.

PEBBLE: You're not sick, Master Clive?

CLIVE: I say, Pebble, how did you feel when you buried Mr
Pebble?

PEBBLE: It wasn't so bad at the time, Master Clive, there was so
much to do. It was after that it got bad, if you understand
me. (CLIVE *nods gloomily.*) I hope you haven't come from a
burying, sir.

CLIVE: No. From the theatre. But it was the same thing, in a
way.

PEBBLE: Was it a sad play?

CLIVE: On the contrary. It was a musical play. Is the bed in my
Den made up?

PEBBLE: No, sir, but it won't take a minute if you don't mind

---

* In production, the original sequences 50 and 51 were substantially shortened and
elided, with lines transposed from the former to the latter. The scenes are
presented here in their final form for ease of reading.

sleeping in blankets. There isn't time to air the sheets. Lady
Margaret has made some changes, Master Clive, you'll see
when –

AUNT M.: (*Off*) Pebble! What is going on there?

[[(CLIVE *signs to* PEBBLE *not to give him away.*)

PEBBLE: Nothing, Lady Margaret.

AUNT M.: You're a liar, Pebble!

(LADY MARGARET HAMILTON *appears on the landing,
carrying a small brass oil-lamp. She is in her night attire.
She is as brusque in conversation as in letter-writing.
She sees* CLIVE.)

AUNT M.: Clive! How dare you come waking up the whole
neighbourhood at this hour of the night. Go to your club!

(CLIVE *smiles and comes running up the stairs to her.*)

CLIVE: All right. I'm going.

(*He scoops his aunt up in his arms before she realizes his
intention.* PEBBLE *passes up the stairs smiling.*)

AUNT M.: Did you hear me, nephew? Go to your club!

CLIVE: Very well. Let's go!

(*He starts down stairs at a great rate, carrying her as if she
were a feather.*)

AUNT M.: (*Highly enjoying it*) Put me down, you fool!

CLIVE: And I can stay?

AUNT M.: I suppose so, since there's no man here to throw you
out.

(CLIVE *at once runs upstairs and puts his aunt down on the
landing again.*)

CLIVE: How are you, Aunt Margaret?

AUNT M.: You may give me a kiss.

(*She offers her cheek. He gives her a big hug.
She is not displeased. She examines him.*]]
Dissolve to:)

177

Interior: 33 Cadogan Place

CLIVE'S DEN
*It contains all the personal belongings which he really cherishes.
It's a sportsman's room. He is a keen fisherman and there is a
gun-cupboard in one corner. There are a number of athletic cups
and shields.*
*Prominent on the wall are half a dozen or so heads of animals
which Clive has shot in South Africa.*
CLIVE *and* AUNT MARGARET *enter the Den.*
[CLIVE: Am I staying?
AUNT M.: I suppose so, since there's no man here to throw you
    out.]
CLIVE: I say? Who put up my South African heads?
AUNT M.: I've no idea.
CLIVE: They don't look half bad, do they?
AUNT M.: No. [Pebble, do stop fussing like an old hen and go to
    your bed.
PEBBLE: Good night, Master Clive.
CLIVE: Good night.
    (PEBBLE *leaves.*)]
AUNT M.: [Now,] Even money that some catastrophe has
    brought you here!
CLIVE: You're on.
AUNT M.: Debts?
CLIVE: No.
AUNT M.: A woman?
CLIVE: Not exactly.
AUNT M.: Explain!
CLIVE: I went to the theatre tonight.
AUNT M.: Alone?
CLIVE: With a girl.
AUNT M.: And pray why is she 'not exactly'?

(*top*) Junge's original design for the Den in Aunt Margaret's house.
(*bottom*) Aunt Margaret: 'Whatever you shoot, there's always room here
for them.'

CLIVE: Oh, it's nothing to do with her.

AUNT M.: Perhaps. [[Who was there?]] (See anyone you know?]

CLIVE: I saw Hoppy with Sybil Gilpin. They're married!

AUNT M.: Certainly. A very suitable match. He has money, she has land. [And neither of them has any brains.] You weren't in love with her, surely?

CLIVE: With Sybil? Oh, no.

AUNT M.: I am glad [of that]. She has muscles like a prize-fighter and she[['s bound to]] ['ll] hit Hoppy one day. [[Come along! I want to show you your Den.]]

CLIVE: (*Judicially*) Hoppy could give her a couple of stone.

AUNT M.: She will soon make that up, I assure you! Who is this girl you took to the theatre?

CLIVE: A Miss Hunter. I met her sister in Berlin.

AUNT M.: Is she nice?

CLIVE: Very. I mean the sister.

AUNT M.: Which sister?

CLIVE: The one that stayed in Berlin.

AUNT M.: (*After a pause, during which she surveys him*) [Then] the one in London is not so nice, I take it?

CLIVE: [(*Pauses*)] No.

(AUNT MARGARET *now knows the whole story.*)

AUNT M.: (*Suddenly she changes her tone*) Now [[look here]] [listen], Clive. I have eighteen rooms here, a bone-idle staff eating their heads off, and when you come home from South Africa, you go straight to your Club.

CLIVE: I know. It's awful.

AUNT M.: [[I had the walls cleared for your heads. Now,]] I want you to remember: wherever you go – whatever you do – you've [always] got a home here! And – whatever you shoot – there's [always] room here for them. Look how much room there is!

(CLIVE *looks around the big cosy room. He looks gratefully at his aunt [[and puts his arm round her shoulders]].*

180

Both of them look up at the heads on the wall.
[Clive casts a growing shadow on the wall.]
We see the heads, each with its plate, bearing the date and
place where the late owner came face to face with the
British acquisitive instinct.
Music starts to play.
The walls become covered with trophies from all parts of
the British Empire:
Trophies: Rhinoceros, Onyx, Lion, Tiger, Indian Elephant,
Sambhur, Tarpon, Mahseer, Crocodile;
Places: British East Africa, Sudan, Rhodesia, Mysore,
Upper Burma, United Provinces, St Helena, Kashmir,
Ganges Delta;
Dates: 1903, 1905, 1906, 1907, 1910, 1912, 1914.
After 1914 the wall is blank.
The camera shows the bare wall, then swings to show a
new trophy. A German spiked helmet, covered in khaki
cloth, of the type used in the Great War.
The inevitable plate says simply: 'HUN. FLANDERS,
1918'.)

THE KHAKI SEQUENCES

Note: The principal reason up to this point for making the
picture in colour is because colour is more successful in evoking
a period which, although some time ago, is still fresh in the
memories of many people. We can claim, of course, the pink
bodies of the General's Staff in the Turkish Baths and the
General's Red Tabs, but these, however attractive, are
decorations. Sights, sounds, but above all, colours, make up the
memories of a generation: more so in the case of the period with
which we have dealt. 1902 was the commencement of the
Edwardian era, full of charm, prosperity, spaciousness and

leisure, to which it seemed there could never be an end.
Our next use of colour is in the first part of the 1918–1919
Sequence which we call for convenience, the 'Khaki Sequence'.
After four years of senseless trench warfare, all the colour and
variety of Europe and its peoples had been reduced to a uniform
dull colour by day and to blackness by night. Khaki was the
colour of clothes, faces, official forms, everything: while the
battle zone itself had been reduced to a consistency as featureless
and as sticky as porridge. By this deliberate elimination of all
colours except Khaki, we hope to point this contrast.

SEQUENCE 52
Exterior: Somewhere in Flanders

A CROSS-ROAD
It is dusk. It is not raining but it has been and it will again.
An Army staff car, 1918 vintage, is approaching along the road,
once a pleasant avenue, now a dreary, cratered embankment
lined with splintered stumps.
The continuous thunder of heavy guns sounds in the far distance.
The car bumps to a stop at the cross-roads.
On the back seat sits COLONEL *(Acting Brigadier)* CLIVE
CANDY. * *He is now a man of forty-two, many ribbons on his*
chest. His moustache is heavy but well cared for, he looks tired
but full of energy and devotion to serve his country. He has a map
spread out on the seat beside him.
His driver, [[MULLINS]] [MURDOCH], *is also his batman. He is*
about the GENERAL's *age; out since Mons.*
The landscape, the sky, the car, the men and their mud-plastered

---

* A script revision memo of 5 July 1942 relies heavily on military protocol advice
  from the film's Technical Adviser, Major-General Sir Douglas Brownrigg. Clive's
  career is clarified and revised: 'Late Wessex Infantry; served South African War

uniforms are all one pervasive scheme of khaki. The only spots of colour are the GENERAL's *Red Tabs.*

MURDOCH: This is Dead Cow Cross-roads, sir.

(GENERAL CANDY *stands up on the back seat of the car and, through his glasses, examines the landscape.*)

CLIVE: (*Mutters*) The question is: whether that is the Church with the double tower, or the 'Estaminet du Pont'?

(*Through his powerful glasses we see the featureless mass of rubble at which he is looking. God knows what it is.* MURDOCH *sits fatalistically.*)

CLIVE: Damn it, Murdoch, you're supposed to know the road!

MURDOCH: I know it at night, sir. In the daytime it looks different.

(CANDY *snorts.* MURDOCH *suddenly sniffs.*)

CLIVE: Eh? Got a scent?

MURDOCH: Yes, sir. (*Sniffs again.*) That's our road. I can smell the two Jerries the Sappers planted.

CLIVE: For'ard then!

MURDOCH: Harkaway, sir!

(*Dissolve to:*)

1899–1902; European War 1914–18; Major-General, retired pay, 1935; re-employed Base Sub-Area Commandant in France 1939; retired pay, 1940; Zone Commander Home Guard 1940–42.' Apparently the rank of Brigadier-General, used during WWI, was changed to Brigadier in 1924, with a resulting change in style of address from 'General' to 'Brigadier' ('causing confusion and heartburning', according to the memo). In 1918, Clive can only be a 'Brigadier-General', the memo notes, and should be addressed in conversation as 'General Candy' – which advice was adopted in the film's actual dialogue, here and elsewhere.

Clive and Murdoch 'somewhere in Flanders'.

SEQUENCE 53
Somewhere in Flanders

EXTERIOR: ESTAMINET DU PONT
We see it in the last dull light of the fading day. The rain has started again, a persistent drizzle. All distinguishing features of the Estaminet have either fallen down or fallen in long ago. It is gradually vanishing into the mud and nobody cares.
MAJOR VAN ZIJL *is waiting outside in the yard as* GENERAL CANDY*'s car drives up. He has a lady's brown silk umbrella against the rain. He is a tough, lively South African of thirty-four, a veteran of the Boer War.*
He squelches over the duckboards to the car.

184

VAN ZIJL: Glad to see you, sir. I've got another umbrella for you.
(*He produces. The* GENERAL *accepts it gratefully.*)
CLIVE: You've a marvellous eye for loot, van Zijl.
VAN ZIJL: Learnt from the English in the Boer War, sir.
CLIVE: (*Chuckles*) Where d'you get 'em?
VAN ZIJL: Off Jerries – eleven of them – brought in an hour ago.
Lord knows where they stole them, they were using them for
camouflage against aircraft.
(*While talking they have left the car, crossed the duckboard
and gone into the Estaminet.*)

SEQUENCE 54
Interior: Estaminet du Pont

BAR
The room is now the Outer Office of Battalion H.Q. MAJOR
VAN ZIJL *is in command.*
*can see vaguely that once this was a pleasant little café, just as
with some filthy old tramp it is not beyond conjecture that he was
once a young, attractive man. The contrast is as great.*
*The room is crowded. Clerks are working and there is a telephone
exchange. Several officers around.*
As GENERAL CANDY *and* MAJOR VAN ZIJL *enter, everybody
stands to attention.*
CLIVE: (*Saluting*) Good evening.
(*He glances round, starts towards the Inner Office, then
stops and speaks to* VAN ZIJL.)
CLIVE: Can we get through to the R.T.O. in Dupuis-sur-
Something?
VAN ZIJL: Dupuis-sur-Crois. The Yanks are down there. How
about it, Paddy?
PADDY: 'Fraid the lines broke between us and 'Mile 14', sir. We
can send a runner.

VAN ZIJL: What message, sir?

CLIVE: Tell him to hold a place on the leave-train. When can I leave here?

VAN ZIJL: Not before dark. They're plastering the road between 17 and 19 with shrapnel.

CLIVE: Right. Will someone look after Murdoch?

VAN ZIJL: Nobby! Paddy, get that runner away!

PADDY: Yes, sir.

CLIVE: If any of you have got an important letter or message home, I'll take it.

CHORUS: Thank you, sir!

(CLIVE *goes across.* VAN ZIJL *follows, calling over his shoulder:*)

VAN ZIJL: Paddy! I'll [[tackle]] [see] the prisoners again presently.

SEQUENCE 55
Interior: Estaminet du Pont

KITCHEN

This was once the large kitchen and chief living room of the café's owner. You would scarcely guess it now. Its present function is office of the Battalion Commander.

The GENERAL *has heard* VAN ZIJL's *last remark. He goes to the fire and stands in front of it.*

CLIVE: What are these prisoners?

VAN ZIJL: Ulans. The Second Regiment. That's all I've got out of them so far.

CLIVE: The Second Regiment of Ulans? I'd like to question them.

VAN ZIJL: (*Secretly unwilling*) Certainly, sir. (*Goes to passage, yells.*) Paddy!

PADDY: (*Off*) Sir!

VAN ZIJL: Bring in the prisoners.

PADDY: Yes, sir.

CLIVE: Any officer with them?

VAN ZIJL: No such luck.

CLIVE: Where did you nab them?

VAN ZIJL: Floating down the river early this morning. I had a boom across and netted them like salmon. They had a hundred pounds of dynamite with 'em. My guess is they were after the new pontoon-bridge below St Mangy.

CLIVE: How the blazes did they get to know about that?

VAN ZIJL: They took one of our patrols prisoner day before yesterday.

CLIVE: (*Stares*) Are you suggesting our fellows talked?

VAN ZIJL: The Germans know how to make them talk.
     (*A little pause follows.*
     CLIVE *is thinking, a fact betrayed by a heavy frown and an occasional 'Hm!' He shakes his head as if unwilling to believe something.* VAN ZIJL *watches him, half affectionately. The slim, dark South African is a contrast to the solid Englishman. He produces a paper from his pocket.*)

CLIVE: (*Finally speaking*) [Well if they are,] They're cracking, my dear chap. It's a sure sign. Nobody starts to fight foul until he sees he can't win any other way. I quite believe Hindenburg, who I hear said the other day that until now Germany has used her arms with honour – (*After a slight pause.*) I admit he said nothing about her legs.
     (VAN ZIJL *has unfolded the paper, which is printed in German.*)

[[VAN ZIJL: This bears you out, sir.

CLIVE: What?

VAN ZIJL: It was on one of the prisoners.

CLIVE: Let me see it.

VAN ZIJL: It's in German.

CLIVE: Oh! Well, read it.]]

187

(*The door opens and the eleven German prisoners march down the passage and into the room under an escort with fixed bayonets. The prisoners have none of the colourful appearance of the Ulans of 1902. All the same they are defiant although not arrogant, as Nazi prisoners would be. They remain grave and serious all through the scene. Outside it is almost dark and the rain has got heavier. The wind has got up.* [[*When the prisoners come in an Orderly brings in three or four candles stuck in bottles and one oil-lamp with a cracked and smoky chimney and no shade. Another Orderly blacks out the windows. The escort lines the prisoners up against the wall.*
During all this action, VAN ZIJL *reads aloud from the German paper to the* GENERAL.)

VAN ZIJL: It's an appeal from the 'Erster General Quartier-Meister', from old man Ludendorff himself, to his loyal troops. It starts: 'Soldiers, stand fast or Germany will lie in the dust. Should the enemy discover that our Mannzucht – (*He searches for the word*) our morale is broken, all is lost, you will have fought and suffered in vain and the Homeland will hear the tramp of the invader.' What do you think of that, sir?

CLIVE: (*Grim smile*) What else? (*He is watching the prisoners as he listens.*)

VAN ZIJL: (*Reads*) 'Have you heard the British say that Germany has fallen? Is this to be? Nein und abermals nein! (*He mocks the style.*) Thus far they have seen only German faces, shall they now see only our backs? Stand, or the Fatherland is doomed and you with her!'

CLIVE: (*Thoughtfully*) There's a rumour that the Kaiser abdicated yesterday.

VAN ZIJL: Again, sir?
(CLIVE *smiles and walks over to the line of prisoners. They have heard* VAN ZIJL *reading Ludendorff's appeal but they have given no sign of having understood.*]]

GENERAL CANDY *walks down the line, examining each prisoner closely. He stops and walks back to a commanding position in front of them.*)

CLIVE: Do any of you know Oberst Kretschmar-Schuldorff? (*No answer.*)

CLIVE: Don't play deaf! He was an Oberst in your Regiment the last time I heard of him – Oberst Kretschmar-Schuldorff, Second Regiment of Ulans! (*No answer.*)

CLIVE: Which of you can speak English? (*No answer.*

VAN ZIJL *bursts out, addressing one of them:*)

VAN ZIJL: You! You spoke English an hour ago! Answer the General!

PRISONER: I do speak.

'We don't use the same methods that I hear you use on your prisoners.'

CLIVE: Ah! Now [[I want to tell you something]] [listen to me]. We don't use the same methods that I hear you use on your prisoners. But I assure you that we have means to get what we want. (*Pause.*) What was this explosive found on you intended for?

PRISONER: I don't know.

CLIVE: (*Blusters*) Don't lie!

PRISONER: I don't know.

(VAN ZIJL's *face as he listens is a study.*)

CLIVE: You took three of our men prisoner two days ago.

PRISONER: No.

CLIVE: Then how did you know about the bridge?

PRISONER: I know nothing about a bridge.

CLIVE: (*Bellows*) Then why were you carrying dynamite?

(*No answer.*

GENERAL CANDY *draws a long breath.*

Fortunately PADDY *comes in.*)

PADDY: All right to go now, sir. Your car's waiting.

VAN ZIJL: Won't you stay for dinner, sir?

CLIVE: What have you got?

VAN ZIJL: Macaroni. We found it in the cellar.

CLIVE: Beastly stuff!

VAN ZIJL: And the usual corned-horse.

CLIVE: Thanks. I'll take my chance in Dupuis. Pity I've got to go. I'd like another [[try]] [shot] at those prisoners.

VAN ZIJL: (*Shepherding him*) I've got the idea, sir. I'll tackle them for you.

CLIVE: Right! Make your report to Brigade.

[VAN ZIJL: Very good, sir.]

(*Dissolve to:*)

SEQUENCE 56
Somewhere in Flanders

EXTERIOR: ESTAMINET DU PONT

[[*Very dark*,]] *wind and rain. The officers are seeing* GENERAL CANDY *off.* [[*All hold ladies' umbrellas over their heads and carry electric torches.*]]

CLIVE: Dirty night! I prefer Natal to Flanders! Don't you, van Zijl?

VAN ZIJL: I have seen nights like this on Commando, General, even in Natal.

CLIVE: (*Laughs*) Good luck with your new enemy!

VAN ZIJL: Goodbye, sir. Let's hope the show's over by the time you're back.

CLIVE: Not much chance of that.

PADDY: Do you know the road, driver?

MURDOCH: Blindfold, sir.

CLIVE: He only lost his way three times coming here! Carry on, Murdoch.

(*The car drives away.*

[[*The others look after him, smiling.*)

VAN ZIJL: Good old Sugar Candy!

PADDY: Did he get anything out of the prisoners?

VAN ZIJL: Not a sausage.

PADDY: Shall I lock 'em up again?

VAN ZIJL: Oh, no. *Now* we put the screws on!

PADDY: Didn't you this afternoon, sir.

VAN ZIJL: No, my lad. Not with Sugar Candy coming. He has a tender heart. Now, listen! Take four men . . .]]

Interior: Estaminet du Pont

KITCHEN
[[*The prisoners stolidly wait the return of the officers. Their guards survey them impartially.*
TOMMY: When's the war going to end, Jerry?
PRISONER: Who knows?
TOMMY: Your Kaiser has a rough idea.]]
(MAJOR VAN ZIJL [[*comes in. He*]] *goes straight up to the English-speaking prisoner who looks at him in a very different way than he looked at* GENERAL CANDY.)
VAN ZIJL: (*Crisply*) [Now] Listen! I am in command here now and I know how to deal with you scum. I am not a simple English gentleman but a simple South African and I assure you that I have means to get what I want. (*His paraphrase is deliberate and he is obviously thinking in the 'taal'.*) What was the dynamite for? How many of you got away? What happened to the three men you took prisoners? Thirty seconds to reply!
[[*(Pause.)
VAN ZIJL: If you do not understand the questions I have a squad of interpreters outside, whom you will understand. (*Outside in the yard we hear the tramp of men.* PADDY's *voice shouts: 'Squad! Halt! Order-Arms!' There is a crash as they ground arms on the stones.*
VAN ZIJL *sits down at his desk. He looks at the men in*

---

* The idea of Major van Zijl successfully interrogating German prisoners by means of threats had been singled out in the Ministry of Information's Report as implying 'that Germans can only be defeated with their own weapons' (p. 33 above). Since it had been identified as suggesting 'confusion of mind on the part of the authors' and would continue to be highly controversial, this series of sequences was eventually cut – and the menace implied by van Zijl's final speech may indeed be more effective. Several surviving stills, however, indicate that at least some of these sequences were shot (see p. 195).

front of him, playing with a sjambok which lies on the desk.
He glances at his watch.)

VAN ZIJL: Right! Cooper!

COOPER: Sir!

VAN ZIJL: The three men nearest the door. Take them out and
shoot them! Lieutenant Casey is in command of the firing
squad!

(PRIVATE COOPER *stares.*)

VAN ZIJL: Jump to it!

COOPER: Yes, sir! (*To the prisoners*) Come on! You three!
(*They go out. The two remaining Tommies exchange
uneasy looks. So do the prisoners.*)

VAN ZIJL: (*To the* PRISONER *who speaks English*) Shall I
repeat the questions?
(PRISONER *makes no answer: he is listening.*
*A command rings out: 'Fire!' There is a volley, other
ominous sounds. Footsteps are heard leaving the yard and
coming back to the kitchen.*)

VAN ZIJL: (*Looks again at his watch, then says to the prisoners*)
Thirty seconds! Shall I repeat the questions?

2ND PRISONER: You cannot shoot us – there is an international
convention about prisoners!

VAN ZIJL: Oh, you can speak English, too?
(PRIVATE COOPER *enters and grounds arms. He looks very
grim. Pause.*)

VAN ZIJL: Right! The next three, Cooper!

COOPER: Come on you!

VAN ZIJL: (*Indicating the first English-speaking* PRISONER)
You can take the tall one. I've found another interpreter.

COOPER: You there!

PRISONER: I protest!

VAN ZIJL: Protest rejected.
(*The second three are hustled out.*
The five remaining men are really frightened.
VAN ZIJL *addresses them ruthlessly:*)

VAN ZIJL: International conventions! You think they are useful on this side of the line, don't you?

2ND PRISONER: Please – Herr Kommandant – I want to speak to the others in German.

VAN ZIJL: Go ahead. You have (*Glances at watch.*) thirty seconds.

SEQUENCE 58
Interior: Estaminet du Pont

BAR

The whole room is grinning at the first three prisoners who are standing by the porch. The door opens and PRIVATE COOPER *ushers in the next bunch, just condemned to 'death'. At the sight of their comrades they are so surprised for a moment they can't even speak.*

SEQUENCE 59
Somewhere in Flanders

EXTERIOR: ESTAMINET DU PONT

The front door opens and a torch flashes a signal.

EAGER VOICE: There's the signal, sir.

PADDY: (*Voice*) Right and for God's sake don't point at me. Ready?

VOICES: (*Suppressed laughs*) Yes, sir.

PADDY: (*Yells*) FIRE!

   (*A volley crashes out.*)

'This is against all international law.' [Production still apparently from Sequence 60, no longer in the film.]

SEQUENCE 60
Interior: Estaminet du Pont

BAR

COOPER *grins cheerfully at the* FIRST PRISONER.

COOPER: I'll bet your pals are talking nineteen to the dozen!

PRISONER: This is against all international law . . .

COOPER: Do you want to stand outside in the rain?

PRISONER: No!

COOPER: Then shut up!

    (*Fade out.*)

Exterior: Somewhere in Flanders

RAILROAD CROSSING
Fade in.
It is pitch dark. The rain has stopped for a moment.
The signal, which is at 'green', swings up to 'red'.
We hear the train receding in the distance.
GENERAL CANDY's *car is waiting for the barriers to open. The*
light of the headlamps shines on the mud-stained barriers. They
rise into the air.
MURDOCH *puts in the clutch but the delay has been fatal. They*
are stuck in the deep mud. The wheels turn madly but get no
grip. The GENERAL, *a darker mass in the darkness, shines his*
torch down on the wheels.
CLIVE: (*Shouts*) Sentry!
    (*No answer.*)
CLIVE: (*Shouts*) SENTRY! (*To* MURDOCH) There must be
    somebody there! Who opened the gate? SENTRY!!
SENTRY: (*Weary American voice*) Every perishing car sticks in
    the perishing mud, I'm not a perishing service station!
MURDOCH: (*Shouts*) This is General Candy's car!
    (*Silence.*
    Then feet squelch towards them. CANDY *flashes his torch*
    on his wrist-watch.)
CLIVE: 11.15. How far are we from Dupuis?
SENTRY: Two kilometres, General.
CLIVE: (*Jumping out into the mud*) Now then, Murdoch! (*To*
    SENTRY) Come on, man, come on! Give us a hand! I don't
    want to spend the night here!
    (*They heave and get covered in mud.*)
SENTRY: 'Taint a bit of use, General. You need a truck to get
    you out of this –
CLIVE: Don't waste stamina talking nonsense, my boy. Push!

(*They try again. Useless.*)

SENTRY: (*Breathing calmly and dispassionately*) The ornery son of a gun!

MURDOCH: We'd better give up, sir.

CLIVE: (*Indomitable*) I shall walk to the village. Murdoch, wait here for a truck and then follow me.

(MURDOCH *sighs.*)

CLIVE: (*To* SENTRY) Which way, sentry?

SENTRY: Steer by your nose, General! Follow the telephone poles until you come to a dead horse. You can't miss it. The road forks, you take the left. Left again at the farm. The Jerries killed all the pigs before they retreated. You won't miss them either. They're ripe as Roquefort. The village lies dead ahead. When you smell chloride of lime, you're there!

CLIVE: Hm! (*He trudges off.*)

MURDOCH: How shall I find you, sir?

CLIVE: (*Calls*) Ask at the R.T.O.'s office!]]

(*Dissolve to:*)

SEQUENCE 62
Somewhere in Flanders

EXTERIOR: OFFICE OF THE R.T.O.

The railway station has been shelled so many times there is nothing left of it at all except mounds of shapeless rubble. The rails have always been replaced and that has been all that mattered. Dimly one is conscious of railway lines, ready to trip you up all over the place. Signals, near and distant, are marked by their coloured lamps hanging in the air. But the only trace of any building, let alone organization, is a small hut right on the edge of the network of rails.

CLIVE *stumbles over the rails to the hut.*

His torch flashes on and illuminates a sign: 'R.T.O.'

197

He opens the door, showing a glimpse of a smoky interior, and goes in, shutting the door.

SEQUENCE 63
Somewhere in Flanders

INTERIOR: OFFICE OF THE R.T.O.
[[*A young* AMERICAN OFFICER *is writing at the desk. On a bench are sitting two English soldiers, patiently waiting. One is very young, the other about forty. It is some moments before the R.T.O. (Railway Transport Officer) realizes that* CLIVE *is a General, he is so covered in mud.*]]
[*A young* AMERICAN RADIO OPERATOR *is trying repeatedly to make contact, on behalf of the* AMERICAN R.T.O., *who is also on the radio telephone throughout most of his dialogue with* CLIVE; *while another* YOUNG AMERICAN SERGEANT *sits nearby waiting for news.*]
OPERATOR: 8.35, 8.35 . . . Hello, hello . . . Dammit. (*To* R.T.O.) Lousy line is dead, sir. I can't get Beechwood. (*Continues to try in background.*)
R.T.O.: Keep trying. (*To* CLIVE, *not recognizing his rank*) Yeah, and what do you want?
CLIVE: I am Brigadier-General Candy.
[R.T.O.: I'm sorry, sir. Sit down, take a load off your feet. I couldn't see your brass for the mud. What can I do for you?
CLIVE: Are you a Railway Transport Officer?
R.T.O.: I run trains, if that's what you mean. That is when there *are* any trains to run.]
CLIVE: Did you get my chit?
R.T.O.: [[Chit, sir?]] [(*To* OPERATOR) Jake, will you for the Lord's sake get me through to Beechwood. The General's having kittens. Try the other circuit. You said chit?
CLIVE: Yes.

198

R.T.O.: What's a chit?]

CLIVE: [A] message, man, [a] message! [I want transport to London. It's urgent.]

[[R.T.O.: Sit down, sir?

CLIVE: Thanks. (*He shows his papers.*)]]

R.T.O.: [[I've been on duty since eleven. No chit came in, General.]] [Hasn't been any message through here since I've been on duty. See what we can do for you.]

[[CLIVE: Well – never mind. I've got a spot of leave. Going to London. Want to touch Paris.]]

[R.T.O.: Jake, get R.T.O. at Ami-le-Bon, will you?

JAKE: OK, sir.]

R.T.O.: (*Into telephone*) [[This is R.T.O. Dupuis-sur-Crois. Get me R.T.O. at Ami-le-Bon.]] [Yes, yes, we're trying to get through, sir. We're trying the other circuit right now. Yes, I'll let you know. (*To* CLIVE) A merry little madhouse we've got here, isn't it?]

CLIVE: [Yes, very.] When does my train leave? [[When do I get to Paris?]] Where do I change? And where can I get some food?

R.T.O.: [(*Into telephone*) I thought so. Thanks very much.] [[Just hang on . . . I'm getting]] [Yeah, it's just what I thought, sir, you'll have to get] through to Ami-le-Bon.

CLIVE: (*Explosively*) [[Ami-le-Bon!

R.T.O.: The highway's OK, sir. Let me show you the route. You turn right at Dead Pigs Farm – (*To telephone*) What? Well, check it! The line is broken between 'Mile 14' and the Estaminet du Pont.

CLIVE: Thank you, I know that. Now look here, my boy – I've *been* to that blasted Estaminet –]] I've *come* from Ami-le-Bon to catch a train here! [My motorcar is stuck . . .]

R.T.O.: (*Ringing off*) [[Well, General, that's rich.]] [(*Cuts in.*) What's that? What General? The hell you say? Well, that's that.]

[[CLIVE: I'm glad you think so.]]

199

R.T.O.: We're in the same boat, General. I've come four thousand miles from Pittsburgh to Dupuis-sur-Crois. I checked in yesterday and the war finishes tomorrow.

CLIVE: What do you mean?

R.T.O.: Haven't you heard the news?]]

CLIVE: [[What news?]] [What's what?]

R.T.O.: A German delegation is on the way to see Foch. [They're going] To sue for an Armistice.

[AMERICAN SERGEANT: Yipee!]

CLIVE: [[Old trick]] [Nonsense]. German propaganda. [Old trick to] Put us off our guard.

[[R.T.O.: Maybe. But I came here 'Express' and I have a hunch I'm going back 'Slow Delivery'.]]

CLIVE: [[Well, what about trains?]] [What about my train?]

R.T.O.: [There's] Not a train, a truck, an engine or a driver, General.

CLIVE: (*Stands up*) In this war I've seen ammunition dumps without ammunition, field-kitchens without cooks and railway stations without rails, so I suppose I shouldn't be surprised at anything. (*Raises his voice.*) But let me tell you, young man, that in the Boer War or in Somaliland this sort of inefficiency would not have been tolerated for a second! Not for a second! (*He changes his tone.*) Now where can I get some grub?

[[R.T.O.: (*Has listened without awe but active interest to the General's outburst, as if at a play*) Grub, sir?

CLIVE: Food, man, food.]]

R.T.O.: The 'Crown of Thorns' is [[always]] good for a hand-out at [almost] any hour, sir.

CLIVE: What is it? A pub?

R.T.O.: A – ? (*He hesitates.*)

CLIVE: A-a-dash it, I don't speak your language, sir – a café?

R.T.O.: [No, sir.] It's a convent[[, sir]]. [It's on the way to Ami-le-Bon.]

CLIVE: [[Good. Well,]] show me the way, will you [[– what's

your name – er – Lieutenant]]?

[[R.T.O.: Schmidt. Ensign Schmidt, sir.

CLIVE: Schmidt, eh. German name?

R.T.O.: (*Grinning*) Yes, sir. I've got cousins in Westphalia. My father told me to give 'em hell if I met up with them. This way, sir.]]

[R.T.O.: I think I hear Armstrong coming with the bathtub now.]
(*The two men step out into the darkness.*)
[[(*The two waiting soldiers are left alone.*)

OLD SOLDIER: The General's right – I was in the Boer War and in Somaliland. I remember –

YOUNG SOLDIER: Garn! Them wasn't wars – them was fatigues!]]
[(ARMSTRONG, *a black American soldier, rides up on motorcycle with sidecar.*)

R.T.O.: Armstrong, I want you to take the General over to the Crown of Thorns.

ARMSTRONG: Yes sir. Yes sir, General. I sure will do that. It's kind of damp underfoot, but I'll get you there, General.

R.T.O.: Climb aboard, sir. You're off.

CLIVE: Poor show I couldn't get a train tonight.

R.T.O.: You can step on it, Armstrong. The General's in a hurry.

ARMSTRONG: Sure will do that.
(*They roar off into the darkness.*)

R.T.O.: (*Calls*) Goodbye, General.

SERGEANT: What were those other wars the General was talking about, Captain? The Boer War, the Somy something. I never heard of them.

R.T.O.: Those weren't wars. Those were just summer manoeuvres.]
(*Dissolve to:*)

Exterior: Convent of the 'Crown of Thorns'

ARMSTRONG: Here we are, General, the Convent of the Crown of Thorns. (*Offers to help him out of sidecar.*)

CLIVE: I can manage, thank you.

(ARMSTRONG *rings the Convent bell.*)

[[CLOISTER
The Cloister connects the Refectory with the Main Entrance. Somebody is using the big knocker to great effect on the outer door. A NUN *is hurrying down to answer it.*]]
The night has cleared and there is moonlight.
The NUN *opens the grille and looks out.*

ARMSTRONG: Bonsoir, Sister Josephine.

SISTER: Bonsoir, Napoléon.

ARMSTRONG: I've brought you a real live English General.

[[NUN: Monsieur.

CLIVE: (*Voice*) Ici le Convent, Madame?

NUN: Oui, Monsieur. Vous desirez?]]

CLIVE: Je suis [[une Colonel]] [un Général] anglais.

NUN: Mais entrez, Monsieur!

(*She opens the gate and the General comes in.*)

ARMSTRONG: Goodnight, General. Bonsoir, Sister Josephine.

SISTER: Bonsoir, Napoléon.

CLIVE: Merci, madame, [[je suis – je suis mangé –]] [. . . les Américains . . . j'ai mangé . . .] (*He points to his stomach.*)

NUN: (*With concern*) Monsieur le Général a mangé quelque chose qui lui aurait fait mal?

CLIVE: Oui – mangé –

NUN: Mais venez donc, mon Général.

(*She leads the way down the cloister, the* GENERAL *following.*)

SEQUENCE 65
Convent of the 'Crown of Thorns'

REFECTORY

The NUN *and* GENERAL CANDY *arrive at the door. She opens it and they go in.*

The GENERAL *stands astonished at what he sees.*

Part of the Refectory has been hit by a shell but it is still a noble hall. Long tables run down the huge room and nuns are waiting at table. At the table are sitting nearly a hundred young nurses fresh from England, their bright uniforms and bright faces making the first patch of colour since the Khaki sequence started.

Most of the nurses look up as the GENERAL *enters, then stare at him, muddy and stained, as he stands at the top of the steps.*

He stares at their eager young faces.

He feels suddenly drained of energy.

Meanwhile the NUN *has fetched two women: the* MOTHER SUPERIOR *of the Convent and the* MATRON *who is Transport Officer for the nurses.* [[*The* MATRON *is Scottish.*]]

[CLIVE: Bonsoir, Madame.]

[[MOTHER SUPERIOR: Bonsoir, mon Général, on va vous soigner.]]

MATRON: [Good evening,] Général, you have fallen on your feet.

CLIVE: (*Smiles*) I was beginning to think so.

MATRON: I have sixty-eight young, freshly-trained nurses straight from England all dying to nurse someone. What's the trouble?

CLIVE: (*Startled*) Trouble, Matron?

MATRON: The nun said you had eaten something –

CLIVE: She got it wrong – I *want* to eat. I'm hungry!

MATRON: Oh! (*To* MOTHER SUPERIOR *and* NUN) C'est qu'il veut manger!

(*Everyone smiles. The* NUN *titters. The* MOTHER
SUPERIOR *and the* MATRON *have a hurried conference out
of which the* MATRON *emerges with an invitation.
While they have talked,* GENERAL CANDY *looks down the
crowded tables. He sees a girl.
She is seated about halfway down the table. She has eaten
and, like several of the nurses, has fallen asleep.*
CLIVE *stares and stares. He knows that face and we know it
too. The girl wears her hair differently, she is much younger
than Edith Hunter – but her face is very like Edith's.*
CLIVE *longs to see the colour of her eyes.*
[[*The* MATRON *turns to him.*)
MATRON: It's all right, General, won't you join us? We shall all
be delighted.
CLIVE: Thank you. (*To* MOTHER SUPERIOR) Merci, ma mère.]]

'Clive knows that face and we know it too.'

MOTHER SUPERIOR: (*Smiles*) Sois bienvenu, [[mon fils]] [Général. (*To the* NUN) Il va rester avec nous.] (*The* MATRON *leads the way down the table.* CLIVE *will pass quite close to the girl.*)

MATRON: [That's settled then. We should be delighted to have you join us.] Have you been in the front line? I suppose you have? Before I got this job I was with the Italians. I was lucky. I came through Caporetto without a scratch.

CLIVE: (*Absently*) Good heavens! What insect powder do you use, Ma'am?

(MATRON *laughs heartily.*
As they pass the sleeping girl, CLIVE CANDY *stops involuntarily. Yes, the girl is strangely like Edith Hunter.*
The MATRON *is now at the head of the table.*)

MATRON: (*To the nurse next to her*) Move a bit, my dear – Sit down, General. (*To a* NUN) Une assiette, s'il vous plaît. (*To* CLIVE, *who sits down*) We have macaroni.

CLIVE: Splendid!
(*He still can't take his eyes off the girl.*
He addresses the MATRON.)

CLIVE: Matron! Have you ever seen the Indian Rope trick?

MATRON: (*Surprised*) No, General. Have you?
(CLIVE *nods.*)

NUN: Pardon, Monsieur. (*A plate is put before* CLIVE *loaded with macaroni.*)
(*We see with* CLIVE's *eyes the girl start to wake up. She smiles sleepily.*)

MATRON: It must be an incredible sight.

CLIVE: (*Slowly*) But I never [[met]] [heard of] anybody who saw it unless he [[first]] heard [[that]] he was going to see it [first].

MATRON: I beg your pardon! I don't quite –

CLIVE: You hear about the thing. You hope to see it – and you see it.
(*He eats his macaroni, never taking his eyes off the girl.*

The MATRON *puts* CLIVE's *vague way of talking down to tiredness. The nurses around are all starting to get up and a general exodus starts towards the door. The girl stands up with the others as the bench is pushed back.)*

MATRON: (*To* CLIVE) [Yes, General,] Will you excuse me? [[I have to put my girls to bed. (*She rises.*)]]

CLIVE: (*Trying to see his girl in a sudden panic*) [[Can you – who is that girl, please, Matron? – The one who just got up –]] [One moment, Matron, do you know that girl over there?]

MATRON: [[Do you think you know her?]] I'm afraid [[I can't tell you]] [I don't]. I only met them here at the station. [[I must go, please excuse me.]] [(*She rises.*) Come along, everybody, come along.

NURSE: (*To her exhausted neighbour*) Come on, Wynne.] (CLIVE *is standing now,* [[*his fork still in his hand. He is strangely near panic. He turns to his neighbours who are also going. He just manages to stop one of them. Already all the others are streaming towards the door. The* NURSE *he has stopped looks at him with frank interest.*)

CLIVE: Tell me, who was that girl who was sitting there?]] [(*As the nurses leave,* CLIVE *speaks to a* NUN.)

CLIVE: Où est le matron?

NUN: La Matrone? A qui vous avez parlé? Restez. Je vais la chercher.

CLIVE: (*To one of the nurses*) Nurse, do you know the name of the girl who was sitting at the end of that table?]

[[YORKSHIRE NURSE: Whereabouts, General?

CLIVE: (*Moving down to the place*) Here. She was sitting here asleep.]]

YORKSHIRE NURSE: Dark or fair?

CLIVE: Fair.

YORKSHIRE NURSE: I don't remember. (*Pause.*) Can you describe her better?

CLIVE: She's – fair. I couldn't see the colour of her eyes. [Slim.]

YORKSHIRE NURSE: Sorry. It might be anyone. [[I was asleep myself.]] Excuse me, General.
CLIVE: (*A last attempt*) Where do you come from tonight? What detachment are you?
YORKSHIRE NURSE: Yorkshire. West Riding, most of us. Good night, General.
(*She hurries away.*
Fade out.)

[[SEQUENCE 66
Interior: Estaminet du Pont

KITCHEN
Fade in. The door is opened from inside by MAJOR VAN ZIJL. GENERAL CANDY *comes out under full steam, with a face of fury. In his hand he holds a typewritten report. He needs a shave and a wash.*
VAN ZIJL: Good morning, General Candy.

SEQUENCE 67
Interior: Estaminet du Pont

BAR
The door is opened from inside by LIEUTENANT PADDY. GENERAL CANDY *comes out as in previous scene.*
PADDY: Nice day, sir.

SEQUENCE 68
Somewhere in Flanders

EXTERIOR: ESTAMINET DU PONT

It is a fine morning. The GENERAL's *car is waiting. It looks like a heap of mud after the night's adventures.*
MURDOCH *is talking to the sentry.*
As the GENERAL *appears,* MURDOCH *jumps to the rear door of the car and opens it. The sentry salutes.*
GENERAL CANDY *snaps an acknowledgement at the sentry, ignores* MURDOCH, *opens the front door of the car, hurls himself into the seat beside the driver and slams the door.*
MURDOCH, *seeing his mood, shuts the rear door and runs round to the driver's seat.*
CLIVE: Come on, Murdoch, come on!
MURDOCH: Yes, sir.
CLIVE: Ami-le-Bon!
MURDOCH: Yes, sir.
    (*The car drives off.*)]]

SEQUENCE 69
Exterior: Somewhere in Flanders

CROSS-ROAD

The car is immobilized. The GENERAL *is pacing impatiently up and down.* MURDOCH, *in an ostrich-like position, cleans the plugs. Finally the* GENERAL *stops and speaks.*
CLIVE: (*For the tenth time*) How long now?
MURDOCH: (*For the tenth time*) Not long, sir.
CLIVE: You've said that ten separate times.
MURDOCH: I know, sir.
CLIVE: Well, hurry! The train leaves at 10.30.

MURDOCH: I know, sir.

CLIVE: [[It's 9.30 now.]] I need extra time in Ami-le-Bon. I'm going to G.H.Q.

MURDOCH: I know, sir.

CLIVE: [[Don't talk]] [Stop talking] like an infernal parrot, Murdoch. How do you know?

MURDOCH: I was told, sir.

CLIVE: Who told you?

MURDOCH: Major van Zijl's batman, sir.

CLIVE: What did he say?

MURDOCH: That you were up in the air, sir, because the Major had got valuable information from the Jerries – the prisoners, sir.

CLIVE: (*Controlling himself*) Your misinformation, Murdoch, is typical.

MURDOCH: Thank you, sir.

[[CLIVE: The reason I am 'up in the air', as your informant grotesquely describes a very natural emotion, is because this information was obtained by intimidation! By mental torture! By firing squads! By the same methods that the Boches use! If we are fighting gangsters that is no reason why we should behave like gangsters, too.

(MURDOCH *remains silent*.)]]

CLIVE: (*Reads report*) Bah! Four pages of 'confessions'! Not worth the –

(*He breaks off. Something in the report has caught his eye. He reads it with interest.* MURDOCH *straightens up and wipes his hands. He has finished. He watches his officer. Insert: item in the official report* [(*only the name is visible*)]. [['On being questioned about their senior officers, the prisoners admitted that, among others, Oberst*]] Kretschmar-Schuldorff [[had been taken prisoner by the British, and was believed now to be a prisoner of war in England . . .']]

CLIVE *is so interested in this news that he quite forgets*

209

how it was obtained.)

CLIVE: Hm! Kretschmar-Schuldorff! There can't be two of them with a name like that, eh, Murdoch?

MURDOCH: No, sir.

CLIVE: You have no idea what I'm talking about.

MURDOCH: No, sir.

CLIVE: Haven't I told you about that time I was in Berlin in 1902?

MURDOCH: Oh, yes, sir. When you grew your moustache.

CLIVE: And yet you[['ve never heard]] [can't remember the name] of Kretschmar-Schuldorff. You know, [[Murdoch,]] you should bequeath your brain to Guy's Hospital, [Murdoch].

MURDOCH: I remember, sir. He married the girl.
(CLIVE *suddenly remembers the girl of the previous night. He is silent for a moment. Then he speaks in an entirely different tone, which very few people have heard.*)

CLIVE: Last night, Murdoch, I saw a girl – a nurse straight from England . . . I've never seen a more striking resemblance . . .

MURDOCH: She must have been a very common type of girl, sir – the young lady in Berlin, I mean.

CLIVE: She was a most *un*common – what the devil d'you mean, Murdoch?

MURDOCH: (*Stolidly*) There was that girl in the film, sir. You remember, you went nine times. And there was that girl in the group out of the Bystander! We lost it in the big Push. And there's – (*Without changing tone*) a despatch rider coming, sir!
(*A* DESPATCH RIDER *roars up and salutes.*)

D.R.: General Candy?

CLIVE: Yes. (*Signs pad.*)

D.R.: Urgent message from Major van Zijl, sir. Came over the wire from 'Mile 14'; they mended the line, sir.
(CLIVE *reads it.*)

D.R.: Any answer, sir?

CLIVE: No. No answer.

(*The* DESPATCH RIDER *wheels and thunders away.*
MURDOCH *looks queerly at the* GENERAL.)

MURDOCH: Anything wrong, sir?

(CLIVE *shakes his head.*
They are alone in the immense landscape, battered and
trampled by four years of senseless, stalemate war.
CLIVE *takes a flask from his pocket, unscrews the little cup*
and fills it with brandy. He hands this to MURDOCH.
CLIVE *stands holding the flask.*)

CLIVE: Murdoch – the war is over.

MURDOCH: Is it, sir?

CLIVE: The Germans have accepted the terms of the Armistice.
Hostilities cease at ten o'clock. (*He looks at his watch.*) [[It
is now a quarter to ten.]] [It's nearly that now.]

[[MURDOCH: (*Struggles with words, then gives up. They drink.*)
God bless us, sir.

CLIVE: Yes, Murdoch, may God bless us in peace as He has in
Victory.

(*He turns full of emotion and walks a step or two.*
He turns and listens.
Far away, born on the wind, there comes the sound of a
mighty cheering, louder and louder as every moment
passes.
CLIVE *turns to* MURDOCH. *He is exultant.*)]]

CLIVE: Murdoch! do you know what this means?

MURDOCH: I do, sir. Peace. We can go home. Everybody can go
home!

CLIVE: For me, Murdoch, it means more than that. It means
that Right is Might after all. The Germans have shelled
hospitals, bombed open towns, sunk neutral ships, used
poison-gas – and *we won*! Clean fighting, honest soldiering
have won! God bless you, Murdoch.

[MURDOCH: Sir!]

(*They both drink.*

[Sound of birdsong. Both look up to the sky.
Fade to black.])

SEQUENCE 70
Interior: Yorkshire Cloth Mill

A large and busy mill. Going closer to the machines, we see the
last lengths of khaki cloth vanishing off the looms: cloth, wool,
cotton materials, all finishing.
In the dyeing vats the khaki dyes are emptied away: new
beautiful dyes appear: the looms are busy again. Gay patterns,
bright tweeds are appearing.
The first length of cloth off the looms is for a bridal gown.

END OF KHAKI SEQUENCES
Dissolve to:
Insert: The Yorkshire Telegraph and Argus, *June 6 1919.*
Bradford.

'NO MORE KHAKI FOR LOOMS
FIRST PEACETIME CLOTH A
BRIDAL GOWN
After an interval of four years the first piece of white brocade
has come off the looms in the famous Mills of Mr. Christopher
Wynne, head of the well-known West Riding family. The cloth
is destined for the bridal gown of Miss Barbara Wynne, only
daughter of Mr. and Mrs. Wynne, whose marriage to Brigadier-
General Clive Candy, V.C., D.S.O. will shortly take place.
General Candy is staying at The Hall.'
Dissolve to:

Exterior: The Hall

*A beautiful, large garden. The great pile of 'The Hall' in the distance.
The tiny figure of the* HOUSEKEEPER *on the terrace. Faintly her
voice is heard calling: 'Barbaraa! – [Lunch is ready.] Miss
Barbaraaaaaaaa!!'*
In another part of the grounds, BARBARA WYNNE *and* CLIVE
CANDY *are talking together. A great sweep of country is visible
beyond a great yew hedge.*
They have the copy of the Yorkshire Telegraph and Argus *with
them.*
BARBARA *is, of course, the same girl whom we have seen in
nurse's uniform in the Convent of the 'Crown of Thorns'. She is
dressed in what, in 1919, was considered a ravishing creation:
rather like a badly tied sack.*
CLIVE *is in uniform. He is a full Brigadier now. He looks very
strong and fit, far less than his forty-three years.*
Distantly we hear 'Barbaraaaa!'
CLIVE: Oh dear.
BARBARA: (*Laughing*) Don't listen [to her]! (*Accusingly.*) Now!
    [You listen to me.] There I was asleep! You never saw me
    before – you never [even] spoke to me then – how could you
    be so sure?
CLIVE: Can I ask you a question first?
BARBARA: You're wriggling! All right, fire away!
CLIVE: How can *you* be so sure? I'm twenty years older than you
    – and I'm a soldier. When other people are thanking God the
    war is over, I am going to the War Office to ask: Where is
    another war where you can use me?
BARBARA: (*Seriously*) You asked me that once [before] and I told
    you [[why]].
CLIVE: I'm asking you again because I want to hear it again [and
    again].

(*He says this so charmingly that she has to answer.*)

BARBARA: I'm marrying you because I want to join the Army and see the world. I'm marrying you because I [[like seeing]] [love watching] you play polo. I'm marrying you for fifty reasons that all mean that's how I imagined my future husband!

(CLIVE *looks at her.*)

CLIVE: Same here! That's how I imagined my future wife!

(BARBARA *looks at him. It is one of the moments that come seldom in life and extend indefinitely until some outside influence breaks them.*

The beating of a big gong comes from the house.

BARBARA *sighs.*)

BARBARA: The gong is the final appeal. We must go, darling. We have the Bishop for lunch.

CLIVE: I hope he's tender.

(*They start up the garden, hand in hand.*

Dissolve to:)

SEQUENCE 72
Interior: The Hall

DINING ROOM

A very fine room, full of good, solid stuff and good, solid people. The BISHOP *is making a little speech.*

MR *and* MRS WYNNE, BARBARA *and* CLIVE *are listening.*

BISHOP: ... and now [[let me]] [in conclusion, I should like to] say a few words to Brigadier-General Candy. We in the Church Militant can admire the heroes of the war. But in our hearts we are men of peace. Therefore, I am glad to have met you as I did for the first time on a simple and heart-warming occasion [[and not]] [rather than] at some military celebration. When I first heard that a Brigadier-General of

214

the British Army was arranging a ball for the benefit of
those nurses from the West Riding who took part in the
four years' struggle, I said [to myself]: There is a man
whose heart is in the right place. (*He refers to slip of paper.*)
And I am glad to announce that one result is that a total of
£131.2.6 will be handed over to the War Nurses'
Benevolent Fund.
(*During the* BISHOP's *speech,* CLIVE *and* BARBARA *have
glanced at each other several times.* CLIVE *is guiltily rolling
bread pills. At the finish, after a little hesitation, he gets up
and stumbles into a speech replying. He starts to tell his
story as a good joke but as he sees it is falling flat, he gets
more and more self-conscious, while as he speaks the faces
of his listeners get more and more embarrassed. Only*
BARBARA *is unperturbed.*)
CLIVE: [[Your Grace]] [My Lord Bishop], I want to make a

The spoils of peace: a pre-wedding lunch with the Wynnes.

confession. You see, I first saw Barbara in Flanders on the last night of the war. (*He glances at* MRS WYNNE.) She was a nurse among seventy other nurses – I never knew her name – but I found out that most of the nurses came from Yorkshire – the West Riding – and of course she was a nurse – [[well]] [so], I thought – Yorkshire's a big place – [[Your Grace]] [My Lord Bishop] – so, I thought, how can I find a nurse in Yorkshire? You – understand who I'm driving at – I suppose – what I mean? –
(*There is a painful silence. The* BISHOP *does not rise to the occasion. But* BARBARA *does. She reaches for* CLIVE's *hand and holds it, smiling up at him.*)
BARBARA: I understand exactly what you mean, darling!
(*Dissolve to:*)

SEQUENCE 73
Exterior: 33 Cadogan Place

A car of the period drives up and stops outside. It is an open car, piled with luggage and dogs.
BARBARA *is driving.* CLIVE *sits beside her. They both look radiantly happy. She wears a wedding ring.*
They both look up at the house; she critically, he affectionately. It is the first time she sees it.
BARBARA: That window is the Den!
CLIVE: Wrong. Next floor is the Den. That's the bathroom.
(*The window in question opens and a large Union Jack on the end of a pole is poked out of the window and socketed into its place.* MURDOCH's *head appears behind it. He sees them below, ejaculates: 'It's them!' and disappears.*)
BARBARA: Is yon grey head Murdoch?
CLIVE: (*Nods*) His idea of greeting the conquering hero, I suppose.

Home is the hero: Clive and Barbara (with Michael Powell's dogs).

BARBARA: I shall like Murdoch – and I [[feel]] [know] I shall like this house. Clive, let [[it]] [the whole house] be our Den, into which we can always crawl, whether we return with rich spoils or badly mauled from our rovings! Or just to change our spots! [[Do promise!]]

CLIVE: [[(*Looks at her*) I do.]] (*He kisses her.*) Aunt Margaret would have loved you for that!
(*They go on talking as idiotic lovers do.*)

BARBARA: It is a fine solid-looking property – (*Mischievously*) like you. Clive, [[please don't ever]] [you mustn't] change and don't ever [[give up]] [leave] this house.

CLIVE: No fear. Even if there is a second Flood, this house shall stand on its solid foundations and we'll have a private lake in the basement.

BARBARA: That's a promise. You stay just as you are . . . till the floods come . . .

217

CLIVE: (*Raising his hand, repeats*) . . . till the floods come . . .

BARBARA: (*Pointing into the area*) . . . and this is a lake . . .

CLIVE: (*Repeats solemnly*) . . . and this is a lake!

(MURDOCH *appears at the entrance and stares in surprise at* CLIVE *standing there with his hand raised. He runs smartly down the steps. His manner, like his costume, is an Armistice one: half-military, half-civil.*)

MURDOCH: Sorry, Ma'am! – Mrs Candy – I was [[up]] [at] the top [of the house] – I wasn't expecting you so early, sir.

BARBARA: So you are Murdoch!

MURDOCH: Yes, Madam.

CLIVE: The first time I've ever heard him answer anything but: 'Yes, sir!' Well, Murdoch, this is [[my]] [the] wife.

(*They shake hands.* MURDOCH *has his own ideas of what a wife will want to know and he has his report all ready for her as they all go into the house, carrying luggage, etc.*)

MURDOCH: Everything is under control, Ma'am. I've had the telephone installed, sir. (*To* BARBARA.) The agency has got a lot of cooks for you to see, Ma'am, but I bought plenty of vegetables and flour and potatoes. [(*They go in.*)] And all the tradespeople have called and will call again for [your orders] –

[[(*By this time they have entered the house.*)]]

SEQUENCE 74
Interior: 33 Cadogan Place

HALL

BARBARA *listens to* MURDOCH *with grave attention but* CLIVE *has no tender regard for his feelings. He interrupts him.*

CLIVE: That's all right, Murdoch, but we're not staying this time. Off tonight.

MURDOCH: (*Very disappointed*) Yes, sir?

CLIVE: Paris for eight weeks. When we get back we'll give a big party and put our feet up for a bit.

MURDOCH: Yes, sir.

BARBARA: I'm [so] sorry, Murdoch. (*She makes a friend.*)

MURDOCH: (*Grins ruefully*) [[I'm]] [We're] used to it [[Ma'am]]. [[(*To* CLIVE) I got your letters from the Club, sir – they're on the little tray.]]

(CLIVE *crosses to the table.* MURDOCH *continues to* BARBARA:)

MURDOCH: I told the porter that the Brigadier wouldn't be using the Club so much in future, Ma'am.

BARBARA: And what did he say?

(MURDOCH *hesitates.*)

BARBARA: [Go on, Murdoch,] I can bear it, [[Murdoch]].

MURDOCH: [[Yes, Ma'am.]] He said: 'They all say that at first!' – Ma'am.

(BARBARA *laughs.* MURDOCH *smiles respectfully and withdraws with the dogs.*)

CLIVE: I say, Barbara – ! (*She crosses to him.*) Here's an answer from the Prisoners of War Committee –

BARBARA: Have they found him?

CLIVE: (*Very excited and pleased*) Yes. Theodor Kretschmar-Schuldorff, Oberst, 2nd Regiment of Ulans of the Guard. That's him! Camp VII, Hardwick Hall, Derbyshire. Poor old Theo! (*He stares at the paper, pulling at his moustache.*) (BARBARA *knows what is going on in his mind.*)

BARBARA: Darling!

(CLIVE *looks up, worried. His face lights up as he sees her expression.*)

BARBARA: Let's postpone Paris . . . I'd love to meet him –

(*Dissolve to:*)

Exterior: Prisoners of War Camp

[*Pan down from blue sky to barbed wire and on to:*]
*A notice, roughly printed by hand on a sheet of cardboard, is
nailed to a tree:*

107-TES KONZERT

DES PHILHARMONIE-ORCHESTERS

DES GEFANGENENLAGERS IV

FÜR DEUTSCHE OFFIZIERE

IN ENGLAND

PROGRAMM

FRANZ SCHUBERT: UNVOLLENDETE SYMPHONIE

[[LUDWIG V. BEETHOVEN: FÜNFTE SYMPHONIE]]

MENDELSSOHN: FINGALS HÖHLE

DIRIGENT: OBERLEUT. JOS. V. SCHONTHAAL

ANFANG: 3 UHR NACHMITTAG

EINTRITT: 6 ENGL. PENNIES

*While the notice is being read, we hear the tragically sweet melody
of the Second Movement of Schubert's 'Unfinished Symphony'.
The camera moves off the notice [[to the tree above.
It has wide-spreading branches, all loaded with German
officers, listening to the music.
We see some of their faces.
We see, from their angle in the tree,]] [to a sentry on guard duty,
and on to] the main audience and the orchestra itself. All are
German officers. The orchestra plays on a raised bank, a natural
rostrum. The audience covers the smooth lawns that run down
to the river, which is crossed by two bridges, with an island in
the middle. There is a Guard House on the island and the bridge
is heavily wired with barbed wire above and below and English
sentries are stationed on the bridge.*

The prisoners sit on benches or on the grass, many are standing,
all are listening intently to the music. There must be 400 or 500
of them. The orchestra has about forty pieces.
We see an ORDERLY *coming towards the concert from the main*
building. This is a fine old country house which has been taken
over. It is now surrounded by huts and all kinds of
administrative buildings. The main offices are in the house itself.
The ORDERLY *carries a message-pad. He comes amongst the*
audience as discreetly as possible. [[*He is obviously looking for*
someone and, as obviously, cannot spot him. He decides to ask
one of the officers, who is leaning against a tree. The officer
questioned looks around, then shakes his head and taps the leg
of another officer in the tree above him. He whispers to him.
The officer in the tree has a bird's-eye view. He spots the wanted
man and the information is passed on in whispers to the ORDERLY.
The ORDERLY *gingerly crosses through the audience. Nobody*
looks at him.]]
He finds his man – OBERST KRETSCHMAR-SCHULDORFF – *and*
touches him on the shoulder.
[ORDERLY: Message, sir, from the Commandant's office.]
 (THEO *turns to the* ORDERLY. *Of course, he, too, is*
 seventeen years older. He still bears the scar which he got in
 the duel. The ORDERLY *gives him the message-pad.*
 THEO *reads the message. He is surprised at its contents but,*
 without any hesitation, he shakes his head very firmly.)
[THEO: No answer.]
 (*He gives the message-pad back to the* ORDERLY *and turns*
 once more to listen to the music.
 The ORDERLY *is rather at a loss. After a moment's*
 hesitation, he starts all over again, emphasizing the
 importance of the message.
 THEO *loses patience with him. He answers almost*
 savagely:)
THEO: (*Louder than he had meant to*) No [answer]!!
 (*Heads turn. Voices go: 'Sh-sh-sh.'*

The ORDERLY *beats a retreat.*
Dissolve to:)

SEQUENCE 76
Interior: Prisoners of War Camp

OFFICE OF COMMANDANT
The tall french windows are open and the music can be heard in the distance.
The Commandant, MAJOR DAVIES, *is an elderly man and a bit of a philosopher.*
CLIVE *is in a new suit of tweeds with a regimental tie.* BARBARA *wears a summer dress and hat which, in 1919 and in 1919 alone, was considered lovely.*
The ORDERLY *knocks and enters – alone.*
MAJOR DAVIES: (*Drily*) Well?
ORDERLY: He says 'No [answer]' sir.
CLIVE: He said 'No [answer]'? (*He frowns incredulously.*) What else?
ORDERLY: Nothing, sir.
BARBARA: He refused to come?
ORDERLY: If that was the message, Ma'am. (*He hands the pad to* CLIVE.)
(BARBARA *reads it, passes it to the Major.*
Insert: message. 'Dear Theo, I am in the Commandant's Office. I want to see you, "very much". Clive Candy.')
BARBARA: Why is 'very much' [[in quotes]] [printed like that]?
CLIVE: It was a joke we had . . .
MAJOR DAVIES: (*To* ORDERLY) Where was the Oberst?
ORDERLY: Listening to the [[orchestra]] [band], sir.
MAJOR DAVIES: All right, Higgins.
(ORDERLY *goes.*)
BARBARA: I [[thought, suddenly]] [was thinking], how odd they

222

are! How queer! For years and years they are writing and dreaming wonderful music and [[wonderful]] [beautiful] poetry and then [[suddenly]] [all of a sudden] they start a war, shoot innocent hostages, sink undefended ships, bomb and destroy whole streets in London, killing little children – and then, dressed in the same butcher's uniform, they sit down and [[play]] [listen to] [[Beethoven]] [Mendelssohn] and Schubert. There's something horrible about that, don't you think so, Clive?*

(*Such abstractions are caviare to the* GENERAL *but he is impressed by* BARBARA's *speech. He nods and grunts agreement.*)

CLIVE: Hm – mm – [[something in that – good deal in fact –]]
(*It is the first time there is something 'blimpish' in his manner.*)

[[CLIVE: Perhaps I should have written in German.

MAJOR DAVIES: He understands English. They have all learnt English while they were here.]]
(*The symphony ends. Distant and prolonged applause.* CLIVE *stands up.*)

CLIVE: Major Davies, would you mind if we went down and had a try? Perhaps it was because of the music – there's an interval now.

MAJOR DAVIES: [[Certainly, you may]] [By all means] try (*Apologetically*) but Mrs Candy had better [[stay]] [remain].
(BARBARA, *who has risen, sits again. She and* MAJOR DAVIES *understand each other.* CLIVE *nods and moves to the windows.*)

CLIVE: (*Half to himself*) Can't understand it. I've written to him before the war and he has written to me . . .

* Barbara's speech about German culture and music originally came at the end of sequence 78, but was brought forward when that sequence was largely cut.

(*He vanishes out on the terrace.*)

MAJOR DAVIES: They stopped English lessons on the 11th of
November.

BARBARA: On Armistice Day?

(MAJOR DAVIES *nods.*)

SEQUENCE 77
Exterior: Prisoners of War Camp

*In the interval of the concert, the audience has broken up into
groups, individuals are pacing up and down, some are smoking
and talking.*

*There is no loud chatter or laughter. The general effect is serious,
even solemn. Depression hangs over the stiff-necked assembly.*

CLIVE *comes down from the house, walking quickly, looking
about him for* THEO.

*He comes among the groups of officers. Nobody takes direct
notice of him.*

*The orchestra starts to tune up. People start to move back to
their places.*

CLIVE *stops one group and addresses a senior officer.*

CLIVE: Oberst Kretschmar-Schuldorff?

OFFICER: (*After a sharp stare*) [[Behind you.]] [Over there.]

(*He moves off.* CLIVE *whirls round.*

He stands directly in between THEO *and his place.* THEO *is
advancing straight towards him, separated by two or three
groups, also moving to their places.*

Seeing CLIVE, THEO *stops. Not a muscle of his face or light
in his eyes betrays his thoughts.*

CLIVE, *on the contrary, advances with a broad smile that
overflows his whole being. He is coming to his friend. He
puts out his hand . . .*)

CLIVE: Theo!

224

Theo refuses Clive's greeting.

(THEO *turns and walks away.*
It is the greatest shock CLIVE *has ever had. He stands*
petrified, staring after his friend.
THEO *throws away his cigarette, treads on it and returns to*
his place in the audience. Nearly everyone has settled
himself. CLIVE *is left standing alone.*
[[*The Conductor takes his place amid polite applause.*]]
[*The music starts again.*]
CLIVE *shakes his head as if he still can't believe what has*
happened to him. He looks ten years older.
He turns and slowly walks away.
THEO *never looks after him.*
The orchestra plays the opening chords of [[*Beethoven's*
Fifth Symphony]] [*Mendelssohn's Hebrides Overture*].
CLIVE *goes on towards the house. He again shakes his head.*
For the second time, there is something 'blimpish' in his

225

behaviour.
He stops and looks back, almost as if he expected to see the
figure of his friend, hastening after him.
But the lawn between him and the distant audience is
empty.)

[[SEQUENCE 78
Interior: Prisoners of War Camp

OFFICE OF THE COMMANDANT
Distantly we hear the [[*Fifth Symphony*]] *Hebrides Overture,*
which continues without a break.
Since CLIVE *left, tea has been served.*

BARBARA: Do you find something rather disturbing about these
concerts – or don't you mind?

MAJOR DAVIES: I'm not musical but I get used to them. This is
the 107th.

BARBARA: (*Smiles*) You misunderstand me, Major – or do you?
(*The* MAJOR *looks at her.*) What I mean is that we know
that the Germans in peacetime are a tidy law-loving people
of poets, philosophers and composers; and then –
(CLIVE *appears at the window. He has recovered himself a*
little. He comes in.)

CLIVE: Well, it's true. I saw him and he wouldn't speak to me.
(*He looks at* BARBARA *and sits down.*) I wouldn't have
believed it possible. He was as close as I am to you and he
turned away without saying a word. You could have
knocked me down with a feather! (BARBARA *gives him his*
tea. He stirs it.) I kept on looking back, you know. I
couldn't believe he wasn't joking. (*To* MAJOR DAVIES)
What on earth is wrong with him?

MAJOR DAVIES: The same thing as all the others. They call it
'Ehre'. The literal translation is 'Honour' but actually I

suppose it means 'Dignity'.

CLIVE: What 'Dignity', what 'Honour'? Who has hurt his
'Ehre'? They lost, we won. What of it. We've been defeated
too sometimes. Fortune of war!

BARBARA: (*Smiles*) Good old sporting spirit. Always time for a
return match.

CLIVE: I was taught to be a good loser. (*He stirs his tea.*) When
are they going to be repatriated?

MAJOR DAVIES: In six to eight weeks.

BARBARA: What will you do then, Major Davies?

MAJOR DAVIES: Take a holiday, Mrs Candy – where they don't
speak German!

CLIVE: If you're passing through London, drop in!

BARBARA: When we're back from Paris, I'm making Clive give a
party for his friends. If you can, do come.

MAJOR DAVIES: Thank you. I'll try. I'd like to talk to you about
Germans, both of you. You were going to say something
rather interesting just now – something about peacetime
and war – ?]]*

SEQUENCE 79
Interior: 33 Cadogan Place

HALL
Fade in.
*An invitation card falls on a tray, which already contains a score
of similar cards.*

---

* The climax to this scene was Barbara's speech about German culture, now in
sequence 76.

Insert: the card reads:

> 'Brigadier-General Clive Candy
> *requests*
> *the pleasure of the company*
> *of*
> *Major John E. Davies, M.C.*
> *to a Bachelor Dinner Party*
> *on Tuesday, 26th August* 1919
> *at 8 p.m.*

33 Cadogan Place,
S.W.I.   R.S.V.P.'

MAJOR DAVIES *is just being helped out of his coat by*
MURDOCH. [[*Behind him the hall clock is striking nine o'clock.*
He is no longer in uniform, he wears a tweed suit and looks
what he is, a distinguished, wise and cultured elderly
gentleman.]] [*He is in uniform.*]

CLIVE *comes eagerly out of the dining room to meet him. From*
beyond we hear the unrestrained conviviality of an exclusively
male dinner party. CLIVE *wears a dinner-jacket.*

[CLIVE: Ah, Davies.

DAVIES: Hello, Candy. I hope your wife will forgive me.]

CLIVE: (*Smiling*) [[Awfully sorry, old man.]] [I'm afraid] You
    haven't read the invitation properly.

MAJOR DAVIES: (*Vaguely: glancing at card*) Ah, [[so it is,]] a
    Bachelor Party. If I'd realized that your charming wife
    wouldn't be here, [[I'd never have hurried as I did]] [I
    shouldn't have been in such a hurry].

CLIVE: We'll find you something.

MAJOR DAVIES: Thanks, I had dinner on the train. I've come
    straight from Victoria.

CLIVE: On leave?

MAJOR DAVIES: No. Duty . . .

CLIVE: Come and have a glass of port.
    (*While talking, they have walked towards the dining room*
    where the hum of conversation has got louder. As they go

in, the telephone in the hall rings. MURDOCH *answers it.*
He has a special voice for answering the telephone, full of
old-world courtesy.)

MURDOCH: This is Brigadier-General Candy's residence . . .

[VOICE: May I speak to the General?]

MURDOCH: And who, may I ask, is speaking? . . .

[VOICE: This is Oberst Kretschmar-Schuldorff, speaking from
Victoria Station. And tell him I'm leaving tonight.]

MURDOCH: Would you mind repeating the name, sir . . .

[VOICE: (*Slowly*) Theo Kretschmar-Schuldorff.]

> (*He obviously hasn't got the name but is too polite to say*
> *so. He puts down the receiver and goes to get his master.*
> *We go close to the receiver. The man at the other end of the*
> *wire is whistling – the Mignon Aria.*
>
> CLIVE *and* MURDOCH *come from the dining room.)*

CLIVE: Couldn't he 'phone tomorrow? Where's he speaking
from?

MURDOCH: Victoria Station, sir. He's leaving tonight he said.

CLIVE: *What* name?

MURDOCH: It sounded like Wretch-Bar Something, sir –

CLIVE: Kretschmar-Schuldorff! Murdoch, that brain of yours
ought to be in a bottle!

> (*He snatches up the receiver and mouthpiece, he listens,*
> *grins, whistles in reply, laughs. He has quite forgotten the*
> *impression he had been given at the prison camp, he is so*
> *pleased to be friendly to his friend again.*)

CLIVE: Theo! [[You old son-of-a-gun! Where are you? . . .
Victoria? What are you doing there?]]

FIRST CLASS REFRESHMENT ROOM

THEO *is using the telephone behind the counter of the refreshment bar.* [[*Beyond him we see the busy bar and the whole big room, crammed with talkative and excited German officers.*]] THEO *himself is in a very different humour than when we have last seen him. He is going home. His uniform coat hangs over his shoulders. He talks good English now, with an accent.* [[*By him is* LIEUTENANT CARTWRIGHT, *the officer-in-charge.*]]

THEO: [Yes, it's me, Theo. How are you my friend? Yes,] I'm
   going home – if there is such a thing left in Germany.
   [[How are you, my friend? . . . Good . . .]] Oh, there are

Junge's design for the First Class Refreshment Room at Victoria Station:
probably not filmed.

scores of us here. [Can't you hear them?] We have an extra
train, it leaves at 11.30. . . . Yes, we are under guard, Clive!
May I still call you Clive, now you are a General? . . .
[CLIVE: Cut the cackle. What have you to say for yourself?]
THEO: (*He listens and laughs*) Listen! I am sorry! [I'm terribly
sorry.] That is what I wanted to tell you. About our meeting
at the Camp. I was a silly fool. [I had to tell you before I
left.] And now I must ring off . . .

SEQUENCE 81
Interior: 33 Cadogan Place

HALL
CLIVE, *at the other end of the wire, glances at the clock.*
CLIVE: [[Wait a minute! Don't hang up! It's only a quarter past
nine, now, I want to see you . . . Who says I can't? I've got
the G.S.O.I. in charge of all military transport here to
dinner, as well as your Camp Commander.]] [Major
Davies. Come here a minute, will you? (*To* THEO)] I'll send
you back to Derbyshire if you're not careful! – Now you
just sit tight and we'll come and get you.
[THEO: All right, all right, I won't run away.]
[[CLIVE: You've got to come and have a glass of port! You can't
leave England without having a glass of my port. Where did
you learn that perfect English of yours?]]
(*Dissolve to:*)

[[SEQUENCE 82
Victoria Station

FIRST CLASS REFRESHMENT ROOM
THEO *is overwhelmed by* CLIVE'*s open delight and flood of talk.*
He answers his last question.
THEO: Where do you think I learnt it? I had plenty of time . . .
   Well, all right. I shall not run away.
   (*He glances through the smoke and over the heads . . .* * *at*
   the clock.
   The time is 9.15.
   Dissolve to: the clock. The time is 9.25.)

SEQUENCE 83
Victoria Station

FIRST CLASS REFRESHMENT ROOM
A SENTRY *is standing on guard at the door, to keep people*
away. On the door is a sign, such as: 'O.H.M.S.'
The SENTRY *sees someone approaching across the station. He*
springs to attention, shoulders arms, salutes.
It is MAJOR DAVIES, MAJOR-GENERAL BLOMFIELD *and*
BRIGADIER-GENERAL CANDY *who are bearing down on him,*
all smoking cigars and all unmistakable senior officers, although
in dinner-jackets (except MAJOR DAVIES).
MAJOR DAVIES: Lieutenant Cartwright inside?
SENTRY: Yes, sir.
BLOMFIELD: Ask him to step outside, sentry!
   (*The* SENTRY *smartly grounds arms, turns, goes and opens*
   the door. We see a glimpse of the crowded room, thick with
   smoke.)

---

* One or two words obliterated here on the original script.

232

SENTRY: (*Calls*) Lieutenant Cartwright, sir!
  (*He sees him coming, returns to his post, snaps to attention,
  reports:*)
SENTRY: He's coming, sir.
BLOMFIELD: (*Testily*) At ease, man, at ease!
  (*The SENTRY stands at ease.*)
CLIVE: Sorry to have dragged you out like this, Piggy.
BLOMFIELD: From an excellent glass of port, too!
  (*LIEUTENANT CARTWRIGHT appears. He is quite shaken
  by the senior officers.*)
MAJOR DAVIES: Ah, Cartwright – this is Major-General
  Blomfield – Brigadier-General Candy – (*They shake hands.*)
  We want one of your prisoners, Cartwright. Oberst
  Kretschmar-Schuldorff is an old friend of the Brigadier's.
  Where's Smollett?
CARTWRIGHT: Went to get some dinner, sir.
BLOMFIELD: Call the Oberst out. I'll be responsible. You can
  have me and the Major as hostages.
CARTWRIGHT: That will be all right, sir.
  (*He vanishes into the room.*)
CLIVE: Now look here – I can't leave you two.
BLOMFIELD: Don't worry – you can't finish the port by 11.30.
  (*The door is opened by CARTWRIGHT and THEO appears, a
  doubtful smile on his face. He carries his suitcase and
  greatcoat. CLIVE goes to him and this time THEO doesn't
  turn away.*)]]

SEQUENCE 84
Interior: Taxi

[[*They are travelling through brightly-lit London streets.
CLIVE sits opposite THEO to see him better.*]]
[*They are sitting side by side.*] Both are friendly, but THEO is

233

more reserved.

CLIVE: [[Theo!]] You Prussian stiff-neck! The only way is to kidnap you!

[[THEO: (*Gesture*) What can I do?

CLIVE: (*Introducing*) Oberst Kretschmar-Schuldorff – Major-General Blomfield – Major Davies, you know.

THEO: (*Smiles*) Intimately.]]

CLIVE: (*Examining him*) [Now, let's have a look at you.] You've worn well, old chap. Still got my mark on you, I see. (*He touches the old scar.*)

THEO: And you still need a moustache!

[[MAJOR DAVIES: Well, if you two are going –

THEO: Going where?

CLIVE: Home. Come on! I've a taxi waiting.
    (*Dissolve to:*)]]*

CLIVE: When were you captured?

THEO: July '16. [[Nearly three years in prison.]]

CLIVE: You were lucky. You missed the worst of it.

THEO: [[Nevertheless]] I would prefer to have been unlucky.

CLIVE: [That's what you think.] (*Changing subject.*) Have you heard from home? Have you any children? How is Edith?

THEO: Which shall I answer first? Edith is [[well]] [all right], as far as I can tell. (*He passes across one of a bundle of* [[Red Cross postcards]] [photographs] *he has in his pocket.*)
    (CLIVE *looks at them.*
    [[*Insert: typical Red Cross postcard from Germany filled in and signed by Edith in German.*]])

[CLIVE: Boys, eh? Now that one's exactly like Edith.

THEO: Karl? Yes, he is, isn't he?]

THEO: [[We have]] [I almost wish we had] no children. [[It's better we haven't.]] What future can children have in a beaten country?

---

* The opening section of dialogue in this sequence originally formed the end of sequence 83, set in Victoria Station, which was otherwise cut.

CLIVE: (*Tolerantly*) [Oh] You Germans are all a bit [[mad.]] [crazy. You wait till you meet] Barbara [[will]] [– she'll] tell you what's what.

[THEO: Who's Barbara?]

CLIVE: [[Did I tell you I was married? By the way, old man, you're going to get a bit of a shock when you see Barbara –]] [My wife. Oh, of course, you don't know I'm married. You'll get a bit of a shock when you see her.]

THEO: (*Politely puzzled*) [Shock?] I am sure she is charming.

CLIVE: (*Chuckles*) [[She's more than that! You'll see! She's out now – taken her mother to the theatre. But she'll be back in time.]] [I don't mean that. You wait and see. Of course, you won't see her. She's gone out to the theatre with her mother. Never mind.]

(*The taxi stops outside the house.*)

[[SEQUENCE 85
Exterior: 33 Cadogan Place

They get out, THEO *clinging to his bag and coat.* MURDOCH *appears.* THEO *looks up at the house as* CLIVE *pays the taxi.*

THEO: Very respectable, your house! Your streets and houses have so much dignity – but even more draughts!

MURDOCH: (*Wresting his bag and coat politely but firmly from him*) Good evening, sir.

CLIVE: You're right about the draughts, my boy. That's what blows us English out of our houses and all over the world – eh? – eh? (*Roars with laughter.*) I must tell that to Barbara! (*They go in.*)

Interior: 33 Cadogan Place

HALL

They enter. THEO *looks round.*

CLIVE: D'you like it? It was left me by my Aunt. Murdoch: leave
    the Oberst's things there and have a taxi at eleven. Come
    on, Theo!

THEO: Won't that be too late?

CLIVE: Now leave everything to me. I want you to meet some of
    the men you've been fighting with!
    (*They vanish into the dining room.*)]]

SEQUENCE 87
Interior: 33 Cadogan Place

DINING ROOM

*The room is thick with cigar-smoke. Over a dozen gentlemen,
who are sitting around the polished table, rise politely as* CLIVE
*comes proudly in with his guest. They wait, without any
appearance of curiosity, to be introduced.*

CLIVE: Gentlemen, this is [my friend] Oberst Kretschmar-
    Schuldorff. (*There is a murmur of acknowledgement.*) [Sir
    Archibald Blair, shining light of the Foreign Office. General
    Beveridge . . .

BEVERIDGE: How d'you do. I've heard about you, Oberst.]

CLIVE: Major-General Taylor-Grant – General Keen – Major
    Michael Cornish and his brother Major John Cornish –
    [[Rear]] Admiral Sir Merton Barrow of the so-called Senior
    Service – Commodore Brandon-Crester, ditto – [Major
    Davies you know.

THEO: Intimately.]

CLIVE: [[Sir Terence Blair, from the Colonial Office – Lord
     Clement-Selby, Lieutenant Governor of Gibraltar]]
     [Colonel Hopper, aide to the Governor of Gibraltar] – Sir
     William Rendall, [[First Secretary to the Viceroy]] [on the
     Viceroy's staff] – George Metcalf of Uganda – Sir John
     Bembridge, just back from Jamaica – Colonel Mannering,
     [known to the press as] the uncrowned king of Southern
     Arabia – Mr Christopher Wynne, of Bradford, England, my
     father-in-law. [Embodiment of all the solid virtues.]
     (*Like a hailstorm this collection of names, ranks and titles,
     representative of an Empire upon which the sun never sets,
     descends upon* THEO.
     *A chair is pulled forward. Everyone sits. Everyone is
     anxious to make the German feel at ease.*)
CLIVE: [[Drink, Theo?]] [Sit down, Theo. What will you have to
     drink?]
THEO: (*Seeing it there*) Port [please].
     (*More than one hand reaches out to pass the decanter
     round to him. As the decanter was only three feet to his left,
     it has to go right round the table.*)
[VOICE: It has to go round the clock.]
     (CLIVE *pushes boxes towards him.*)
CLIVE: Cigar? Cigarette? [They're both on the table – thousands
     of them.]
THEO: Cigarette, please.
[[CLIVE: Turkish! Virginian!]]
[BLAIR: I don't suppose you remember me, but we met in Berlin
     in '02. (*He is the former Second Secretary.*)
THEO: Oh, did we?
     (*Another guest appears behind them.*)
CLIVE: Ah, Barstow. (*To* THEO) Colonel Barstow of the Royal
     Air Force.
BARSTOW: Don't get up.]
TAYLOR-GRANT: I'm glad you're on your way home at last,
     Oberst.

Clive introduces his friends: 'Like a hailstorm this collection of names, ranks and titles, representative of an Empire upon which the sun never sets, descends upon Theo.'

THEO: Thank you, sir.

TAYLOR-GRANT: Can't imagine anything more awful than to be a prisoner of war in England.

THEO: I don't think it can be much good anywhere, General.

TAYLOR-GRANT: [[But]] [Oh], my dear [[Oberst]] [fellow], in this country people are always poking their noses into everything. Did you get any letters from spinsters?

THEO: (*Smiles*) [[No.]] [Yes, we did.]

TAYLOR-GRANT: [[Shows you had a sensible Commandant. Lots of Camps were pestered by them.]] [I thought so.] They started a campaign to write to prisoners of war – not our chaps, mind you!

THEO: [[We were spared.]] It was not so bad – we had books,

[[camp-]]concerts, lectures . . .

SIR TERENCE BLAIR: I am sure your Camp [[had perfect administration]] [was well run]. German organization is [[the best in the world]] [very thorough].

CLIVE: [[We nearly had a lot! Ha! Ha!]] [Bit too thorough for us!]

WYNNE: Was the [[food]] [cooking] good?

THEO: [[Quite good.]] [It was English cooking. (*Laughter.*)] [VOICE: A sense of humour!]

TAYLOR-GRANT: My daughter, Joyce, started a campaign to better the food for German prisoners in England.

WYNNE: I remember the Government was also [[accused of]] [charged with] over-feeding them.

[[CLEMENT-SELBY: I was taken to one of those Food Economy meetings during the shortage. The Ministry of Food speaker asked her audience point-blank if there was anyone present who wanted the prisoners' ration reduced. Nobody answered. Then a woman stood up and said that only when we ourselves were starving, which was very far from being the case, should we be justified in starving prisoners of war. Then the speaker asked whether, if any of the audience saw a starving German prisoner, he would not at once share his food with him? They laughed, and then they cheered.]]

CLIVE: Oh, we're not too bad. [Drink up, gentlemen.

THEO: (*Proposes toast*) Your health.]

TAYLOR-GRANT: [[Where did you leave Davies and Blomfield?]] [What have you done with old Tiger Blomfield?]

CLIVE: At [Victoria, in the bar of] the Grosvenor. [[They're]] [He's] hostage[[s]] [for the Oberst].

BEMBRIDGE: Now where is the sense in guarding officer-prisoners nearly a year after the fighting is over?

THEO: I imagine it is more to [[defend]] [protect] us.

CLIVE: [[Defend]] [Protect]? Against what?

THEO: People.

[[CLIVE: What people?]]

HOPPY: How do you mean?

THEO: Your people. They cannot be adjusted from war to peace as easily as you [can], gentlemen.

[VOICE: (*Off*) I think you'll find that's not true.]

CLIVE: Do you [[think]] [mean to say] our people would attack you in that uniform?

THEO: [[It is only natural.]] I tried to *kill* Englishmen [in this uniform]. [[I'm an enemy.]]

TAYLOR-GRANT: [[Oberst, you're quite wrong.]] [My dear fellow, that's rather a gloomy point of view, isn't it?]

CLIVE: You've got the wrong end of the stick, old man. The war's over. There's nothing to bear malice about. You're a decent fellow and so are we!

THEO: I'm not a decent fellow! I'm a beggar, like the [[other 800 officers in our camp]] [rest of all the professional soldiers in our army]. A beaten country can't have an army. What are we going to do?

[METCALF: I imagine there'll be a lot to do.

THEO: But not for us.] We know a [[little]] [bit] about horses, we can be stable-boys.

[CLIVE: You'll feel different when you're home again.

THEO: Home! But what will home be like? Another prison camp?

CLIVE: Who says so?

THEO: Aren't we] [[We are]] going to have foreign troops occupying our cities [for years?]. [[You set us prisoners free but we shan't be free because our whole country is going to be a prison camp.]]

BEMBRIDGE: I've never heard a man more wrong than you are! We don't want to make beggars out of you!

WYNNE: We are a trading nation, we must have countries to trade with.

BLAIR: [[We don't want you out of it. It simply can't be done.]] [Surely you realize that the reconstruction of Germany is essential to the peace of Europe?]

TAYLOR-GRANT: [[And where do you get this idea that we are going to keep millions of men under arms to occupy your country?]] [I can't see our tax-payers keeping an army in your country. Can you, Candy?]

CLIVE: [Of course not.] Read the papers, man! The English papers! [[I]] [We] can't ask you to be [[my]] [our] friend, if [[I]] [we] rob you and humiliate you first. That's how we all feel. We want to be friends!

(*Dissolve to:*)

[[SEQUENCE 88
Victoria Station

PLATFORM

It is 11.27.

A special train is at the platform, crowded with German officers, every window is full of typical faces.

A large crowd has invaded the platform. They are pressing newspapers, books, magazines, boxes of chocolates on the officers, shaking hands and waving.

Voices shout: 'Cheerio!' 'Goodbye, Jerry!' 'We don't want to lose you/But we think you ought to go!' 'Cheer up, Jerry, you couldn't help losing the ruddy war!'

THEO *and his escort move with difficulty along the train. They have all come to see him off – the Major-Generals, the diplomats, the famous sportsmen . . .*

People give THEO *a cheer. They are quick to recognize the type of men who are seeing him off. It looks like an occasion. Some of the crowd slap him on the back. Complete strangers push packages of cigarettes into his pockets.*

CLIVE, *who has him by the arm, looks proudly at him.*

CLIVE: How is the old German scepticism?

THEO: (*Shakes his head*) Fabelhaft! (*He has no English words for it.*)

(*Some officers hail* THEO. *He stops at their coach.*)

THEO: Here I am!

CLIVE: Give my love to Edith! Tell her – no, don't tell her anything! Come and see us sometime in London, or wherever we are!

(*A whistle blows.* THEO'*s luggage is passed in.* CLIVE *shakes him warmly by the hand.*

THEO *looks out at the smiling faces. He shakes his head in amazement.*)

THEO: Just like when we went to war . . . !

(*The train starts moving.* THEO *waves. Everyone waves.* CLIVE *is beaming. He turns to the nearest of his friends, which happens to be* MAJOR DAVIES.)

CLIVE: Well, I think we made an impression on him!

(MAJOR DAVIES *reserves judgment.*)]]

SEQUENCE 89
Railway Compartment. L.C.&D. Railway

THEO *is speaking to seven of his brother officers who listen with great attention.*

THEO: [[Es ist unglaublich! I have to say it in English, the German language has no words for it.]] 'We want to trade with Germany,' said one! A General said: 'We don't want to keep an army just to occupy your country!' A General! They are *children*! *Boys*! playing *cricket*! They win the shirts off our backs and now they want to give them back, because the game is over! War is the most unpopular thing in England! They are already organizing pacifist societies, their newspapers are anti-militarist – Here can we get to something! [[This is our chance! Their]] [This child-like]

242

stupidity is a raft for us in a sea of despair! Do you know
what my friend, [[Brigadier-]]General Candy said? He said
– [We'll soon have Germany on her feet again.]
([[*He breaks off as the door to the corridor slides open and
the friendly face of* LIEUTENANT CARTWRIGHT *appears.*]]
[*Close-up of railway lines – trains passing fast.
Dissolve to:*])

SEQUENCE 90
Interior: 33 Cadogan Place

CLIVE'S DEN
CLIVE *and* BARBARA *are having a drink before going to bed. It
is quite late. She is still in evening dress. He is wearing a smoking
jacket.*
CLIVE *has just come to the end of the story of the evening's
events.*
CLIVE: [[. . . so I told]] [The last thing I said to] him: 'My dear
old chap, [don't you worry,] we'll soon have Germany on
her feet again!'
BARBARA: (*Major Davies would understand her expression*)
And he believed it?
CLIVE: Theo? I believe so. I hope so. [[Don't you?]]
[[(BARBARA *stands up. She bends down and kisses him.*)]]
[(BARBARA *leans back reflectively.*)
BARBARA: Darling, don't hum.
CLIVE: Was I humming?
BARBARA: Yes, it's a little habit you've got.
CLIVE: (*Pauses*) What'll I do if I don't hum?
    (*They laugh and hold hands in front of the fire. He kisses
    her hand.
    An album of snapshots, Embassy invitations, mementos.
    Insert:* Times *death notice. 'Clive Candy wishes to thank all*

Barbara and Clive's sole moment of domestic bliss – a scene largely improvised.

kind friends who have written to sympathize with him in his irreparable loss. He hopes to answer them all personally in due course.'
The album's pages are all blank after this.]
The camera moves up to the trophies on the wall.
[New ones start to appear, dated up to 1938.
A map of Germany, focusing on Munich.]
Dissolve to:)

Insert:
[[*A mimeographed letter, with handwritten dates, saying roughly the following (wording to be checked):* 'Sir (or Madam), You are requested under the Enemy Aliens Order 1920 to appear before Tribunal 132. (In Pelham School, Pelham Close, N.W.9.) on Monday Nov. 6th 1939 between 11–12 a.m. Aliens' Registration Book and National Identity Card have to be produced.']]
[*BCU typewriter typing letter, dated November 1939, summoning* THEODOR KRETSCHMAR-SCHULDORFF *to a Tribunal hearing.*]
Dissolve to:

[[SEQUENCE 92
Tribunal

WAITING ROOM
The Tribunal sits in a requisitioned school. This room was a classroom, but has been transformed into a waiting room. Benches and chairs line the walls. The room is full of nervous, gloomy people of all ages and sexes, waiting to be called. In the next room, their fates are being decided. The door to it opens and a uniformed policeman comes out with the papers of two men.
POLICEMAN: (*Calls*) Mr H. Bruck and Mr S. Bruck.
   (*The two brothers hold up their hands and answer: 'Here!' They stand up as the* POLICEMAN *comes to them and hands back their books and Identity Cards.*)
POLICEMAN: You can go.
S. BRUCK: ⎱
H. BRUCK: ⎰ Thank you.

POLICEMAN: (*Turns and calls*) Mr Theodor Kretschmar-
Schuldorff!
(THEO *stands up. He is an old man now, about sixty-five. But*
he still carries himself like an officer. He goes into the
Tribunal.)]]

SEQUENCE 93
Tribunal

This was also a classroom. It is smaller than the other but there
is plenty of room. Behind a desk are seated two men: one is the
JUDGE, *the other an inspector from Scotland Yard (in mufti).*
Beside the desk sits a middle-aged Englishwoman from the
Refugee Committee. She also interprets, if necessary. In a
corner, near the door, is a plain wood table, where a uniformed
policeman sits. He has lists and rubber stamps, comes from the
'Local' Police Station and stamps the papers after the
interrogation. *
The tone of the inquiry is impersonal at first, but later becomes
more sympathetic. The JUDGE *has the Home Office file of the*
person interviewed in front of him; it is pretty fully documented
but he prefers to use it only as a check on their own stories.
The inspector does not speak unless asked.
THEO *enters, comes to his place, clicks his heels together (such*
customs die hard with a German), bows very gently and waits to
be questioned. When he speaks he is unafraid, like a man who
has nothing to lose by the truth.
JUDGE: Mr Theodor Kretschmar-Schuldorff?
THEO: [[Yes.]] [Here.]
JUDGE: Sit down.

---

* The Powell papers include a sheet giving precise details of layout, dress worn and
procedure for the Aliens' Tribunals.

THEO: Thank you.

JUDGE: Your Registration Book and Identity Card, please.

THEO: Please! (*He has them in his hand and passes them over.*)

JUDGE: [Sit down.] When did you arrive in this country?

THEO: On the 6th of June [[19]]35.

JUDGE: From?

THEO: Paris, France. I [[came to]] [arrived in] Paris on the 15th January 1934.

JUDGE: From Germany?

THEO: Yes.

JUDGE: Why did you leave Germany?

THEO: My outlook of life is against [[Nazism]] [the Nazis].

JUDGE: Most refugees left Germany early in 1933, when Hitler came to power . . .

THEO: I had nothing to fear from Hitler. At least I thought so. It took me eight months to find out I was wrong.

JUDGE: Rather a long time.

(THEO *is silent.*)

JUDGE: Don't you think so?

THEO: Please, I mean no offence – but you in England took five years.

(*The policeman in the corner looks up, but no fire descends from heaven. The* JUDGE *merely remarks.*)

JUDGE: (*Drily*) Quite right. (*Pause.*) Have you been in England before?

THEO: Yes. I was a prisoner of war in the last war.

JUDGE: (*Looking in file*) I see you were an officer. When did you leave the army?

THEO: In 1920 – eight out of ten officers had to retire when the German Army ceased to exist – I mean as a large army . . .

JUDGE: You prefer the existence of a large army?

THEO: [[No]] [Not any more]. In 1920 I chose a new profession – Military Chemist – I worked for thirteen years in a factory at Mannheim.

JUDGE: Are you married?

247

THEO: My wife is dead. [[(*Pause.*) In 1933.]]

JUDGE: Children?

THEO: Two. I have no connection with them. They are good Nazis – as far as any Nazi can be called good.

(THEO's *frankness has made an impression on the* JUDGE; *but, at the same time, he has decided to intern him. The presentation of the facts has been too unvarnished.* THEO, *of course, senses this.*

JUDGE: [[Well,]] I'm afraid, Mr Kretschmar-Schuldorff, that doesn't sound very much in your favour.

THEO: (*Wryly*) I have tried to answer correctly.

JUDGE: (*Sympathetically*) [[No doubt, but –]] [Personally, I don't doubt your good faith. But I am here to safeguard my country's interests. You may be an anti-Nazi. You may not be. In times like these, one enemy in our midst can do more harm then ten across the Channel. If you were here to work for the enemy, what would you tell me now? Exactly the same – and that our enemy was your enemy.

I know this is hard on those who are really with us. But it should be their best assurance that this time we mean business. If you are a friend, our precautions are your precautions and our interests are your interests. Because our victory will be your victory.] Is there anything you would like to add?

THEO: (*Sees that the* JUDGE *wants to help him*) If you won't mind, sir?

[[JUDGE: Go ahead.

THEO: Since I have lived in foreign countries, I am very cautious.]] In earlier years the most important principle of my life used to be: Never lie, always speak the truth.

JUDGE: [[An excellent]] [A very good] principle. I hope you still keep to it.

THEO: I have not told a lie. But I also have not told the truth. A refugee soon learns that there is a great difference between the two.

(*He pauses. The* JUDGE *nods.*)

THEO: The truth about me is that I am a tired old man who [[has come]] [came] to this country because he is homesick. (*He smiles.*) Don't stare at me, sir, I am all right in the head. You [[see]] [know that], after the war, we had very bad years in Germany. We got poorer and poorer. Every day retired officers or schoolteachers were caught shoplifting. Money lost its value, the price of everything rose except of human beings. We read in the newspapers that the after-war years were bad everywhere, that crime was increasing and that honest citizens were having a hard job to put the gangsters in jail [[where they belonged]]. Well, [I need hardly tell you that] in Germany, the gangsters [[started to put]] [finally succeeded in putting] the honest citizens in jail.

[[Do you know, sir, who were the first pillars of the Nazi Party? The dirt of the people, the lazy ones, the drunkards, the scum of the country. Ask, sir, all these people who come here before you. They will remember them. In every business there was one who had no talent and no desire to work or to learn; and one morning he appeared with a brown shirt on and a revolver in his holster. Then they were joined by the huge army of easy-going people who always say: 'I am an engineer and I understand engines: that's enough for me!']]

My wife was English. She would have loved to [[return]] [come back] to England, but it seemed to me that I would have been letting down my country in its greatest need, and [so] she stayed at my side. [[When at last she would have come]] [When in summer '33, we found that we had lost both our children to the Nazi Party, and I was willing to come], she died. Neither of my sons came to her funeral [Heil Hitler] . . . and then in January [[1934]] [1935], I [[came up alone]] [had to go] to Berlin on a mission for my firm. I drove up in my car. I lost my way on the outskirts of the city, and suddenly [[I recognized]] the landscape

249

[seemed familiar to me. Slowly I recognized] the road, the lake and a nursing home, where I spent some weeks recovering [[many]] [almost forty] years ago.

I stopped the car and sat still remembering. [You see, sir,] in this very nursing home, I met my wife for the first time . . . and I met an Englishman who became my [[best]] [greatest] friend [[all those years, although we have only met twice since then – in 1919]]. [And I remembered] the people at the station [in '19], when we [prisoners] were sent home, cheering us, [treating us like friends] . . . and the faces [[round a polished table]] of a party of distinguished men who were kind and [[did their best]] [tried their utmost] to comfort me when the defeat of my country seemed to me unbearable . . . And very foolishly I remembered the [[English]] countryside, [the gardens,] the green lawns [[where I spent the long months of captivity]], the weedy rivers and the trees she loved so much. [And] a great desire came over me to come back [[here]] to my wife's country. [[At first I couldn't get a permit. But I tried – and tried again.]] [And this, sir, is the truth.

(*Silence in the schoolroom after* THEO's *long speech. The* JUDGE *rises and walks round the table.*)

JUDGE: Haven't you got anyone in this country who knows you well, a British citizen?

THEO: The doorman at the chemical works where I offered my services. The police officers at the Aliens Department at Bow Street.

JUDGE: (*To policeman*) Sentry! (*To* THEO) Don't you know Major-General Clive Wynne-Candy?

THEO: Yes, I used to know him.

JUDGE: Did you ask him to come here and testify on your behalf?

THEO: Yes, I did send him a letter, but I suppose he . . .
(*The door opens and* CLIVE *appears.*]
[[*During his last words a disturbance has started outside*

*and has gradually grown in intensity, doors are slamming,
voices are raised and, as everyone looks around at the
door, it bursts open and, flanked by awed policemen,*
MAJOR-GENERAL WYNNE-CANDY *enters the room*]]. *He
is, of course, three years younger than when we met him
in the Turkish Bath at the beginning of our story, but he is
physically much the same and he is much more self-
assured and pompous now, before the disappointments of
the next three years have deflated him. He talks very
loudly and goes straight to the* JUDGE *as the only person
worthy of his attention, beside* THEO.)

[[CLIVE: By gad, sir, Lord Prendergast was right! He told me
I'd never find this blasted school! My card, sir! (*He flings
his card down on the table.*)
(*Insert: visiting card.* 'Major-General Clive Wynne-Candy,
V.C., D.S.O. 33 Cadogan Place, s.w.1. Boodles Club.']]
CLIVE *has grabbed* THEO, *pleased and bewildered*[[,
turned him to the light and slaps him on the back]].)

CLIVE: [Theo, my dear chap,] Let me have a good look at you,
[[old bean – my old German bean – eh? – dashed good!]]
(*Roars with laughter.*) By gad, you've kept your figure
better than I have! (*He slaps his tummy.*) Bit of a bay
window, eh? [[But there's life in the old dog yet! (*He turns
to the* JUDGE.) Sorry, sir, to butt into your court-martial,
unpardonable intrusion and all that sort of thing, but I
only got down from the North yesterday and I'm off to
France – well, mustn't say when, but damn soon! – Found
this idiot's letter waiting for me, put Sherlock Holmes on
his track, got his address – (*To* THEO) don't think much
of your choice in digs, old chap – they said you had to
come here – the war, I suppose – so I dropped Buggy
Prendergast at the Club – he'd had enough – and came
along myself to take you home with me – (*To* JUDGE) if
it's all right with you, sir.
(CLIVE *obviously takes it for granted that it is.*)

Clive comes to Theo's rescue at the Tribunal.

THEO: I'm afraid, Clive, that I can't come with you.
CLIVE: Why not?
THEO: They are going to intern me.
CLIVE: (*Explodes*) Pooh! Ridiculous!
(*He turns on the poor* JUDGE, *who starts to assert himself*.)
JUDGE: My dear General, the law is the law. This is a civil court
and you have already disturbed it. I have the greatest
respect for your –
CLIVE: (*With great charm*) Gad, sir, I'm awfully sorry. I come
bursting in like a bull in a china shop! You're absolutely
right, sir, you're absolutely right! I apologize!
(*He extends his hand, the* JUDGE *has to take it.* CLIVE
shakes it vigorously and points to THEO, *who is looking
admiringly at his friend's easy authority*.)
CLIVE: I know him well, sir, and I'd go bail for him anywhere.

You can have all the credentials you want. I know everybody in London who *is* anybody! Is this a Home Office or a Foreign Office do? Can I use your telephone? Hullo! Hullo! Operator! (*Jerking at* THEO.) He's just exactly the opposite of the men we ought to be interning! Hullo! Operator!]] [You see, sir, I wouldn't be surprised if this fellow really dislikes us. He comes to England twice in his life: the first time he's a prisoner and the second time he's about to be one. May I talk to him, sir? I haven't seen him for nineteen ... er ...

THEO: Twenty.

CLIVE: Twenty years and a bit.

JUDGE: Afraid not here, General. We have many Kretschmar-Schuldorffs waiting.

CLIVE: You mean to say that I've travelled eleven miles from – mustn't say where – and you won't allow me to have a word with a condemned man?

JUDGE: Well, you don't have to go back this minute, do you?

CLIVE: Tomorrow morning, sir, and infernally early too.

JUDGE: Well, you can talk to him all day and all night till midnight – Aliens' Curfew, you know.

CLIVE: And can I take him with me?

JUDGE: If you say you know him.

CLIVE: Do I know him?

JUDGE: And will stand surety for him.

CLIVE: With everything I have, sir.]

(*Dissolve to:*)

SEQUENCE 94
Interior: 33 Cadogan Place

DINING ROOM
CLIVE *and* THEO *are sitting on after dinner, smoking in*

companionable silence. There is an enormous difference between the two men. For CLIVE *very little has changed; for* THEO *everything: he has seen less than* CLIVE *during the years but he has experienced more. He is a wise man now. He speaks with a little smile about the most important things. His attitude is that of a man very little concerned with life's troubles. He has nothing to lose because he has lost everything.*

Outside it is quite late. It is winter. The windows are shuttered.

[[*After a moment* THEO *looks at his watch.*]] [*Clock chimes.*]

THEO: It's time I was going. [[I must be home by midnight.]]

CLIVE: [[Why midnight?]] [The night is young yet.]

THEO: [Don't you remember?] Curfew for aliens.

CLIVE: (*Blimpish nod*) Ah – yes . . .

[THEO: I have to be home by midnight.

(MURDOCH *comes in. He is about the same age as his master and has become, over the years, the perfect butler.*)

MURDOCH: Don't forget, sir. You have to be up for 6.30.

CLIVE: Early parade, eh?

MURDOCH: Yes. (*He leaves.*)

THEO: How lucky you are.

CLIVE: Yes, they put me on the retired list in '35. But I knew they'd want me again. Back I went on the active list like a shot. (*Changes the subject.*)] I mean, why don't you stay here? I've eighteen rooms. (*Bellows.*) Murdoch!

THEO: Thanks, Clive, but I don't think I had better. I would need a special permit anyway.

(MURDOCH *comes in.*)

MURDOCH: You called, sir?

CLIVE: All right, Murdoch, it was nothing – no! [[As you were!]] (*To* THEO) Stay a little longer, I'll send you back by car. Murdoch, tell Miss Cannon to be here at quarter to twelve.

MURDOCH: Yes, sir. (*He goes.*)

THEO: Who's Miss Cannon?

CLIVE: [[Johnny]] [Miss] Cannon, my driver. [[A.T.S.]] [M.T.C.]

THEO: [Do you] Remember, Clive, we used to say: 'Our army is fighting for our homes, our women and our children'? Now the women are fighting beside the men. [[In Germany,]] the children are trained to shoot. [[Only remains]] [What's left is]: the 'home'. But what is 'home' without women and children?

CLIVE: (*Nods, then says suddenly*) You never met my wife. Do you want to see [a picture of] her?

THEO: Very much . . . (*They both laugh as they stand up.*) . . . do you remember when that was all I could say in English?

CLIVE: You got further with it [then] than I ever got.

THEO: In what respect?

CLIVE: My dear fellow, don't tell me you [[never knew]] [didn't know] . . .

THEO: What?

CLIVE: [[That I – dash it, don't]] [you] make me blush!

THEO: But I don't know what you are talking about.

CLIVE: Well – I thought it was written all over my face when I left Berlin in [[19]]02.

THEO: Don't forget, I never saw [[you]] [your face] after you left.

CLIVE: (*It is a great secret*) I was in love with [her –] your wife.

THEO: (*Slowly*) She never told me . . .

CLIVE: She never knew.

THEO: But [[when I told you]] [I seem to remember] – that last day [in Berlin] – [[that I loved her]] – you seemed genuinely happy . . .

CLIVE: Dash it – I didn't know then. But on the train I started to miss her – it was worse on the boat – and by the time I was back in London – well, I'd got it properly. My Aunt Margaret got on the scent [[right]] [straight] away, women have a nose for these things. Besides I did a stupid thing! First night back I took out her sister . . .

THEO: Aunt Margaret's?

CLIVE: Edith's.

THEO: (*More puzzled*) Martha?

CLIVE: Yes. Martha.

THEO: But what was stupid about that?

CLIVE: (*Gruffly*) Thinking her sister would be like she was.

THEO: [Like] Edith?

(CLIVE *nods.*)

[CLIVE: Yes.]

THEO: (*Tenderly*) [[Anyway]] [Well], you got over it.

CLIVE: That's just it, I [[didn't]] [never did get over it]. Theo, this may sound a damn silly thing to say to you but I never got over it. [[I suppose you could]] [You may] say she was my ideal – if you were some [sort of] sickening long-haired poet – all my life I've been looking for a girl like her – so now you know –

THEO: (*Quite thunderstruck*) I never thought it possible that an Englishman could be so romantic . . . (*Pause.*) and your wife – you don't mind my asking? You loved her . . . ?

CLIVE: Yes . . . dreadfully. She was exactly like Edith. I'll show her to you . . .

(*He takes* THEO's *arm and leads him out of the room. Dissolve to:*)

SEQUENCE 95

Interior: 33 Cadogan Place

CLIVE'S DEN

The walls are completely crowded with trophies except in one spot which, until now, we have not seen. A painting hangs there, covered by a curtain.

CLIVE *pulls a cord and the curtain slides aside. It is a painting of Barbara at the time of her marriage and very much like her.*

THEO *looks at the painting for quite a little time before he speaks.*

THEO: (*Quietly*) She's very lovely.

CLIVE: Isn't she like Edith? Eh? See the resemblance?

256

(*Now actually it is quite hard for* THEO *to see any resemblance at all.* CLIVE'*s memory of Edith is different from* THEO'*s. She has always stayed young to him as he last saw her.* THEO *continues to stare at the picture.*)

THEO: (*Answering* CLIVE) Yes . . . there is something very striking . . . But you mustn't forget, I saw Edith thirty-one years later than you. We grew old together – you understand?

CLIVE: (*Blimpish agreement*) Hm! – yes – [[suppose so]] [of course] – but she was [[very]] [exactly] like her –

THEO: (*Looking round*) It's a strange place to hang such a lovely picture.

CLIVE: She wanted it. I call this my Den, you know. She knew I always used to come back here, we had a joke about it – all my stuff is here. It would be an awful gap without her . . . ([[*He pulls the curtain back over the painting.*]] *Goes to the side-table.*)

CLIVE: Have a peg – what?

THEO: (*Looks at his back*) It must be terrible to lose someone very dear to you in a foreign country.

CLIVE: (*Pouring out drinks*) It wasn't a foreign country. It was Jamaica.
(*Dissolve to:*)

SEQUENCE 96
Exterior: 33 Cadogan Place

CLIVE *stands in the half-open door, a bright light streams from the hall.* THEO *is beside him in an overcoat of obvious Continental cut.*

MURDOCH *stands half-way with a torch. The car,* JOHNNY CANNON *at the wheel, is waiting.*

CLIVE *shakes hands warmly with* THEO.

THEO: [[God bless you. Come back safely, Clive.]] [Bye, Clive.

257

Have a nice journey.]

CLIVE: [[Nothing to worry about!]] [Don't worry about anything.] Everything under control.

[[THEO: I hope it is as you say. (*He goes to the car.*)]]

MURDOCH: Will you close the door, sir, please.

CLIVE: Oh, shut up, Murdoch.

   ([[*But he closes it all the same and looks around.*]]
   THEO *gets in beside the driver. He opens the window as*
   MURDOCH *fusses around.*)

THEO: Good luck, Murdoch.

MURDOCH: Thank you, sir, but the General isn't taking me. I stay [[here and do A.R.P.]] [to look after things here.]

CLIVE: (*Bellows*) You know the way, [[Miss Cannon]] [Angela]?

JOHNNY: Yes, sir.

[[THEO: (*As the car moves*) Good hunting. There's just room in the Den for Hitler's moustache!]]

[MURDOCH: The door, sir, please.]

CLIVE: Did you see the Warden?

MURDOCH: I am the Warden of this District, sir.

SEQUENCE 97
Interior: General's Car

JOHNNY CANNON *seems to be a very efficient, matter-of-fact girl, judging by her voice. Neither can see the other in the black-out.*

[[THEO: You don't mind my sitting beside you?

JOHNNY: No, sir.]]

THEO: It must be difficult driving in the black-out.

JOHNNY: [[It looks more than it is.]] [It's not as bad as it looks, sir.]

   (*After a pause* THEO *goes on talking.*)

THEO: I suppose you've done a lot of night-driving?

JOHNNY: No, sir. (*She realizes she must explain this.*) I never drove before the war.

THEO: What made you learn?

JOHNNY: My boy-friend taught me. But not at night. [[(*She laughs.*)]]

THEO: Is he a good driver?

JOHNNY: First-rate. He's one of the Bentley boys. [[But]] just now he walks [on his two flat feet]. He's a private. In training.

(*Pause.*)

THEO: What was your job before the war, Miss Cannon?

JOHNNY: Photographic model.

THEO: Interesting work.

JOHNNY: [[It was all right]] [Not bad]. A bit hard on the feet. How did you know my name, sir?

THEO: [[I heard]] the General [told me about you].

JOHNNY: Oh, [[of course.]] [Did he? Mind if we try to beat the lights, sir? (*Brakes sharply.*) Sorry, sir, couldn't make it.]

THEO: Do you like being [[his]] [the General's] driver?

JOHNNY: Who wouldn't? He's an old darling. I could have done a hand-stand when he chose me. [[It was at an inspection.]] [D'you know] He picked me out of seven hundred girls to be his driver. Some odds [[700 to 1!]] [wasn't it?]

(*A car is approaching with a badly fitted mask, the light points higher than it should.*)

JOHNNY: Look at that headlight. He ought to be reported.

(*The headlight flashes for a moment on her face. Only for a moment.* THEO *stares, startled, at the girl by his side. He knows now why the General chose her out of seven hundred girls. It is the same face.*

Edith – Barbara – and now this girl.

The other car has passed.)

JOHNNY: (*Grumbles*) That's what causes accidents. (*To* THEO) Long odds, weren't they, sir?

THEO: (*In a reverie*) I beg your pardon?

JOHNNY: Seven hundred to one! Makes me a bit of an outsider. (*She chuckles.*)

THEO: What is your first name, Miss Cannon?

JOHNNY: Angela.

THEO: Lovely name. It comes from 'angel' [doesn't it?].

JOHNNY: I think it stinks. My friends call me 'Johnny'. (*She peers out.*) Is it this crossing or the next [,sir]?

THEO: [[I'll get out here]] [Oh, this will do]. [[Many thanks.]] (*He opens the door and gets out. They have stopped by a traffic light.* THEO *holds out his hand. She shakes it firmly.*)

THEO: Goodnight, Angela.

JOHNNY: Goodnight, sir.

THEO: I'd like to see your boy-friend one of these days.

JOHNNY: Me too! [Goodnight, sir.]

(*She laughs.*

THEO *vanishes into the darkness.*

Fade out.)

SEQUENCE 98
British Broadcasting Corporation

Fade in.

Insert: the usual contract form of the British Broadcasting Corporation. The details: 'Major-General Clive Wynne-Candy, V.C., D.S.O., will give the Sunday night Postscript on June 16 1940. Title: Dunkirk – Before and After'.

A DIRECTOR'S OFFICE

The contract (or a copy) is lying on the desk of one of the Directors of the B.B.C.

[[*Beside the contract is a telephone, which is buzzing discreetly. Behind the desk sits*]] the DIRECTOR [*sits on a low chair,*

nervously]. *He is a charming diplomatic man, doing his best in a
very awkward and responsible job. He is about forty-five.* [*With
him is a* SECRETARY.]
The office is underground. The light is crude and glaring.
[*The telephone buzzes.*]
[[DIRECTOR: Yes?]]
    [(*The* SECRETARY *answers it.*)]
[[LOUDSPEAKER: General Wynne-Candy has just passed
    through the entrance hall, sir.]]
[SECRETARY: He's on his way down now.]
DIRECTOR: [[Thank you.]] [For the love of Gielgud, go and stop
    him as he gets out of the lift. If you let him put one whisker
    inside the studio, you are out!
SECRETARY: (*Echoes*) . . . out.
    (*Dissolve to:*)]

SEQUENCE 99
British Broadcasting Corporation

UNDERGROUND CORRIDOR
*Crude functional architecture. Crude glaring lighting. An
impression of great depth and strength. Many people are
bustling to and fro with papers. The lift has just arrived down.*
CLIVE *comes out with several others. He looks tired and worn,
but otherwise all right. He glances at the ultra-modern clock on
the wall. It shows* 20.45. CLIVE *is accompanied by a* GUIDE.
GUIDE: This way, [[sir]] [General].
    (*But a girl who has been waiting at the lift now steps
    forward. She is the* DIRECTOR'S SECRETARY.)
SECRETARY: General Wynne-Candy?
CLIVE: (*Turns a terrifying eye on her*) [[Mm! –]] [Yes.]
[GUIDE: This way to Studio 5, sir.]
SECRETARY: Mr Herbert Marsh would like to see you, sir.

261

CLIVE: Never heard of him!

SECRETARY: [[One of the directors.]] [Yes, but he's heard of you sir.]

CLIVE: [[Mm! – Mm – Ah, yes!]] [Oh, has he? Good. (*Following her.*)]

SECRETARY: [It's] This way [to Studio 5], sir. [(*Pointing in opposite direction.*)]

CLIVE: Lead on!

(*They start walking.*)

CLIVE: When does my [[– ah!]] broadcast start precisely?

[GUIDE: Well almost at once, sir.]

SECRETARY: [[The Postscript, sir? About]] [At] 21.20. [, sir].

CLIVE: [[Lots]] [Plenty] of time [[– good –]]!

[GUIDE: Excuse me, miss.]

SECRETARY: Oh, shut up. (*Steering* CLIVE.)

CLIVE: Regular rabbit warren, eh?

SECRETARY: Yes. (*Hurrying him.*)

CLIVE: Beehive of industry. D'you like working here?

SECRETARY: Oh, very much. You meet such interesting people.

CLIVE: You can tell that from the programmes.]

(*They arrive at a door: 'H. Marsh, Acting Director'. Without knocking, the* GIRL *opens the door.*)

[SECRETARY: (*Opening door to* MARSH's *office*) General Wynne-Candy.]

(CLIVE *walks innocently in. She closes it with relief behind him.*)

SEQUENCE 100
British Broadcasting Corporation

A DIRECTOR'S OFFICE

MR MARSH *is prepared to be very friendly. He stands up.* CLIVE *comes in speaking.*

CLIVE: I don't think I've met you, sir.

DIRECTOR: [[I have never had the]] [No, I'm afraid I've not had that] pleasure. Won't you sit down? Cigarette?

CLIVE: (*Accepting*) Very snug quarters here. And deep!

DIRECTOR: (*Smiles*) We need to be these days.

CLIVE: Quite agree! Back to the Stone Age, what? (*He puts down his cigarette.*) Think I'll leave this, if you don't mind. Bad for speaking. Makes my throat dry.

DIRECTOR: [[There may be some difficulty]] [General, I'm afraid we've been having a bit of trouble] about your broadcast [[,General . . .]].

CLIVE: [[Can't be worse than Dunkirk.]] [Well, I'm used to trouble. I'm a soldier.]

DIRECTOR: [[We have been advised at the last moment that your broadcast is considered]] [Yes, the – um – authorities think it's a little] ill-timed and [[must be]] [that it might be better] postponed . . .

CLIVE: (*Stares, goes purple*) [[Considered? Considered? Who is considering? Why?]] ['Think it's a little ill-timed.' Who has been saying that? Why?]

DIRECTOR: [[I'm afraid]] [Well], General, [you know] that in time of war [[it is]] –

CLIVE: Don't talk to me about war! (*He stands up.*)

DIRECTOR: (*Quietly*) No. [Of course,] That would be [(*Pauses*)] grotesque.

CLIVE: I have been asked to describe in this broadcast my views of the cause of the Retreat and its aspects for the future. There they are! I have been serving my country for forty-four years. What was your position before this one, sir? What? A lawyer! (*The* DIRECTOR *has murmured 'Lawyer'.*) Well, I was a soldier. And before that, I suppose you were at college. And I was a soldier. And I was a soldier when you were a baby, and before you were born, sir, when you were nothing but a toss-up between a girl's and a boy's name – I was a soldier then! (*He suddenly*

263

stops, collects himself, stares at Mr Marsh.) I'm deeply
sorry, sir. I know it's not you.
DIRECTOR: (*Who has listened patiently*) No. I'm afraid [[not]]
[it isn't].
CLIVE: I will make the necessary enquiries through the War
Office. I'll have a light for this cigarette now, if you please.
[[Thanks. Pity I sent my car away.]]
(*Dissolve to:*)

SEQUENCE 101
Interior: 33 Cadogan Place

DINING ROOM

THEO *and* JOHNNY CANNON *are listening to the radio.* (*June 16
was the day Pétain came to power.*)
MURDOCH *is making the black-out. The table is laid for two
people with a cold supper.*
The News finishes. There is a pause.
ANNOUNCER: (*Rustling paper*) [That brings us to the end of the
news and] Tonight's Postscript [which] is given by Mr J. B.
Priestley. Mr Priestley . . .
(MURDOCH *turns sharply. The others react.* THEO *is not
surprised.*)
JOHNNY: What can have happened?
THEO: I was expecting it.
JOHNNY: Why?
THEO: I've read his speech.
(*We hear the front door bang. Meanwhile the radio is
silent.*)
MURDOCH: The General!
(*The* GENERAL's *return is a great surprise.* JOHNNY *leaps
to her feet. She has no business to be here. She looks wildly
around.*)

264

'Tonight's Postscript is given by Mr J. B. Priestley . . .'

ANNOUNCER: (*On radio*) [[We apologize to listeners for]]
[Sorry about] the short delay. Here is Mr Priestley.
(*Without a qualm,* MURDOCH *turns Mr Priestley off before
he has said a word.*)
JOHNNY: Murdoch! Where can I go? The General mustn't find
me here! Murdoch!
THEO: Let me handle it, Angela . . .
JOHNNY: No fear. Let me out of here!
(*The* GENERAL *comes in. He is not angry; only
disappointed.*)
CLIVE: Hullo, Theo. If supper's ready, you can serve it,
Murdoch.
JOHNNY: I'm very sorry, sir.
CLIVE: Hm? Why?
JOHNNY: I shouldn't be here – I –

265

THEO: I asked Miss Cannon to come in. She was anxious to hear your broadcast.

CLIVE: Cancelled! At the last minute. Pity we hurried like we did, Angela. (*To* THEO) We didn't leave the War Office until [[twenty-five]] [five and twenty] to nine.

MURDOCH: There's a War Office letter here, sir. It came this afternoon.

(CLIVE *holds out his hand.* MURDOCH *gives him the letter. He opens it.*)

CLIVE: Paul Reynaud [has] resigned. Pétain is Prime Minister.

THEO: Bad news.

CLIVE: What? (*He has started reading the letter.*) Oh, yes – bad news.

MURDOCH: Sherry, sir.

CLIVE: (*Looking up*) Ah – yes! (*Goes on reading.*)

[[(MURDOCH *pours out drinks, looks enquiringly at* JOHNNY. *She shakes her head. He pours one for* THEO, *puts down the decanter and goes out.* THEO *picks up the decanter and pours a drink for* ANGELA. *She doesn't think it proper to drink with the* GENERAL *and shakes her head violently.* THEO *smiles.*)]]

[MURDOCH: Sherry, miss? (*She grimaces to dissuade him. To* THEO) Sherry, Mr – , sir?

THEO: Yes please.]

THEO: (*In a low voice*) How is your fiancé?

JOHNNY: (*Same tone*) He's not my fiancé.

THEO: [Beg your pardon. How is] Your boy-friend?

JOHNNY: He's getting a commission.

THEO: Congratulations.

JOHNNY: [[I think]] I ought to go [you know].

(*She looks towards* CLIVE. *He is still reading. He turns back to the first page and starts re-reading the whole thing.* THEO *and* JOHNNY *continue to talk in low tones.*)

THEO: (*Nod towards* CLIVE) [[Wait a little longer.]] [No, stay a bit.]

JOHNNY: [[O.K.]] [Down the hatch. (*Pause.*)] Any news about your application?

THEO: Turned down. Enemy alien.

JOHNNY: But you're an expert! Why didn't you ask *him*. He knows everybody.

THEO: He was [[in France]] [away].

(MURDOCH *brings some soup and bottled beer.*)

MURDOCH: Dinner is served, sir.

(CLIVE *mechanically folds the letter. He is only half listening.*)

CLIVE: Ah – yes.

JOHNNY: (*Stands up*) I'm going now, sir. Will you [[need]] [want] the car [any more]?

MURDOCH: I've brought another cover, sir.

CLIVE: (*Absently*) All right. Sit down, Angela. Theo! (*They glance at one another.*) Sit down, both of you.

JOHNNY: Never mind, Murdoch. (*To* CLIVE) Thank you, sir, but I had dinner.

THEO: Have another, Angela.

JOHNNY: No, really – I –

CLIVE: (*In a normal voice at last*) If you're worried about sitting down with your General, then stop worrying. I'm not a General any more.

THEO: (*He knows better than anyone what tragedy this means for his friend*) Clive! What has happened?

CLIVE: Retired [again]. Axed! They don't need me any more.

MURDOCH: I'm sorry, sir. (*Passing the sherry glass to* CLIVE.)

THEO: [[[(Holds out his hand to seize his friend's)]]] I know how that feels.

CLIVE: No you don't!

THEO: I was barely forty-five when it happened to me.

CLIVE: Different kettle of fish! [[Your country was]] [You were] *made* to do it. [But] We're not finished – nor am I! Just starting! (*Bites moustache.*) – I've often thought – somebody like me dies – special knowledge – awful waste – Well, am I dead? Is my knowledge worth nothing? Skill

... experience – eh? You tell me –

THEO: It's a different knowledge they need now, Clive. The enemy is different. [[The defenders must be]] [So you have to be] different too.

CLIVE: [[Have you gone]] [Are you] mad? I know what war is!

THEO: I don't agree. I read your broadcast up to the point where you describe the collapse of [[your own sector in]] France. You commented on Nazi methods, foul fighting, bombing refugees, machine-gunning hospitals, lifeboats, lightships, baled-out pilots, by saying that you despised them, that you would be ashamed to fight on their side and that you would sooner accept defeat than victory if it could only be won by those methods.

CLIVE: So I would!

THEO: Clive! If you let yourself be defeated by them, [just because you are too fair to hit back the same way they hit at you,] there won't be any methods but Nazi methods! If you preach the Rules of the Game while they use every foul and filthy trick against you, they will laugh at you! They think you're weak, decadent! I thought so myself in 1919. [[Filthiness! That is their secret weapon!]]

CLIVE: (A little shaken) I[['ve]] heard all that in the last war. They played foul then. And who won it!

THEO: I don't think *you* won it! *We* lost it! But you lost something, too. You forgot to learn the moral. [[Because victory was yours]] you failed to learn your lesson twenty years ago, you have to pay the school fees again! Some of you will learn quicker than others. Some will never learn it. [Because] You have been educated to be a gentleman and a sportsman – in peace and in war. But, Clive, [[my dear fellow]] [dear old Clive], this is not a gentleman's war. [[This is a life and death struggle, with your backs to your cliffs against the hordes of barbarism.]] [This time you are fighting for your very existence against the most devilish idea ever created by a human brain – Nazism.] And if you

268

lose there won't be a return match next year, perhaps not even for a hundred years! (*He pats* CLIVE'*s* [[*hand*]] [*shoulder*].) You mustn't mind me, an alien, saying all this. But who can describe hydrophobia better than one who has been bitten – and is now immune?

CLIVE: (*He is defeated. He knows Theo is right but cannot say so*) Well, you see, Angela – eh? Even one's best friend lets one down . . .

(JOHNNY *has been the silent witness of the scene. She is too young to be detached. Her respect for the* GENERAL *makes it quite painful for her to listen. She, of course, agrees entirely with* THEO. *She does not know where to look until directly appealed to by* CLIVE. *She looks miserably up at him and at* THEO.)

JOHNNY: I don't think so, sir.

CLIVE: (*Grunts*) You, too, eh? Kick a fellow when he's down – what?

JOHNNY: (*Weak smile*) Nobody would ever kick you, sir. [[You'll have]] [You've just got] to change over, that's all.

CLIVE: Change over? To what? (*He already speaks in a stronger voice.*)

JOHNNY: Well – [[some other]] [a new] job [[,sir]]. It's easy enough for a man.

CLIVE: Hm! Think so, do you? Swop horses in midstream – eh?

JOHNNY: (*Daring*) A lot of people had to in this war, sir. It's better than drowning.

THEO: Bravo, Angela! I shall call you Johnny in future! She's hit the nail on the head! I don't know you. You shouldn't give up so easily, my boy. Is this the same man who took Berlin by storm forty years ago? Look at me! Nobody wants me but do I give up?

CLIVE: (*Depressed again*) Nobody wants you – and you're an expert. I don't know anything but soldiering – (*Looks at letter.*) – not even that, apparently.

JOHNNY: What about the Home Guard, sir? They [[must have]]

[need] leaders. They are just becoming an army. If we are invaded, they['re] [[will be]] our first [[line of]] defence – [[all]] the papers say so.

THEO: There you are! You know everybody, you could get them arms and instructors and equipment! [[I wish I could join.]] What a grand job, forming a new army.

CLIVE: (*Looks from one to the other with great suspicion*) EH? – HOME GUARD – ?

MURDOCH: (*Entering*) Yes, sir. I was going to tell you myself, sir. (*He looks reproachfully at* JOHNNY *and puts down some cheese and the Cona.* CLIVE *gapes at him.*)

CLIVE: You're drunk, Murdoch. Tell me what?

MURDOCH: That I'd joined the Home Guard, sir.

CLIVE: You?

MURDOCH: Yes, sir. (*He is about to clear away when he realizes no food has been touched.*) Anything wrong with the soup, sir?

CLIVE: (*With gathering momentum*) How should anyone know if nobody's touched it. Take it away, [[Private]] [Lance-Corporal] Murdoch!

MURDOCH: (*Proudly*) Sergeant Murdoch, sir. (*Gathering up cold soup.*) What have you been doing, sir, all this time?

CLIVE: (*Seizing carving knife and steel, sharpens it*) Nothing, you blockhead, except *talk*! (*Seizing carving fork.*) But *watch now*!
(*He starts a murderous assault on the cold chicken.*
Fade out.
[*Explosion and star-burst on screen.*]
Fade in.
Insert: 'In Memoriam' column in The Times. 'MURDOCH – *In proud and loving memory of John Montgomery Murdoch, my friend and comrade in two great wars, killed by enemy action in an air-raid of* [[April 20]] [Oct.] *1941.* *Clive Wynne-Candy.'*
Dissolve to:)

SEQUENCE 102
Exterior: 33 Cadogan Place

The house we know so well has received a direct hit and lies in ruins, although those on either side are hardly touched.
The Demolition Squad are working on the ruins, amongst clouds of dust.
One of them pulls out a frightening object, coated with dust, from the rubbish.

1ST MAN: [[Crikey! This is a bit of all right!]] [Hello! What's this?]
(*He shakes and bangs the hairy object which gradually reveals itself as the pride of Clive's Den: 'Buffalo Head' – 'Nigeria' – '1924'.*)
[[2ND MAN: Upsadaisy! (*He has hold of a long curved thing.*) Give us a hand, Marmaduke!

33 Cadogan Place destroyed.

271

(*They both pull and, in a cloud of dust and clatter of
rubble, a rhinoceros'*]] [*a boar's*] *head emerges. Both regard
it solemnly.*)

1ST MAN: Hi, missus. Two basins, for me and me old chum.
(*Scares her with boar's head.*)

[[1ST MAN: Who *is* the bloke that lived here, Harry? Huxley?]]
(*They deposit their finds on a growing pile of dusty trophies
on the pavement. On the steps a shooting-stick is stuck in a
flowerpot, a large card clipped in it. One of the men reads it
out aloud.*)

2ND MAN: [See this? (*Reads.*)] Major-General Clive Wynne-
Candy – [[Boodles Club]] [moved to Royal Bathers' Club,
Piccadilly.

1ST MAN: I should think he needed a bath after this lot. Good
luck to the old bastard.]
(*Dissolve to:*)

SEQUENCE 103
Interior: Royal Bathers' Club

HALL
CLIVE *hurries towards the exit. He is now a General in the
Home Guard and wears their insignia. He is full of enthusiasm
for his new career. He wears a coat, it is still chilly.
The* PORTER (*the same rugged individual whom we have seen
confront* SPUD *at the opening of our story*) *salutes him.*

CLIVE: Still here?

PORTER: Just going, General.

CLIVE: Don't be late!

PORTER: I won't, sir.

CLIVE: By gad! what on earth's that?

PORTER: (*Proudly*) Gun, sir. [[My]] brother's a gamekeeper.
(*It is an old but serviceable double-barrelled 12-bore shot*

gun.)

CLIVE: That's the ticket! Load with No. 4! We'll soon have rifles
– tommy-guns, too. Know which end is which – eh?

PORTER: (*Keen*) [Oh] Yes, General.

CLIVE: [[Hah!]] [That's right.]

> (CLIVE *bustles out. The* PORTER *hurriedly takes his Home
> Guard armband and steel helmet from a hook. He has no
> proper uniform – these were the early days.*)

SEQUENCE 104
Exterior: Royal Bathers' Club

The car is waiting. JOHNNY CANNON *is still his driver.* [*She is
talking to another uniformed woman driver.*] [[*She holds the
door for him, then slips into the driver's seat.*]]

[CLIVE: Break it up, chaps. (*To other driver*) Good afternoon.
(*Gets in.*)]

[[JOHNNY: Where to, sir?

CLIVE: War Office.]]

> (*The car moves off down St James's Street.*)

SEQUENCE 105
Interior: General's Car and London Exteriors

CLIVE *is talkative. He scowls menacingly.*

CLIVE: By gad, we'll have proper weapons or I'll know the
reason why! I won't leave their damn doorstep! I'll make a
sit-down stroke – or a stay-in strike – or whatever they call
it! I'll show 'em! Angela! Eh?

> (ANGELA *smiles at the volcano. He can't see her.*
> *The car turns down by St James's Palace into the Park. The*

sentry salutes. CLIVE *nods.*)

CLIVE: A real army – eh? The men are all right – keen as mustard!
– Organization, General Staff, Offices, General
Headquarters – that's what we [[need]] [want] and, by gad,
we'll get 'em! D'you hear, Angela?

JOHNNY: Yes, sir.

CLIVE: [[One thing at a time.]] Give me [[a]] [one] year [– six
months]! I'll show 'em!

[[*Dissolve to:*
W. H. Smith newsstand, lined with copies of Picture Post, *all
featuring* CLIVE'*s portrait on the cover. The leading article is
by* CLIVE, *entitled 'Home Guard: Britain's First Line of
Defence'. Martial music. Another article is credited to Zone
Commander Wynne-Candy, dated 19 September 1942.*]
Dissolve to:)

SEQUENCE 106
G.H.Q. Home Guard, Marble Arch

*The Union Jack flies above the building. It is 1942: a year later.
At the entrance, two [[smart and formidable]] [young] sentries
are guarding the door. [[Each has rows of medal ribbons and
their combined ages would total about 140 years.]]
A sign says:* G.H.Q. HOME GUARD.
*General Wynne-Candy's car comes out of the park gates. Beyond
we see Hyde Park.
Camera pans with the car past the Marble Arch.
The General's car stops outside the Home Guard H.Q. The two
[[smart Methusalehs]] [young soldiers] slope arms.*
JOHNNY *jumps out and opens the car door.*
CLIVE *wears a lightweight uniform as it is now summer, he is in
very good spirits. We are back on the afternoon of the day on
which we first saw him.*

274

CLIVE: (*To* JOHNNY) Take the afternoon off.

JOHNNY: Thank you, sir.

CLIVE: Club – 7.30.

JOHNNY: Very good, sir.

> (CLIVE *goes in. The* [[*Methusalehs*]] [*young soldiers*]
> *present arms* [[*like guardsmen – which they were*]]*.*)

SEQUENCE 107

Interior: G.H.Q. Home Guard, Marble Arch

STAFF ROOM

Maps, street plans, Home Guard manifestos cover the walls and
tables.

About twenty staff officers of the Home Guard are waiting
around a huge table. We recognize some faces from the first
Turkish Bath sequence.

The door opens. MAJOR-GENERAL WYNNE-CANDY *has arrived.*
Everyone stands up.

He proceeds to the armchair on one side of the round table. He
waves them to their seats. He himself remains standing. He is
full of energy, radiates enthusiasm. He is obviously a born
leader and organizer, extremely popular.

CLIVE: Gentlemen! This is Der Tag! What! (*Laugh.*) [[I've been
conferring with the G.O.C. of the 6th Army Corps.]] This is
the most vital and comprehensive exercise in which the
Home Guard have yet taken part. Defence of London!
We've trained for it. We can tackle it! We'll put up a good
show, eh? [[I know you're all as keen as I am.]] We'll show
these youngsters there's life in the old dog – eh? Gentlemen!
War starts at midnight!

275

'We'll show these youngsters there's life in the old dog – eh? Gentlemen!
War starts at midnight!'

SEQUENCES 108 & 109
Exterior: Western Avenue

SPUD WILSON's *pocket commando thundering towards*
London.
It is more 'westerly' than when we picked them up at the
beginning of the story.

ROADHOUSE
SPUD's *commando pulls in off the road.*
A car is drawn up outside the Roadhouse: a military car, which
we know well: GENERAL WYNNE-CANDY's *car.*
SPUD *jumps from his truck, also* STUFFY. SPUD *looks at his*
watch.

SPUD: [[Quarter to six! Mark time! I've got a date with Mata Hari!]] [Five minutes easy, Sergeant.]
(*He goes into the Roadhouse.*)

Interior: Roadhouse, Western Avenue

LOUNGE

JOHNNY *is* [[*sitting having tea*]] [*playing darts*]. *Nobody else is in the hideous modern lounge* [*except a bored waitress, watching* JOHNNY].

SPUD [*enters, glancing at dartboard ('No. 9 – doctor's favourite') and orders 'Tea for two' as he*] *goes straight to her and kisses her. They make a good job of it.*

SPUD: Hullo, Johnny.

JOHNNY: Hullo, Spud.

(*A* WAITRESS *comes in and waits for an order.*)

SPUD: [[Tea – and the bill with it. I've got to go.]] [Got to go in a minute.]

JOHNNY: (*Disappointed*) [[Rightaway?]] [Why?]

SPUD: [[Yes.]] Got a job on.

JOHNNY: [[Where are you going, you liar?]] [Oh, you would have.]

SPUD: (*Taking her arm, leading her to the window*) Come [[here!]] [along, have a look.]

(*He takes her across to the doors. As they go they talk.*)

[[JOHNNY: I feel a criminal.

SPUD: So you are. Why?

JOHNNY: Using Army petrol.

SPUD: You ought to be shot. Probably will be.]]

(*They have reached the door. He opens it and points.*)

[SPUD: See that?

JOHNNY: What, those trucks?]

SPUD: My private army!

JOHNNY: [Well,] What about it?

SPUD: You remember [[when I rang you this morning]] [what you told me last night – amongst other things]?

[JOHNNY: Yes I do. And I wish I hadn't told you.

SPUD: Why do you think I wanted the [[dope]] [low-down] on 'Sugar' Candy's movements?]

JOHNNY: [[Of course.]] [Well, why did you?] What's the mystery?

SPUD: We're off to see him!

JOHNNY: Who?

SPUD: The Wizard!

JOHNNY: What for?

SPUD: Because of the wonderful things he does. We're going to teach him Total War!

JOHNNY: [[How?]] [Shut up, Spud. What do you mean?]

SPUD: Capture him! War starts at midnight! We're going to bag him hours before that. Nazi methods. You know.

JOHNNY: You're not a Nazi!

SPUD: [[The Home Guard isn't]] [We're not] training to fight Englishmen!

JOHNNY: You can't do that, Spud!

SPUD: Can't I? [[Watch me!]]

JOHNNY: [[How can you do such a thing to him?]] [I won't let you do it.] He's such a dear old man . . .

SPUD: So will I be when I'm over the hundred! [(*Turning.*) Ah, tea. (*Goes to table.*)]

JOHNNY: [[I won't let]] [How can] you do it! I know what this would mean to him!

SPUD: You can't stop me, Johnny. [[Inside]] [Within] an hour the Wizard will be the captive of my bow and spear – not to mention three dozen of the toughest troops between here and [[Tobruk]] [New Zealand]. [[Now where's that girl with the tea?]] [Come on, drink this.]

[[(*While he has been looking lovingly out at his private*

278

army, JOHNNY *has been looking desperately around.*
There is no chance of escape. Her eye falls on a heavy
ash-tray on the table. She seizes it in her fist. It makes a
formidable weapon and is quite concealed in her hand.
As SPUD *turns, she walks back with him, pleading:*)]]
JOHNNY: Spud! Don't you see? I gave you the information.
It's mean to take advantage of it!
SPUD: (*Callously*) Don't be a sissy! In war anything goes!
[[You have to use the first weapon that comes to hand!]]
[(*They circle each other, warily.*)]
[[JOHNNY: All right!]]
[WAITRESS: Hey, stop that!]
([[*She knocks him cold with the ash-tray.* SPUD *falls with*
a crash. She bends over him for a second in great
distress.]] [*She knocks over a chair deliberately. He trips*
over it and falls unconscious.])

Johnny(Angela) discovers Spud's plan to teach Clive Total War.

JOHNNY: (*To the unconscious* SPUD) Oh, darling! [[You asked
    for it!]]
    (*She flashes across the room and out of the door.*
    [[*A scream rings out: the* WAITRESS *has returned with the tea.*]]
WAITRESS: [[Help! Murder!]] [He's dead!]

SEQUENCES 111 & 112
Roadhouse, Western Avenue

EXTERIOR
[[JOHNNY *nips into the General's car and is off as hard as she can
go. She nearly runs over* STUFFY GRAVES, *who tries to stop her.
(This intercuts.) The troops invade the Roadhouse.*]]

LOUNGE
SPUD*'s army invade the lounge.* TOMMY *is the first to reach*
SPUD, *who is already sitting up groggily.*
[STUFFY: Spud!]
SPUD: She got me!
STUFFY: Who?
SPUD: Mata Hari! [[Stop her!]] [Come on!] Quick!
    (ROBIN *rushes out.* TOMMY TUCKER *examines* SPUD*'s
    head.*)
[[TOMMY: You need a field dressing on this.
SPUD: (*Grimly*) She'll need a field dressing somewhere else when
    I catch up with her.]]
    (ROBIN *and* STUFFY *appear at the door.*)
STUFFY: [[Not a hope!]] [Well, any luck?] She's half way to
    London [by now].
    (SPUD *suddenly bursts into action.*)
SPUD: [[Come on! We've got to get her! She wants]] [She's gone]
    to warn the Wizard! (*They all sweep out like a pack in full
    cry.*) [Come on, get my tin hat. Get after her, quick.]

280

WAITRESS: (*Cries*) Who's going to pay for the tea?

TOMMY: [[(*Shouts*) Charge it to E.P.T.!]] [The Sergeants' Mess.]
(*Kisses her.*)

WAITRESS: Mr Marshall!

CAR

ANGELA *driving with a smile.*

SEQUENCES 113 & 114
Interior & Exterior: Royal Bathers' Club

[CLUB EXTERIOR

ANGELA *enters the club.*]

[[CORRIDOR

JOHNNY *gains the safety of the corridor, stops for a second and listens. We get a suggestion of the scene from her angle.*]]

CLUB INTERIOR: PORTER'S DESK

PORTER: Really, miss, it's quite impossible.

ANGELA: Get on the phone, then. Go on, man.

PORTER: Very good. (*Telephones.*) Head Porter speaking. His driver wants to speak to General Wynne-Candy. Yes, it's . . .
(ANGELA *dives under the* PORTER's *desk as* SPUD *and Co. enter.*)

SPUD: (*Off*) Is Major-General Wynne-Candy in the Club?

PORTER: (*Off*) No, sir. The General left an hour ago with Brigadier-General Caldicott and Air Vice-Marshal Lloyd-Hughes.
[(*This is now the same scene as at the beginning of the film.*)

SPUD: Did he say where he was going?

PORTER: Excuse me, sir, what is your business with the General?

SPUD: I have a message for him – an urgent message.

281

PORTER: If you will give me the message, sir, I will see that the General gets it.

SPUD: But dammit all, man – ! (*Suddenly changes tone.*) Are you in the Home Guard?

PORTER: Why, sir?

SPUD: (*Low voice*) The password is 'Veuve Cliquot 1911'!

PORTER: (*Salutes*) The General and his staff are in the Turkish Baths, sir.

SPUD: (*Blows whistle*) Right!
(*The men come in, carrying rifles and bayonets, and go up to* SPUD *and the* PORTER.)

SPUD: (*To* SERGEANT) You're in charge here. Stay with him. (*To* PORTER) Don't leave your desk or use the 'phone. You're a prisoner of war.

PORTER: But war starts at midnight.

SPUD: Ah ha, that's what you think. Sergeant, that girl under the desk: she's a prisoner too.

SERGEANT: Sir!

SPUD: Corporal, follow me. Brute force and ruddy ignorance.

JOHNNY: (*Under the desk*) Hello, hello. Well warn him then. Can't you understand? Tell him to hide . . .]

[[EXTERIOR
JOHNNY *pops out of a side entrance. She sees* SPUD's *army with the two men going into the club, as in the First Sequence. Nobody sees her but her own car is surrounded. She stops a taxi, opens the door and looks back, listening.*

SPUD: (*Off*) The Turkish Baths, Northumberland Avenue.

JOHNNY: (*Promptly, to her taxi-driver*) The Turkish Baths, Northumberland Avenue. Quick! Matter of life and death! (*Dissolve to:*)

SEQUENCE 115
Exterior: Turkish Baths

JOHNNY *in the telephone box.*
From her angle we see SPUD's *army arrive.*
SPUD *and his men pour into the building.*
The SERGEANT-MAJOR *(as ordered) is coming towards her. She
is still trying to get through. She tries to get out but too late. The*
SERGEANT-MAJOR *puts his hand against the door and keeps her
in.*
JOHNNY: What are you doing? Stop it! How dare you? Help!
   Police! (*To telephone*) Porter! Hullo! Hullo!

SEQUENCE 116
Interior: Turkish Baths

CUBICLES
STUFFY *is coming from one of the cubicles. He has the famous
brown pigskin case in his hand. He stares towards the end of the
corridor.*
SPUD *has appeared, dripping wet and in a hurry. He comes
from his cold plunge with the* GENERAL.
STUFFY: Been in?
SPUD: (*Nods*) Defence in depth. Have you got it?
STUFFY: All serene.
SPUD: Here are your orders. That's their secret code! Get on the
   blower and contact their H.Q. Orders have got to go out to
   all Posts to let the Enemy through the barricades. From
   midnight on! Spin 'em a yarn. It's a trick! Grand Strategy!
   Be Clever!
STUFFY: (*His eyes gleam*) What a dish!
SPUD: Jump to it. I'll be with you in a sec.

(He vanishes. STUFFY, *exultant, rushes to the* PORTER's *booth.)]]*

SEQUENCE 117
Interior: Turkish Baths

HOTTEST ROOM
The naked General Staff guarded by SPUD's *men.*
The sweat is pouring off them. SPUD *is speaking.*
SPUD: [[I'm sorry,]] Gentlemen – the war will soon be over.
   We agree that it's nice to win the last battle but [[we'd
   sooner]] [we much prefer to] win the first!
   (Nobody says a word. He has the grace to look a bit
   ashamed of himself.)
SPUD: You will be kept prisoner in this building until 6 a.m.
   (Fade out. [[Fade in:)

BIG BEN
The time by Big Ben is 7.00. It is a lovely summer morning.]]

SEQUENCE 118
Exterior: 33 Cadogan Place

We hear Big Ben continuing to strike in the distance. The
railing round the private gardens has been removed some time
ago.
On a bench is seated GENERAL CLIVE WYNNE-CANDY. *He is*
alone. He sits waiting. The birds are singing in the trees.
A car approaches and stops near the gardens. [[The GENERAL
stands up; it is not so simple standing up this morning.]] The
car is his own. THEO *and* JOHNNY *are the only occupants.*

[[CLIVE *crosses the grass and steps into the road over the stumps of the former railings.*]]

ANGELA: (*To* THEO) It's all right, sir. He's still there.

CLIVE: [[(*Looking down at the stumps*) You couldn't do that either in my time. (*He means step over the vanished railings.*) Hullo, Theo!]]

THEO: Hullo, Clive!

CLIVE: [[Nice of you to come.]] [Hello, Theo. I'm glad you've come.] I couldn't have stood anyone else.

THEO: That's all right.

CLIVE: You heard, I suppose?

THEO: [Yes,] Johnny told me.

CLIVE: And?

THEO: [I think] It was a dirty trick but I can't help finding it a bit funny too.

CLIVE: It is. That's the worst of it.

Clive accepts defeat gallantly.

THEO: What [[will happen – officially]] [do you think is going to happen now]?

CLIVE: [[I suppose]] [Officially] this young [[officer]] [fellow] will be [[court-martialled]] [brought before a court of inquiry] and the Exercise [[will be]] repeated on some other date. [[(*With a change of tone.*) They won't find the Home Guard so easy next time!]]

JOHNNY: (*Uneasily*) Will [[he be court-martialled]] [there be an inquiry, sir]?

CLIVE: [[Yes.]] [No, there won't. I'll see to that. Where is he now?]

[[THEO: Will you give evidence?

CLIVE: Have to.]]

JOHNNY: [[What will happen to him?]] [Spud, sir? He's with his men. They're marching into London.]

CLIVE: (*Gruffly*) [[He'll be all right.]] [Did you see them?]

THEO: [[When we crossed]] [Yes, we saw them come across] the Cromwell Road [[we saw them coming]]. The whole Army. With bands.

CLIVE: (*To* ANGELA) Did you see 'em, Angela?
(JOHNNY *nods.*)

CLIVE: (*To* THEO) How [[do]] [did] they look? Eh?

THEO: [Well, Clive,] I must say, [[Clive]] [they] . . .

JOHNNY: (*Simultaneously*) [Oh,] They looked [[grand]] [OK]!
(*From a great distance we hear the sound of military bands approaching nearer and nearer.*
[[CLIVE *points towards*]] [*They go to*] *where his house once stood.*)

CLIVE: They've cleaned up my place [[quite]] [rather] nicely.

JOHNNY: (*Looks*) Oh! They've built an emergency water [[supply]] [tank] too!
(*They all cross the street. There is the low wall, with 'E.W.S.' and the life-belt, so well known to Londoners. They lean on the wall.*)

[CLIVE: I've been thinking this over all night. I don't want to get

286

this young fellow into trouble. I think I'll invite him to dinner instead. Wasn't I just as much of a young fool as he is? Of course I was.

THEO: Yes, but I wonder if he's going to be such a grand old man as you are.

CLIVE: When I was a young chap, I was all gas and gaiters with no experience worth a damn. Now, tons of experience and nobody thinks I'm any use. I remember when I got back from Berlin in '02. Old Betteridge gave me the worst wigging I ever had. And when he invited me to dinner, I didn't accept – often wish I had. Yes, I think I *will* invite him to dinner. And he'd better accept, d'you know!]
(*We see the huge tank of deep water where the house once stood.*
The band sounds very loud and martial: they all listen.)

JOHNNY: [[They're coming this way.]] [Yes, sir, here they come.]
[(*Sound of marching.*)]

[[CLIVE: (*Grunts restlessly*) Hm! Better go!
(THEO *puts his arm round* CLIVE.)

THEO: Isn't it all the same who's going to win this war: the old or the new Army?]]
(*A little pause.* CLIVE *stays where he is. The sound of the band and the rumble of the machines is very close.*
The morning wind makes little waves on the tank.
Suddenly CLIVE *smiles.*)

[BARBARA'S VOICE: . . . promise to stay just as you are until the floods come . . . and this is a lake . . .]

CLIVE: (*Slowly*) Now here is the lake – and I still haven't changed . . . (*He shakes his head, his smile grows broader*) . . . Hopeless!

[JOHNNY: Sir?]
(*The music blares out.*
Somewhere close by the New Army is passing[[: *tanks, guns, trucks, men, fast-moving . . . hard-hitting*]].

[*Pan from* JOHNNY *to* THEO *and finally* CLIVE, *who salutes.*
Dissolve to tapestry of opening credits.])

The End.

CONTEXT

RESURRECTION

Playing the Game

The newspaper articles and reports reproduced here were all collected by Michael Powell during the preparation of The Life and Death of Colonel Blimp. *One (the 'Forum' article) is mentioned in his letter to Wendy Hiller quoted earlier. Together, they evoke the intense public debate over Britain's 'blimpery' and veneration of sportsmanship and the amateur which formed the immediate background to* The Archers' *film.*

HOUSE OF COMMONS DEBATE
ON THE WAR SITUATION

Following a number of changes in Government personnel, which included the appointment of Sir Stafford Cripps as Lord Privy Seal and the promotion of Sir James Grigg (one of LDCB's most trenchant critics) from Permanent Secretary to Minister at the War Office, a general debate was held on the conduct of the war in late February 1942. The last day's proceedings contained several references to 'blimpery'. The following exchange was reported in The Times *on 26 February.*

'MR PETHICK-LAWRENCE (Edinburgh, E, Lab) said that the debate had emphasised the essential unity of the nation. Some of the critics desired to impress on the Government – and he sympathised with it – that if they were to carry the country with them in the war effort they must set about abolishing "blimpery" in all fields of action.

'The essence of blimpery was a refusal to entertain new ideas, and a determination to keep the bottom dog permanently in his place. (Hear, hear.)

'MR BEVERLY BAXTER (Wood Green, U) – Isn't the essence of blimpery to keep the top dog in his place? (Laughter.)

'MR PETHICK-LAWRENCE said there was the evidence of the Beveridge Report that a great deal of blimpery remained in the Army. He hoped the new Minister for War, whom he knew well as a man of great drive and courage, would prove equal to the task of getting rid of blimpery.'

Sir Stafford Cripps began his reply by saying he 'could assure Mr Pethick-Lawrence that from now on they had said "Good-bye" to blimpery.'

THE FORUM: 'WE AND THEY' [ANON]

When upper-class people talk politics and strategy, they say 'We shall make such-and-such a peace when We win,' or 'We shall reform colonial administration.' If one asked: 'Who do you mean by We?' they would reply with astonishment 'Why, of course, Us, the whole country.'

They assume that every other Englishman means the same things when he says 'We' in similar contexts. However, when one has lived for some months with working-class people in the Army, Civil Defence, or a factory, one discovers that this We is not as universal to the English as members of the well-to-do classes assume. When the poor say 'We' they mean the workers. When they say 'They' they mean, as a rule, the rich. Occasionally they say: 'I wonder what sort of peace They'll make this time.' Recently the poor have been thinking, and saying, that They have made a pretty good mess of the colonies. As for the workers themselves, they do not accept any responsibility; they consider themselves the passive victims of the bosses. If they are not to-day in a revolutionary mood, this is largely because they cannot conceive of themselves playing an active role in society under any circumstances whatsoever.

'Two Nations'

The different emphasis put on personal pronouns by two different classes in society may seem extremely unimportant. Actually it is the clue to poor morale on the Home Front. Our propagandists are almost exclusively people with nice accents – who imagine that when they say 'We' they are speaking for the whole people – talking to people who mentally substitute the pronoun *They* every time they hear the note of the M.P.'s, the B.B.C. announcer's, the officer's, or the Ministry of Information lecturer's, voice. The result is that after three years of war, millions of ordinary people are apathetic, and many thousands live in wilful ignorance of the atrocities committed by the Nazis, refusing even to interest themselves in the fact that the workers living under German rule are much worse off than here, and only brightening up when they hear fifth-hand Russian propaganda. Why? Because when the propagandists tell them about German brutality they shut their ears and say: 'Ah, *They* are trying to get me to support *Their* war.' It is quite clear that there is only one kind of war which the people will whole-heartedly support: *Our* war – the kind of war they believe is being fought in Russia.

What can be done about this gulf between We and They? In the first place we must have a policy which really convincingly shows the mass of the people that the war is for them, and that the future is for them also. We do not need promises, because our society should not consist of one class in a position to offer promises and bribes to another. We need a declaration of basic principles and of aims. The fulfilment of these aims, such as the winning of the war and the establishment of a new social order after the war, can be achieved only by the will and the effort of the whole people; therefore, there is no ruling class in a position to make promises any more than Stalin, say, could promise the

293

results of the Five Year Plan, which depended on the workers themselves. We need essentially, something to correspond to a Five Year Plan of Reconstruction for all, by all.

Education, not Propaganda

To achieve this there must be a mass educational movement to take the place of our existing kind of propaganda, to get the people to see the tasks that they are undertaking, the role that they need to play, the nature of citizenship in the modern democracy. The fact is that our apathetic population has got, in the next five years, to change the world. This cannot be achieved by passive audiences lectured to by Ministry of Information lecturers. It can only be done by the whole consciousness of society rising to a higher level of intelligent understanding. A movement of this sort can only come from below, though, of course, it can be helped by people who are already what is called educated. But if they are to join this educational movement they should not come from a level of life completely different from the people who are to be educated; they should themselves belong to the factory, the Army, the Civil Defence Unit. There should be a great extension of the Army Education scheme into civilian life. We need in the factories, in Civil Defence, and in every street, some democratic function corresponding to the Political Commissar who explains to the workers the relation of their immediate tasks to the far aims of society.

The Will to Learn

Fortunately, there are signs that people are ripe for such a mass movement of Short Term Education. The enormous success of the Brains Trust, which stimulates discussion in the majority of listeners, could hardly have been achieved before the war. In the Fire Service a Discussion Scheme, conducted voluntarily by leaders who are also occupied in training themselves to conduct the discussions, has met with a remarkable success. Though the meetings are voluntary, they are at most stations attended by between 75 per cent and [*illegible*] of the personnel. One result of these discussions has been an increase in the demand among firemen that they should work in factories and learn to use firearms. Our propaganda should be revolutionised to consist not of haranguing, but of extensive education in the tasks to be achieved if we are to have sufficient faith in our own future to win the war and the peace.

The source of 'The Forum', described as 'a medium for free discussion by a variety of writers', has not yet been identified.

'STOP PLAYING THE GAME!' BY LORD WINSTER

Mr Mason, in his recent book, retells the story of Francis Drake being found playing bowls on Plymouth Hoe by an officer who had arrived in some haste to inform him that the Armada was off the Lizard. 'We have time enough to finish the game,' was the comment of Drake.

Mr Mason agrees that the story is circumstantial, but says the answer is 'too racial to be forgotten. The Englishman's confidence in himself as against the foreigner, his trust in his improvisation, his instinct that the men who can pull a game out of the fire are the men who can do the same for a war, are all expressed in it.'

If such an attitude of mind, which has already done an immense amount of harm, is too racial to be put into cold storage until the war is over we may have a long war. It will be as well to get the fetishism of games complex out of the national system until happy days are here again. Hitler does not play bowls, he plays bombs. The *Herrenvolk* do not say 'well played' and shake hands with the loser. To be found playing a game when Hitler is about means big trouble. To go on playing games after his presence has been reported means a long goodbye.

Hitler and his associates do not play at anything in war-time.

They do not even take time off to watch games or to attend innumerable public luncheons and dinners. They seem to be on the job the whole time; they have the uncomfortable type of mind which finds running a war to be enough to get on with and in itself quite an absorbing occupation.

Stalin does not play games, and oddly enough it is Stalin alone, so far, who has made Hitler sit up and take notice. In the Far East the Japanese, who do not play games, are engaged with the Chinese, who do not, either, and with the Americans and ourselves, who do. The Chinese are still going strong after five years, the Americans and ourselves not so well, although Americans and British are, I presume, men dear to the heart of Mr Mason as able to pull a game out of the fire. On the other hand, when we play Americans at polo, golf or tennis, they very rarely allow the game to get into the fire for us to pull out.

It was depressing to read that the chairman of the Council of National Associations for Civil Defence had remarked that 'Civil defence as we and the public know it is pretty well dead,' until one read in a pamphlet issued by the Home Office to Civil Defence workers, that 'given good facilities and the necessary equipment cricket will probably be popular in the summer.'

It was cheering to read that Lord Gort had said at Gibraltar that 'the Germans have a five-legged horse and none of the legs is sound,' until one remembered that in the operation against his Army which ended at Dunkirk, the Germans did not use horses but tanks, which seem to have been quite sound enough for the job in hand.

Mr Mason may be right in his postulate that we can have confidence in ourselves as against the foreigner, although, of course, the Russians and quite a lot of other foreigners are on our side.

It may be assumed, however, that just as the Japanese by their association with the Axis are honorary Aryans, so even non-games-playing foreigners lose something of their foreign-ness by association with us and become honorary games-out-of-the-fire pullers and really quite decent fellows.

But Mr Mason's axioms that men who can pull a game round can pull a war round and that in war improvisation is the thing are more debatable. Improvisation does not seem to have gone so well in Crete, where, when the inevitable clash came after we had had the island for six months or so, General Freyberg reported that his troops had no blankets, cutlery or cooking utensils.

There are, however, two sorts of improvisation, one rendered necessary by neglect, the other deliberately trusted to. In Crete ours appears to have been of the first category. The Germans who crash-landed, or landed by parachute or glider bringing not only no cooking utensils but no dessert knives and forks, no table napkins and no finger bowls with them, were relying on the second. They won.

The instinct for games and sport is very strong in us. Their ritual and etiquette are an admirable social training. The self-discipline necessary for success is useful. Improved health and physique are valuable assets. The publicity and money sides of highly organised competitions are bad and breed vanity, jealousy and dishonesty.

There is a distinction between games and sport, a sport probably breeds better qualities than games. But is there not something beyond games and sport which breeds better qualities still, viz, adventure?

Mr Meade in a book of great charm, 'Approach To The Hills', discusses the rise after the last war of a new school of thought in climbing 'the greatest revolution that the ethics of mountaineering have yet undergone.' The Alps had become exhausted with no novelty or uncertainty left. 'The only solution is to alter the rules of the game and the young generation will not hesitate to do so – dangers must be courted, chances must be taken, uncertainty can be improvised – the word impossible is to have no meaning to the new mountaineer – it is not for him to wait upon the weather. For him mountaineering is to be the same thing as war.'

Perhaps one hears in these words a sound of something more in tune with the world into which we have passed than one used to hear at Lord's or Wimbledon, or St Andrews. Something that we have come up against in this war. That sense of adventure, that refusal to admit impossibility, which drove Drake and the Elizabethan seamen on their amazing voyages.

It is here again in the record of climbs in which 'safety first' is flung to the winds, everything that the old school said was impossible is accomplished and the human mind and body pushed to the very limit of what they can endure.

But Mr Meade goes on to say that 'no English names are to be found in the records of this peculiar school of mountaineering . . . its general principles do not appeal to Englishmen . . . yet the new attitude is responsible for some astonishing exploits.' May not the lack of appeal lie in the respect for the age-long rules of the games we play, which all Englishmen are taught to feel, for the conventions they are taught and trained almost to worship? But respect for rules can produce an ugly situation against an opponent who knows no rules and whose attitude of mind is contempt for rules if a thing can be improved or done better another way.

Unlike the winners of our great tournaments, Mr Meade tells us that 'the strange heroes who perform these feats are dismayed' by publicity and that their actions may be the result 'of a new attitude to the conduct of life.' He concludes 'it is possible that those who have a more conventional outlook on life than the new adventurers might find that there is something to be learnt from them.'

Mr Meade seems to have stumbled by intuition upon what is at the back of one factor which we have encountered in this war. But the pilots of the R.A.F. prove every day that the instinct for adventure is still with us if we develop a less hide-bound and conventional social system which will permit the spirit to soar.

Evening Standard, 9 April 1942

'NEED BITTER WAR FILMS: CAN'T GAG ABOUT NAZIS ANY MORE' BY ROBERT GESSNER

Further afield, Powell and Pressburger were no doubt encouraged by an article in Variety, *from a former Hollywood scriptwriter turned New York University professor, which cited their* 49th Parallel/The Invaders *as an example to be followed in trying to educate the American public on the deadly threat posed by Nazism.*

The time is here when we can no longer delay a reconsideration of the motion picture industry's attitude toward this war. No one doubts the patriotism and good purpose of the executive producers, but patriotism won't save MacArthur and the Burma Road is paved with good intentions. The ugly fact is that we are in danger of losing the war because the American public is not awake to the menace of Fascism. The ugliest fact of all is that we are at this moment actually losing the war, with the possible exception of Russia, because we were not awakened earlier.

Many institutions which shape or control public opinion may be responsible, but I am concerned in this writing only with the most effective of the channels of communication, the motion picture. Radio and the press have done good jobs, but the human consciousness is not so much influenced by what it hears or reads as by what it sees in pictorial images which have been dramatized. One movie like 'One Foot in Heaven' can induce more people to attend church than all the sermons in the Monday morning papers. The power of the screen places a responsibility upon the studio heads which they must discharge with taste and intelligence and foresight.

To some large measure they are responsible for morale.

Credit must be given for the few pioneer anti-Nazi motion pictures of the pre-war days, but how can we praise the anti-Nazi film of today which in effect diminishes the menace and discounts the nature of the Nazis?

This question troubles the highly placed executives in Washington with whom I have spoken. It troubles the intelligent movie-goer. It disturbs more civilian defense workers than we realize. It concerns all of us.

As a script writer who has worked in Hollywood I can understand how these misinterpretations originate, but as one who is honored to be associated with this 20th century art form as a Professor of Motion Pictures I can not excuse them. Neither, for that matter, would the intelligent producer want to excuse them. I walked out on a script-writing career in Hollywood, even before my first script based on my first book was screened, to study in Europe the nature of the Hitler menace. We all know today what that plague means and how it spreads. We know that the Nazis are not Keystone Kops. This war is no Mack Sennett chase. So why make it one on celluloid?

The basic error, I believe, is in using the war indiscriminately as a background for all types of films. The motion picture has attempted to be topical since the early days when Darryl Zanuck was brilliantly issuing gangster films almost in competition to the headlines. Catastrophies may be surefire background, but the interest is historical in the case of the Chicago fire or the Frisco earthquake; pictorial in the case of a South Sea typhoon or hurricane. The Gestapo do not so easily lend themselves to that type of background, because the menace is real and can strike any hour. We can ridicule Hitler as a symbol, and thereby prove that we are not afraid of what he stands for, but we must give the Gestapo the respect that we would give a rattlesnake.

In one current example we have a troupe of poor players who strut their brief hour on the Warsaw stage and are heard again behind whiskers and stage uniforms as master minds who outwit the [supposedly] 'dumb' Gestapo. A ham Hitler who isn't even convincing to his stage producer is able, however, to fool Hitler's personal guard. Such preposterous scenes, and there are many in the film, jar violently with the bits of excellent comedy. There is a need and a place for comedy, but bombed and devastated Warsaw is not the place. To see a comedy director traipsing over the corpse of Warsaw is a touch indeed. Inasmuch as the film is presented as comedy the Nazi sequences are doubly insidious; the Gestapo chief becomes no more harmful than Ford Sterling, the Keystone heavy. One expects to see bullets explode about the dancing feet of our hero. We are assured that false hair and makeup will win the war. Dr Goebbels and his staff, working day and night to distract us from a total war effort, could not hope for a better idea.

In the past few weeks Americans everywhere have been shocked by the costs of our complacency. The Normandie was demolished, either through neglect or sabotage or both, at a time when a simple barmaid was outwitting on celluloid the best brains of the Gestapo in Paris. German battleships were able to slip half-way up the English channel without being detected at a time when an Oxford archaeologist with the aid of whiskers and a pair of marbles in his cheeks could walk into the Gestapo headquarters in Berlin and run them around like sheep. Pearl Harbor had been caught napping and Singapore collapsed from over-confidence – but fear not: a Parisian piano player or a Broadway Runyonite or a Washington stenographer can outwit the Gestapo any day. One Boy Scout is equal to a corps of the Elite Guard.

Hasn't this complacency already proven disastrous? We cannot afford to be smug and superior in the face of an enemy who capitalizes on our lack of alertness.

The remedy is really simple. It is a question of taste. Slapstick belongs in the backyard where it has always been. Keep comedy out of the concentration camp. It never was there.

No doubt some legitimate need for 'escape' entertainment exists but blood and wine do not mix. We can make plenty of satirical fun out of the would-be Hitlers in our midst, the nightshirt leaders, the peacock uniform nuts, the monkey-wrench Congressman. Pelley, the professional anti-Semite, would be terrific in Technicolor. We can laugh at those fakers, and thereby prevent anybody from taking them seriously.

But when it comes to the real stuff we can take a tip from the English film, 'The Invaders.' In spite of its episodic character, the result of fusing Canadian documentary backgrounds with English studio takes, here the Nazi ideology is in dramatic conflict with our democratic way of life. There is an ironic overtone in this story wherein five and less Nazis make 11,000,000 Canadians look like sleeping beauties by roaming free and easy from Hudson Bay to Banff and back to Niagara before they are caught or shot.

But before Dunkirk the British movies were also winning the war with whiskers. An amateur cricket player could outbat a professional terrorist. It appears, however, that Pearl Harbor as a psychological Dunkirk has proven a dud. For a long time we called this a phoney war; too many still think it remote enough to be taken as a sports contest. They hope MacArthur will make a touchdown.

We are told that the London stage is alive with drama related realistically to the war, including satires against complacency. The people there no longer want to be fooled by politicians or playwrights. I sincerely believe that the same attitude is potential here. We Americans don't want to be fooled by Keystone Kops. Half-truths are not enough when our lives are at stake. The truth may be shocking, but we're a nation that can take it.

There is talent and technique and taste in Hollywood; the military films produced on a cost basis are evidence that abilities can be used effectively. Let the same intelligence apply to the entertainment film. In the final analysis topical backgrounds by themselves mean nothing; badly produced war films make no money.

There are countless untold dramas in the lives of our civilian defense workers, air raid wardens, factory hands. Our very lethargy is a drama awaiting treatment. For melodrama let the G-2 or Naval Intelligence outwit the Gestapo, or vice-versa.

Why not a surprise scene wherein the cocky amateur has his whiskers jerked off and is given the spanking of his life?

Variety, vol. 146, no.1, 11 March 1942

'WAS LOW RIGHT? BY COLONEL BLIMP'
BY DAVID LOW

While LDCB *was in production, David Low published an extended 'Blimp' broadside in the* Evening Standard, *in the ingenious form of an attack on* himself *by the Colonel.*

I am well aware, after some acquaintance with Low, that the ethics of modern journalism do not include a respect for privacy, even in the bath ... I endure Low's offensive habit when reporting my views of depicting me naked on the shallow pretext that Democracy demands the whole truth.

I tolerate his showing me in such absurd shape that people might almost think I was a cartoon of his imagination instead of flesh-and-blood. But recently he wrote of me in your newspaper as though the purpose of my existence was solely to provide a contrast to his own omniscience. WAS COLONEL BLIMP RIGHT? asked Low; and, giving a list of what he calls my past 'stupidities,' answered himself in the negative. Gad: sir, I demand the right to reply. WAS LOW RIGHT?

In so far as Low's cartoons have meaning, it is clear that for years past he has been in favour of Foreign Affairs. In my opinion the cause of the present war can be summed up in two words – Foreign Affairs. Gad, sir, a country like Britain with interests all over the world should mind its own business and keep away from foreigners.

But Low was all for those League of Nations cranks. I considered their international measures to abolish war were a menace to world peace. Try to stop fighting and you're bound to make trouble. If you want peace, the only thing is to let everybody fight. Safety first. Events have proved me right.

Lord Elton very properly admonished Low for his neglect of the military virtues. One virtue, I assert, he is incapable of understanding. I refer to LOYALTY. Democracy, Decency, Liberty and Civilisation are all very well, but Loyalty comes first, Duty to one's side. Gad, sir, even when the Government are going over the edge of an abyss, the nation must march solidly behind them. Lacking this supreme virtue, Low was nearly always wrong and unsportsmanlike in his criticism of pre-war Conservative Governments, especially when they were trying to avoid Foreign Affairs – Manchuria, Abyssinia, Munich and all that.

Hang it, after making an arrangement with an aggressor nation, we had to keep our word and let the victim down. It was the only decent thing to do. Our policy was Safety First. That is to say. Neutrality and down with the dashed Red. We had no quarrel with Hitler or Mussolini. They were obviously the sort of people to whom, if one offered one's hand, one would take dashed good care to get it back again. In short, cads. But in common fairness, you've got to admit they cleaned up the dashed Reds. And there's no doubt that Hitler did a lot for German Youth – physical training, open-air life and all that. Pity they all have to be killed.

Low was completely wrong about Munich, and about Russia. Wrong when he said that Chamberlain made one mistake in not making a military pact with Russia, and another in making a pact with Poland without Russia. He didn't understand the position. The dashed Red armies were no good. Bolshevism had sapped their fighting spirit. The grave danger of making an alliance with the dashed Reds was that it would have lowered our prestige with the enemy. (In mentioning the dashed Reds of course, I distinguish them from the heroic Russian people now defending their Motherland.)

Munich was a great gesture of peace. And Realism. Gad, sir, it stood to reason that if Hitler was conceded Czecho-Slovakia's tank factories, the biggest in the world, he would be satisfied and abandon further ambitions. Anyway, we were not ready.

Who was responsible for that? Low tries to make out that because Conservatives ran the Government from 1931 onwards it was their fault. But he is quite wrong. It was the dashed Reds. Mr Baldwin had to conceal the true facts of the situation in order to beat the dashed Reds at the elections. Munich 'bought time' for us to place ourselves in readiness.

Well, asks Low, why by 1939 were we not in readiness? Simply because the politicians – and Low – had so discussed the weakness of our defences that it had sapped the confidence of the War Office, and arms production had been seriously discouraged by the agitation for Government interference in war industries. Gad, sir, somebody should be shot.

Now a word on the Home Front. According to Low, his pre-war policy was Happiness and Prosperity, while I, he says, opposed Liberty and was 'inconsiderate of the condition of the people.' This is a travesty of the facts. I am a staunch upholder of the sacred British Freedom of the Press, but we can't let the wrong kind of people say, or write what they like, especially with education rampant among the lower classes. Economics and all that. It creates unrest.

Take slumps, for instance. We all know how slumps arise – lack of Confidence. The way to deal with Slumps is to be confident that there will be a restoration of confidence. But how could confidence be restored when people could read about the slump? Low failed to realise that you can't have it both ways. He was wrong. One saw the disastrous effects of unrest among the pre-war unemployed in their failure to appreciate that if the positions had been reversed the wealthy classes would have been quite well-behaved on the dole.

What the lower classes have never understood is that unrest is always created by the dashed Reds only for the purpose of preventing the upper classes from being fair of their own accord. Today it is evident that the wiser course in the pre-war years would have been to have given the unemployed less food and spent more money on keeping them fit.

What of the Future? Hang it, sir. We are at war! Yet some people – including Low – are always agitating about What We Are Fighting For. They pretend to be doing it for the troops, but in my opinion it's not likely to encourage the troops to know what people at home are thinking about what they are fighting for. Gad, sir, the troops are fighting for Civilisation, not for sordid ideals.

I'm all for the Atlantic Charter, of course, except as regards the British Empire. Gad, sir, what we have we'll hold, if we can get it back. We hear a lot nowadays about the Colonies from the dashed Reds. They always try to blacken the administration and whitewash the natives. Self-determination is all very well. Difficulty is that these natives don't understand Patriotism. Give 'em an inch and they want to run their own countries. After all, we are fighting this war to protect the rights of small peoples, so there must be no monkeying with the Liberty of the natives to do as they're dashed well told.

What about the Home Front? Low supports these dashed Nosey Parkers running about planning everything. Absolute anarchy. Fellows always wanting to improve the British way of life. Dashed unpatriotic. These Planners say they are out to avoid chaos. Say what you like about chaos, it provides complete freedom for Enterprise and Initiative. And what is going to be needed more after the war than Enterprise and Initiative?

First, you've got these dashed vista-mongers wanting to tell people what to do with their own land. With six million new houses to build we shall be too busy to plan what they will look like or where we will put 'em. 'The Land for the People,' indeed! Well, aren't the Duke of Westminster and the Marquess of Bute people? Sheer class distinction.

Then there's the Bishops. 'Public Control of Credit, Land and Water!' Dash it, you can't mix religion with business. It's unethical. What this country needs is a religious revival against the teachings of the Archbishop of Canterbury. And now we have this fellow Beveridge wanting to undermine the stability of the country with Security.

The grave danger of Security is that it will sap the sturdy British independence of the working classes. Who's going to have Initiative and Enterprise if he has £2 per week? (I except, of course, those in the higher income brackets.) Everybody knows that insurance discourages thrift even more than saving does.

As for Beveridge's free doctoring proposal, all this compulsory public health will rot the stamina of the nation. They'll be making the doctors into a union next. It should be reported to the British Medical Association. Gad, sir, we are fighting for Freedom, but what with the Post Office, Income Tax, the London Passenger Transport, the Bishops and Beveridge, we might as well be under Hitler. Rank totalitarianism.

Burdened with a colossal national debt, with our invisible exports vanished, our overseas investments sunk and all our markets gone, trading conditions after the war are going to be practically impossible. This is no time for planning. We must stand by the traditions and practices that saw us safely up to the Slump. We must stick to Capitalism as Nature intended us to. No Government interference. We must revive exports by prohibiting imports, thereby inducing a spirit of Healthy Competition bringing stability to industry and recovering British supremacy in world trade. We could whoop up the home markets, too, by strict rationalisation. Costs must be cheapened by reducing wages, thus increasing the purchasing power of the people and creating domestic demand.

True, post-war conditions may involve some Reorganisation for Efficiency. But the best people to handle all that are the Federation of British Industries. It stands to reason private people know more about what is good for the country than members of Parliament, because private people are inspired by the Profit Motive which is the spirit of service.

A lot of bosh is talked by the Reds about the Profit Motive, but you've got to have people making profits or you can't have business development (except in Russia, where they don't understand economics). The great danger of concentrating industrial power under public control is that any adventurer may get a majority of votes and then command the lot. Too dangerous. Much safer to hand the whole thing over to private monopolies that aren't dependent upon votes and can't be interfered with.

Later on, perhaps, the Government might send a commission to the F.B.I. to try to secure their support for Democracy.

It appears certain now that victory will be won as soon as we have defeated the enemy. True Englishmen will never sheath the sword until Freedom is restored and until Low, the dashed Reds and the dashed planners are all locked up. Let us put our backs to the wall with stiff upper lips and all pull together against Government interferences and the future will be before us.

Evening Standard, 15 January 1943

Analysis of the Idea behind
the Story of *Blimp*

This document must have been prepared in late May 1942, since it lists Olivier, Walbrook and Deborah Kerr as already cast – i.e. while Olivier still seemed possible and Kerr had been brought in to replace Hiller. It quotes Stafford Cripps on 'Good-bye to Blimpery' as an epigraph.

The man whose life and death we wish to portray was not called Blimp. He was born Clive Candy, at Cotteridge Court, near Kenilworth, Warwickshire, in the very centre of England in the year 1876. He was educated by private tutor and at Harrow, and passed into Sandhurst in 1894. He passed out with distinction in 1897 and joined a good infantry regiment shortly afterwards. His first major war was the Boer War.

In his youth Clive Candy was full of enterprise and impatience with his elders. His opinions about war were no better and no worse than the principal military figures of his time. He was anxious to succeed in his chosen profession, he saw active service early in his career and was lucky in obtaining promotion and distinction. He kept his eyes open during the South African campaign, he studied Clausewitz and the other military theorists. He was a promising young officer. There were hundreds like him.

Naturally not everyone who was born 66 years ago and who went through the mill of Harrow, Sandhurst and the Staff College is today a Blimp. Many fine houses built during the last 60 years, containing all the latest improvements such as gas-lighting, eccentric plumbing and an enormous bathroom whose water supply had to be pumped up by hand, have since been further modernized and kept up to date. Our story deals with men who have not kept up to date: Clive Candy was one of them.

Of all the peculiarities acquired in youth and through early training which formed his character, the most dangerous was the Sporting Spirit. He was able to exercise this harmlessly at polo, on the tennis-court, while hunting, and even on the croquet-lawns; but the King of Sports to him was War, and it was here that he gave it full play. He was an admirable enemy. Of course his intention was to win but when he lost, he was the best loser in the world. In his opinion defeat was due to bad luck or simply because his opponent's form was better.

This common attitude of mind for a long time failed to prove serious because the stake has always been, say, a colony in South Africa, a concession in Asia, a mandate in the Middle-East, the security of a road in China or of a sea-lane in the Pacific. If we lost one of these, there was always a feeling that a return-match could be arranged the following year. But when one day the stake became the British Isles and the future of England itself, with no prospect of a return-match if we lost; and when Clive Candy and his friends still believed in the Sporting Spirit, it became disastrous.

The opinion might be hazarded that, in the history of Society, no more important revolution took place than the discovery by a human being of the value of a lie. What tremendous advantages the discoverer of this possessed over his simple fellow creatures! So it was with the first country to invent Total War.

In 1902 Clive was far from realising that he had taken part in the last of the Gentlemen's Wars. To him Rules were everything. When, in the War of 1914–18, the Enemy waged unrestricted submarine warfare, bombed hospitals and civilians, and used poison-gas, a glimmer of doubt illuminated his mind, although he continued to fight like a true Sportsman, and never broke a rule until the enemy had broken it first. But this glimmer of doubt vanished when, unexpectedly, we won the War. Nothing could be clearer for him: drawn into a game with card-sharpers and crooks, the honest country gentleman had won the shirts off their backs. Being a Sportsman, his next action was to give the shirts back. His mistake was to think that the Sporting Spirit won the War: the truth was, merely, that the cads lost it.

Our scheme is to contrive a head-on collision between a ruthless young officer of today's New Armies and Clive Candy, now 66 and a Major General. In the scene which takes place between them, Clive suddenly realises how similar he once was to this young officer and how very different he has become. Only he can realise this: the young officer naturally cannot imagine that he was ever any different.

But he was: and our story will show him in his youth and then we will try to show how he became a Blimp; we will try to show how Blimpery is a negative, not a positive state; how a man becomes a Blimp, not by acquiring bad qualities but by failing to acquire good ones; and that Blimps are made, not born.

England is an island entirely surrounded by water. The water in its turn is surrounded by aliens, friendly and unfriendly.

In 1902 Clive Candy was 26, the Boer War was dragging to its close, the Conservative Government was following suit, people were making plans for the Coronation, the Prince of Wales was visiting Berlin for the birthday of the Kaiser, the German Grand Fleet had just come into being, and simultaneously a book had appeared on the Berlin bookstalls by a certain Dr Vallentin, entitled: 'The Huns in South Africa'. By this he meant the English.

At the same time Conan Doyle wrote to *The Times*: '. . . so rancorous is the feeling in Germany against us that we have been unable so far to find a publisher who dare publish a moderate account of the British case although all expenses were guaranteed by us.'

In 1902 Theo Kretschmar-Schuldorff was a young officer of Uhlans. He, like his country, Germany, had a choice of careers before him.

In 1918 he was a prisoner of war in England.

In 1942 he was a refugee from his own country.

In 1902 Lieutenant Clive Candy, V.C., in Berlin at the time of the Prince of Wales' visit, ran foul of the young Oberleutnant of Uhlans, fought a duel with him and consequently became his friend.

In 1918 Colonel Candy told Oberst Kretschmar-Schuldorff not to be downhearted at losing the war: England would soon have Germany on her feet again.

In 1939 this prophecy came true. Old Kretschmar-Schuldorff, a refugee to England, saved from internment by the intervention of General Candy, was able to tell how his two Nazi sons had refused to speak to their own father and to warn the General that this time Germany must be beaten so decisively that she will never forget it.

In 1940 the remnants of the General's command in France were evacuated from Dunkirk and the General lost his job.

A New Army arose with new equipment, a new toughness and a new spirit, an army with which Blimps and Blimpery had very little to do.

During the last forty years other events of importance happened in the world. WOMAN, used for centuries by men as one of their chief slogans for fighting, emerged as a fighter herself. Nowadays this is regarded as a commonplace, in the first World War it was an exciting novelty, in 1902 it was unheard of.

Clive Candy had, of course, a private life. He fell in love three times in the course of his life and, as so often happens, with the same type of girl. The first was a Governess, one of the half-dozen women who dared to leave their own country to get a job. The second was a nurse, one of the thousands of women who went overseas in the last war. The third was an A.T.S. Transport Driver, one of the millions of women in the Services today.

Because he lost his first love, all his life Clive Candy was searching for the same type of girl. He found her twice. Because the other two women looked like the first, he thought they were alike in character, too: he never discovered that there was as much difference between them as between WOMAN of 1902, 1918 and 1942.

COLONEL BLIMP
HAS NEVER LIVED, YET ALL THE WORLD
KNOWS HE IS DYING.
HE HAD ALL THE CANINE VIRTUES.
HE WAS HONEST AND BRAVE AND STEADFAST.
HE NEVER INTENTIONALLY LET A MAN OR WOMAN DOWN.
LET THIS BE HIS EPITAPH.

Script Changes during Production

Blimp *was probably subject to more changes immediately before and during production than most films of its time, largely due to The Archers' concern to achieve the maximum plausibility in their elaborate fantasy in the face of official disapproval and non-cooperation. Apart from numerous details of chronology and military protocol to be verified (see note on p. 182), many of the cuts made in the original script necessitated new transitions and links — which in turn contributed strongly to the film's elliptical texture and its 'structuring absences'. The following undated memo gives a vivid impression of what the production of* Blimp *was like, and how improvisation led to some of its happiest inventions.*

'Colonel Blimp' latest decisions

1. It is decided that the Spud sequences at the start and finish are to remain 'Army' as written so that either co-operation must be obtained or the sequences must be done without. Consider ways and means including possibility of Canadian Army.

2. Any additions to the end of the film to make the link of understanding between the young and old man successful will not, in Mr Pressburger's opinion, involve additional sets but will be in the dialogue. NEW DIALOGUE PLEASE.

3. Although the scene in the Corridor of the War Office is out, there will be a scene outside the door of Betteridge's office

which will include Hoppy. There will be a couple of new lines from Clive and the essential part of the existing scene which establishes that Hoppy goes to the Theatre instead of Clive. DEFINITE DIALOGUE PLEASE.

4. This scene outside Betteridge's office dissolves directly to a new scene with a picture post-card from Berlin addressed to Hoppy in the Hall of the Club. We see the Porter give Hoppy the post-card and read what is written. NEW SCENE PLEASE.

5. Extra lines of dialogue to go into Café scene, explaining that Clive has been to the Embassy and got flea in his ear. (This replaces first Embassy sequence). DEFINITE DIALOGUE PLEASE.

6. The Embassy Sequence following the Café will be preceded by an exterior shot of the Ulans' boots marching across the pavement in the snow and into the Embassy, with a brass plate or mat to establish that it is the British Embassy before dissolving to the Corridor shot. THIS NEW SCENE MUST BE CHECKED WITH MR JUNGE.

7. A proper scheme for the time lapses in Clive's Den should be discussed and definitely outlined by Messrs. Powell, Pressburger, Gray and Junge.

8. The Flanders Sequence still depends upon the model and it is understood that the scene of the car arriving at the Estaminet will be a real exterior combined with a matte shot.

9. It is understood that Ovington Gardens is now the definite location for Clive's house and the address Stanhope Gardens has been approved providing there exists no Stanhope Gardens. The number of the house should be checked with the Production Office. These new points affect the address on the letter from Aunt Margaret which we want to shoot on the set THIS COMING SATURDAY. It is agreed that the

essential long shots and broad action of all sequences relating to Clive's House will be shot at Ovington Gardens as soon as arrangements can be made.